Hard Road to Freedom

Hard Road

to Freedom

The Story of African America

VOLUME ONE

From African Roots through the Civil War

James Oliver Horton and Lois E. Horton

Rutgers University Press
New Brunswick, New Jersey, and London

Library of Congress Cataloging-in-Publication Data

Horton, James Oliver.
   Hard road to freedom : the story of African America / James Oliver Horton and
     Lois E. Horton.
       p.   cm.
   Originally published in 1 vol.: c2001.
   Includes bibliographical references and index.
     Contents: v. 1. African roots through the Civil War — v. 2. From the Civil War
   to the millennium.
     ISBN 0-8135-3180-2 (v. 1 : alk. paper) — ISBN 0-8135-3181-0 (v. 2 : alk. paper)
   1. African Americans—History.   I. Horton, Lois E.   II. Title.
E185 .H643   2002
973'.0496073—dc21   2002068382

British Cataloging-in-Publication data for this book
is available from the British Library.

First printing of the two-volume edition, 2002.

Manufactured in the United States of America

Contents

Illustrations and Maps

Maps

Acknowledgments

In the course of researching and writing this book, we have been fortunate in receiving the advice and guidance of more friends and colleagues than we can adequately acknowledge here. Yet a number of them deserve special thanks. Norbert Finzsch of the University of Hamburg in Germany convinced us to undertake a project with him that resulted in a book on African American history for German readers. We joined him in that venture, and although *Hard Road to Freedom* is a quite different book, that project inspired us to undertake this publication. John Vlach, a friend and colleague, was, as always, willing to help by reading and offering valuable suggestions on the early chapters dealing with Africa and the slave trade. Allen Isaacman also provided important advice in the early stages of the manuscript, and James Grossman read several chapters with his usual discerning and critical eye. Laurence Glasco read portions of the manuscript and offered valuable advice, and Raymond Arsenault listened to our ideas and offered suggestions. At a critical moment, and a late hour, Rod Paulini stayed awake to discuss Chicago politics from the view of a hometown boy.

Denise Meringolo, Stephanie Batiste-Bentham, and Michele Gates-Morese read the manuscript and made helpful suggestions, and with Candice Hewitt, they also put in long, frustrating hours assisting us with the picture research. Finally, we thank Dana Jeffrey Horton-Geer for his encouraging hugs and Alex James Horton-Geer for his ever-present smiles. They will someday be old enough to understand their place in this story.

Hard Road to Freedom

Introduction

People are often surprised, fascinated, even shocked, when they first learn about the history of African Americans. Sometimes outraged, they demand to know why they haven't heard this story before. Why did their textbooks ignore the dramatic tales of the black experience? Why has no one told this story? It is true that until recently, general American history textbooks and courses have paid little attention to this aspect of the country's development, save for a few references to slavery, usually discussed in connection with the period just before the Civil War. But it is not true that the story of black America has not been told.

Black people told their own stories again and again during their time in America. For the past three hundred years, they told it in oral testimony, in written petitions to the government, in autobiographical narratives, in poetry and song, in dance and religious ceremonies. In his autobiography published in 1760, Briton Hammon told of his enslavement in New England, his shipwreck in Florida, his imprisonment by the Spaniards, and his service aboard a British warship. In the many autobiographies that followed, Africans and African Americans recounted their lives in West Africa, and they remembered African history and culture. They described the horrors of capture and enslavement, and the restrictions on those who gained a limited freedom. Published at the end of the eighteenth century, the influential autobiography by the African Olaudah Equiano related how he had been captured and brought to America when he was only eleven years old.[1]

A flood of slave narratives telling the stories of those who had experienced the inhumanity of slavery was published in the early and mid-nineteenth century, becoming a powerful weapon in the fight against slavery during the decades before the Civil War. Some former slaves—Frederick Douglass, Nat Turner, Harriet Jacobs, William Wells Brown, and Jarena Lee among them—wrote or dictated widely read autobiographies that countered proslavery propaganda. James W. C. Pennington, a slave blacksmith and carpenter who taught himself to read and write, wrote two books after he escaped from slavery in 1827. The first, a general African American history called *A Textbook of the Origin and History of Colored People*, was used in the Free African School in Hartford, Connecticut. Since he was still a fugitive from slavery, he had to flee to Britain after his 1849 autobiography, *The Fugitive Blacksmith,* revealed his identity and location. In the 1850s, William Cooper Nell, a free black man and community activist in Boston, published two histories detailing the role of African Americans in the Revolution: *The Services of Colored Americans in the Wars of 1776 and 1812* (1851) and *Colored Patriots of the American Revolution* (1855). Nell hoped to counter charges that black people had no history worth recording and to establish black entitlement to American freedom and citizenship.[2]

Other African American histories followed. Former slave and autobiographer William Wells Brown published *The Black Man: His Antecedents, His Genius, and His Achievements* in 1863. He followed this with several works of fiction and a play dealing with race during the Civil War. George Washington Williams's landmark *History of the Negro Race in America*, published in 1882, influenced most of the important chroniclers of the African American experience who came afterward. Williams carefully documented his work with extensive footnotes, hoping to prevent his account of the role and accomplishments of African Americans from being dismissed as propaganda or wishful thinking. More than a half century later, when John Hope Franklin was preparing his classic study, *From Slavery to Freedom*, he was greatly impressed with Williams's scholarship.[3]

Scholarly African American histories, biographies, and autobiographies continued to flourish in the early decades of the twentieth century. W.E.B. Du Bois published his Harvard University doctoral dissertation, *The Suppression of the African Slave-Trade*, in 1896 and went on to produce a host of important historical and sociological studies. Du Bois's work ranged from a landmark analysis of the Reconstruction period after the Civil War to a study of the black community in Philadelphia that anticipated the mid-twentieth-century social history movement. Carter G. Woodson was born in West Virginia to a former slave and received a Ph.D. from Harvard University in 1912. Determined to raise popular awareness of the contributions of blacks to America, he organized the Association for the Study of Negro Life and History in 1915 and established the *Journal of Negro History*. Historians Charles H. Wesley, Luther Porter Jackson, Lorenzo J. Greene, and L.D. Reddick were among the first black scholars to publish in this journal. In addition to scholarly articles, the journal made many important historical documents available for study.

Meanwhile, such black institutions of higher learning as Howard University, Fisk University, and Morehouse College began offering courses in Negro history. In 1926, Woodson and his organization established Negro History Week. Celebrated at first almost exclusively in black schools and churches, this one-week observance introduced black history into school curricula, encouraged the publication of work dealing with African Americans, and stimulated the black press and a few white newspapers to run related stories. By the 1930s, the federal government aided this work, as the Federal Writers' Project of the Works Progress Administration gathered the recollections of elderly people who had been in slaves before 1865. Until World War II there were few black Ph.D.s in history, by 1940 only eighteen, more than half of whom had earned their degrees at Harvard University and the University of Chicago.[4] Among the recipients were Rufus Clement, Benjamin Quarles. and John Hope Franklin. Along with those still active from the earlier years, these scholars set the stage for a major breakthrough in the study of African American history. Their advances in the field were capped by the publication of Franklin's *From Slavery to Freedom* in 1948.

Black scholars played a critical role in the Supreme Court's *Brown* decision, which struck down the concept of "separate but equal" in 1954, fueling the postwar drive for civil rights. Their work, which laid the foundation for arguments for racial equality by challenging the segregationist assumptions that dismissed the importance of black people to the nation, presented historical evidence placing black people squarely in the center of the American experience. White scholars, too, contributed to this work during the 1950s. Studies focused on the history of slavery were especially relevant to policy discussions during the civil rights era. Kenneth Stampp and Stanley Elkins corrected earlier contentions that slavery was a benign institution, and by the late 1960s, federal social policy advisors debated whether the destructive effects of slavery served as an explanation for twentieth-century African American poverty. Some scholars argued that slavery had robbed blacks of their African heritage, disturbed black family and community values, and left them without culture. The debates inspired a new generation of historians to undertake social history studies to examine the validity of such claims. These young scholars called for a "history from the bottom up" that broadened the vision of American history to include those at the lower socioeconomic levels of society.

During the 1970s studies of slavery established the existence of a slave community, social and cultural space that allowed slaves to resist much of slavery's destructive intent. Studies by such historians as John Blassingame, Herbert Gutman, Eugene Genovese provided convincing evidence of the resilience of African American families and culture. Lawrence Levine's study of black folklore and culture proved conclusively that black people had shaped a remarkably rich social and cultural life and had preserved a considerable African heritage. By the 1980s African American history had moved beyond demonstrating the significance of black contributions and celebrating first blacks. Newer works took up Du Bois's task—the study and analysis of black communities and culture—with modern research techniques and technologies.

Important studies of Boston, Cleveland, Detroit, Philadelphia, Providence, New York and many other black communities began to illuminate the too-often-obscured interior world of black urban America, and a few scholars investigated black rural life. Meanwhile historians produced critical works of political history that drew on the social data to describe and analyze race in America in new and valuable ways. The last generation of African American scholarship has brought us a great distance toward a fuller, more useful understanding of the historical experience of black people. Recent work has added immeasurably to the complexity and texture of the African American story. In 1998, Ira Berlin's *Many Thousands Gone* and Philip D. Morgan's *Slave Counterpoint* explored the differences time and place made for slaves shaping their culture and negotiating their roles as workers, as slavery and the nation evolved together. In our 1997 book, *In Hope of Liberty*, we attempted to add to this scholarship not only by investigating the lives and relationships of northern blacks during the eighteenth and early nineteenth century but also by showing that the African American culture created during that period helped to create the general American culture developing at the time. Our aim in that book was to link the historical experience of blacks to that of other Americans, making the point that no American history happened in isolation from other American experiences. We have tried to continue that theme in this book.[5]

One major undertaking of the most recent work in African American history has been the creation of a narrative that brings together stories formerly told separately. In this first volume of *Hard Road to Freedom*, we begin the account of black people in America, telling their story as an expression of one of the nation's fundamental principles: the pursuit of freedom. The story begins with African cultures and the slave trade in which many Africans lost their freedom. Those speaking out against the trade that dominated New World development and created so much wealth were voices crying in the wilderness of greed and economic windfall. The evolution of slavery in British North America is the recapitulation of the development and codification of racial slavery and the story of cultural resistance to the hardening system.

The age of the Revolution brought the promise of African American freedom, raised along with the colonists' cries of liberty. Whether black men fought for the British or for the independence of the new American nation, they fought for their own freedom. For them the Revolution was an antislavery struggle, which freed more African Americans than did any other act before the Civil War. In its aftermath the nation was regionally divided by the issue of slavery or freedom. In newly formed northern black communities, African

Americans called on the country to live up to its founding principles, while in the South, slavery expanded its territory, tightened its grip, and increasingly stifled dissent. Slaves resisted a hardening bondage, forming communities of support that sustained the hope of freedom in desolate times. They found encouragement in the increasing strength of antislavery voices. Slavery's opponents saw the Civil War as a second American revolution, a blow for freedom that would complete the first. The abolition of slavery was one of the most significant events in all of American history. That it could only be accomplished by a war that cost more American lives than any American war before or since, illustrates the powerful significance of race in the formation of American history and culture. We argue that African American history is American history, and this first volume of *Hard Road to Freedom* brings the African American story to the crossroads of American history.

Chapter 1

Africa and the Atlantic Slave Trade

O laudah, whose name meant "the fortunate one," was born in 1745 to an elder among the Ibo (also called Igbo) people living in Benin, the eastern area of present-day Nigeria, in West Africa. Olaudah Equiano was his full name, although later in his life he would also be called Gustavus Vassa. His first few years were fortunate indeed. Indulged as his mother's favorite, he was the youngest son in a large family of comfortable means in a warm, productive land, "almost a nation of dancers, musicians, and poets."[1] Trade with neighboring settlements linked Equiano's people to a far-flung commercial network, but most daily contacts were local, and most disputes were decided by the village elders. Living more than a hundred miles from the coast, the young boy had no contact with European traders and knew nothing of their society. Through local oral histories, however, Equiano probably had heard stories of his own people, the Kingdom of Benin, and the ancient empires and great civilizations to which it was tied. Beginning in ancient times, African storytellers memorized proverbs and tales from their people's history and could recite them to educate and entertain the villagers. As the archivists of their people, these talented and specially trained men were often trusted govern ment advisers respected for their skill.

Equiano lived in a small corner of a vast continent. Second only to Asia in size, Africa has a land area of 11,700,000 square miles, stretching from the Mediterranean to the Cape of Good Hope, almost six times the size of Europe. Its geographical characteristics vary from the dry Sahara Desert in the north, an area the size of the United States, or the Kalahari Desert in the south to the grasslands of the Sudan to some of the most beautiful tropical rain forests in the world, situated in the central regions of the continent. It is a land infinitely diverse in climate, terrain, wildlife, and human culture. Between 6000 and 2500 B.C.E., a desert gradually emerged in Africa where once a green belt had existed. Equiano knew that his homeland was but a small corner of this vast expanse; that his nation and its people were rooted in an ancient civilization, indirectly descended from those who migrated south from the fertile Sahara as that region became too dry to sustain agriculture.

Long before, in the fourteenth century B.C.E., the Egyptians had retaken much of northern Africa from the darker skinned peoples of Kush, who retreated southward. Archaeological records reveal that the people of Kush established a strong kingdom based on agriculture, commerce, and iron manufacturing. They built urban centers and massive stone structures and dominated the trade routes to the Red Sea and the ivory markets of northern Africa for many centuries. In the third century C.E. their power was challenged by another emerging nation, occupying the region of present-day Ethiopia centered in the commercial city of Axum. Finally, around 350 C.E., the commercial conflict between these two nations became open warfare that ultimately destroyed Kush, scattering its people among other national groups to the east and to the west, toward the Atlantic coast.[2]

The contentions creating critical changes in northeastern Africa during this period included religious conflicts. Christianity was taking root in Egypt and spreading to the south and west, challenging traditional religions in those regions. After Rome became Catholic, most African Christians broke away from the Roman Church and formed the Coptic Church. ("Coptic" comes from a Greek word meaning "Egyptian church.") Over many centuries, as it spread, Christianity faced stiff competition from the many traditional local religions and from Islam, which was particularly influential in the region of the Sudan. In regions where Islam was accepted, oral historians added the Koran to their other recitations; in Christian areas they incorporated the Bible.

In the fourth and fifth centuries, a powerful trading nation arose to the southwest of Egypt. It took the name "Ghana" from the title given to its ruler, and by the eighth century it dominated West Africa. It controlled the trade routes across the Sahara that connected Africa with Mediterranean Europe, its people acting as middlemen between the people of West Africa and the Arabs of the north, and imposing tariffs on salt, gold, rubber, ivory, brass, and the small numbers of slaves that flowed north from the grasslands of central Africa. The tariff collected on this trade increased Ghana's wealth, and the wealth made it militarily strong. By the eleventh century Ghana's rulers commanded an army estimated at two hundred thousand warriors. From the north Ghana received the influence of Muslim merchants, Arabic as a written language, and the Islamic faith. The Muslim influence was apparent in its capital city of Kumbi-Saleh, which had not only a national palace and other opulent state buildings but also a Muslim quarter with twelve mosques and guest accommodations for Muslim visitors; Kumbi-Saleh was a center for education as well.

Ghana's wealth was enhanced still further by the gold brought from the mines of the Senegal River region and by the craftsmanship of its ironworkers, who were skilled at making weapons for warfare. This empire too was constantly challenged by its neighbors, who sought to acquire its wealth. Muslim warlords chipped away at the territory and trade that were the source of Ghana's power, and in 1076 they captured the capital, executing all who refused to convert to Islam. As the result of military losses and successive droughts, Ghana finally ceased dominating its region in the late twelfth century.

The successor state to Ghana was the Kingdom of Mali, which became extraordinarily wealthy and powerful during the thirteenth century. Travelers from the Middle East and southern Europe came in caravans to trade in Gao, Kangaba, Jenne, and other commercial cities of the empire. In the fourteenth and fifteenth centuries scholars came to Timbuktu to study Koranic theology, diplomacy, and law at the University of Sankore. The city and its university became a major center of Islamic learning, offering special education in geography and mathematics. European visitors were impressed with the grandeur of Mali and the grace and adroitness of its rulers. Under Mansa Kango Musa, a devout Muslim who made regular pilgrimages to the holy city of Mecca, Mali reached the zenith of its power between 1312 and 1332. With these pilgrimages Mansa Musa made a mighty impression on rival states. In 1324 five hundred slaves wielding heavy golden staffs heralded his arrival at the gates of Mecca. His camel caravan, escorted by many thousands of his servants, carried thirty thousand pounds of gold.[3] In terms of wealth, governmental organization, and military power, fourteenth-century Mali dominated its region and rivaled any nation in Europe. Centuries later British historian E. W. Bovill wrote that Mansa Musa ruled over a nation as "remarkable for its size as for its wealth, and which provided a striking example of the capacity of the Negro for political organization." J. C. DeGraft-Johnson believed that Mansa Musa "came nearest to building a united West Africa." "Whether you lived in the Gambia, Sierra Leone, the Ivory Coast, the Gold Coast, Togoland, Dahomey, or Nigeria," DeGraft-Johnson asserted, "you could not help but feel the power and strength of the Mali Empire, the empire which sought to fuse all of West Africa into one whole." Thus Mali and its glory were directly connected to Benin's history. Through his ancestors Equiano was linked to all West Africans who were dominated by, and shared in, the ancient kingdom's power.[4]

In the late fifteenth century Mali's power waned, and Songhay (Songhai), a nation in the western Sudan that had been converted to Islam in the beginning of the eleventh century, rose to power. Songhay, with its capital city of Gao on the banks of the Niger River, became a mighty trading nation. Under its control Timbuktu and Jenne flourished, their markets and schools drawing an ever-increasing economic and intellectual traffic from North Africa, the Middle East, Asia, and southern Europe, especially Spain and Portugal. At the height of Songhay's power Timbuktu alone had 180 schools, and white and black scholars at the University of Sankore studied grammar, literature, geography, science, law, surgery, and diplomacy. African scholars from Songhay carried their learning to the educational centers of southern Europe. Its government was a complex structure, comprising elected and appointed officials. Its military was a professional corps distributed throughout the provinces of the nation under the command of provincial governors. Its economy revolved around trade, agriculture, and herding, and its economic success attracted the attention of rival states in North Africa.[5] In 1591 the sultan of Morocco dispatched troops, many of whom were Spanish mercenaries, to attack Songhay. The resulting war was a costly one for both sides. Despite their superior weaponry, which included firearms previously unknown in the region, twenty thousand Moroccan troops fell. However, the warfare weakened Songhay's ability to withstand internal conflicts and pressures from neighboring states, and the empire disintegrated by the early seventeenth century.[6]

Equiano's nation of Benin had gained importance in the fifteenth century, growing from a walled city to a nation state as a result of its conquest of states west of the Niger River. The religion and science of his people reflected the long history of diverse influences in the region. They were not Muslim, although there were strong Islamic influences. Equiano reported that his people had no public places of worship but were attended by "priests and magicians, or wise men." There were strict religious rules governing funerals, food preparation, and cleanliness. The people believed in only one "Creator of all things" but also believed that spirits could affect the world. There was a close link between religion and science. Religious "magicians" also practiced the art of bleeding, much like Europeans at the time (and Americans well into the nineteenth century).

Although religious practices varied widely in West Africa, the importance of ceremonial music and dance was universal. Special dances, songs, or poems marked any significant event, victory in battle, marriage, birth, death, or an agricultural festival. Public dances were highly stylized, with special positions occupied by married men, married women, young single men, and "maidens," representing battle, domestic life, sports, and courtship. Later in his life, after he left Africa, Equiano saw Greeks dancing in ways that reminded him of the dances done by his people.

Benin was an agricultural nation and a land of traders. By the end of the fifteenth century its cloth products were popular with European traders, and its bronze and ivory art was found in Europe. The farmers of Benin were famous for their pepper, and the Portuguese established a trading post to deal largely in this one coveted spice. Africans received copper, coral beads, umbrellas, and guns in exchange for pepper and some slaves taken from the interior as prisoners of war. Increasingly after 1500 the Portuguese became more interested in the slave trade to supply labor for their sugar plantations on the island of São Tome in the Gulf of Guinea, in southern Portugal, on Madeira, and later on Cape Verde and in Brazil. Their plantation system drew on the earlier expe-

Eighteenth-century engraving depicting a celebration near the city of Benin
on the Guinea Coast of West Africa.

Museum of African Art, Smithsonian Institution, Washington, D.C.

rience of Mediterranean sugar plantations in Cyprus, Crete, and Sicily, which
used Muslim war prisoners and Slavic forced labor from the port towns of the
Black Sea. In fact, so closely were eastern Europeans identified with this
forced labor that the word "slave" originated in the ethnic designation of Slav,
only gradually coming to denote bound laborers of African origin. Over the
next three centuries Europeans competed for control of the massive Atlantic
slave trade, which provided much of the labor for their colonization of the
Americas.[7]

Slavery was already well established in Benin and other areas in North
and West Africa before European involvement. Those held in bondage were
generally taken in war, the losers of some battle who might have been killed
but for their capture. Traditionally a slave's value increased with the distance
from the slave's home. Before the fifth century Romans were willing to pay
higher prices for North African slaves because their remoteness from their homeland made them a more secure investment. In the Muslim world slaves at a
distance from their homes were valued as "strangers" who might be provided

with trusted positions because they were thought to have no local loyalties other than to their master. These slaves were often used as special military guards in their master's household or harem. As a logical consequence of this reasoning, as a slave became more familiar with the social customs and the politics of a region, that slave also became less suitable for slavery in that region. This might have critical implications for a slave's children, whose familiarity with the local society might brand them as unfit for slavery.[8]

In Benin slaves became servants, tenders of the livestock, domestic workers, and agricultural field laborers. They were denied the freedoms accorded to others in the society and were subject to harsh punishment for infractions of the rules that governed master-slave relationships. Slaves endured harsh, restricted lives, but they had hope for a better future.[9] Among Equiano's people a slave might rise from that lowly position to become a full citizen, equal in rights and status to any others in the society. Equiano had witnessed many slave sales as a child. Well-armed traders with large sacks traversed his region offering to buy or sell slaves. Before travelers were allowed to transport slaves through Benin lands, however, they were required to certify the lawfulness of their acquisition. Kidnappers were themselves enslaved as punishment for their violations of the rules. Equiano claimed that only war prisoners and criminals were held by his people or sold to passing traders. This was the expectation with which Benin's traders initially participated in the slave traffic with the Portuguese. Their understanding eventually changed, however, but by that time their principles had been compromised by the allure of the guns that came in return for slaves and greatly magnified the military might of Benin.

Equiano explained the process. "When a trader wants slaves, he applies to a chief for them, and tempts him with his wares." "It is not extraordinary," he observed, "if on this occasion [the chief] yields to the temptation with as little firmness, and accepts the price of his fellow creature's liberty, with as little reluctance as the enlightened [European] merchant's."[10] Benin was among the first nations in its region to be supplied with substantial numbers of firearms and horses, which facilitated the expansion of its empire beyond the Niger Delta to Lagos and from the Atlantic coast into Yorubaland.[11]

As with other powerful nations, Benin was constantly challenged by rivals, and as the pressure to maintain a strong military presence was unrelenting, trading slaves for weapons of war increased. Eventually, during the eighteenth century, Benin's power waned so that by the time Equiano was born its military might was overshadowed by competitor nations who controlled more of the area's trade. The Yoruba empire of Oyo largely supplanted Benin in the Portuguese trade during much of the eighteenth century. Oyo and Ashante became two of the most powerful nations of the region, controlling much of the slave trade and defending their commerce against the military incursions of Muslim traders. Their power allowed them to require tributes and taxes from Europeans in return for the privilege of trading in the region. Access to the coast was important for participation in the European trade. Along the coast from the Senegal River in the northwest to Angola in central Africa, European nations established trading posts that grew with the slave trade into a chain of more than fifty forts dotting three hundred miles of coastline. The greatest concentration of forts was along the Gold Coast, reflecting the original impetus for European involvement in African trade. The largest of these forts were called castles, elaborate walled settlements providing accommodations and offices for European traders, storage facilities for supplies, and holding pens for more than a thousand slaves. In 1481 the Portuguese built Elmina, one of the first of the large castles, on the Gold Coast in present-day Ghana. From coastal garrisons like these, European nations contended for control of the slave trade, as African nations contended for internal control of the trade. Elmina fell to the Dutch in 1637; the Cape Coast castle built by the Swedes in 1653 had been held successively by West Africans, the Dutch, and the English by 1665.[12]

Dahomey, a non-Muslim inland nation, broke through to the coast and replaced the coastal traders who had served as go-betweens selling Dahomean goods and slaves to the European coastal traders.[13] Among the people of Dahomey, slaves often filled out the ranks of military forces used to capture more slaves, who were then sold to strengthen Dahomean military power further. Perhaps it was a group from Dahomey who came to Equiano's village while the adults were away in the fields. But it was no military unit that found the eleven-year-old Equiano and his sister alone in their compound. This was a small slave-raiding party of two men and a woman, who seized the pair and took them off into the woods, where they were bound and placed in large sacks. They were taken first to a neighboring state where their own language was spoken, and were sold to a chieftain. Equiano's owner was a blacksmith, and the boy was employed working the bellows at the forge. The children remained in this "very pleasant country" for only a short time before they were sold again and separated. Equiano was eventually taken to the Atlantic coast, where he was shocked by his first encounter with Europeans. "Their complexions . . . differing so much from ours, their long hair, and the language they spoke (which was very different from any I had ever heard)" reinforced his fear that he would be killed by these "white men with horrible looks, red faces and long hair" whom he considered "bad spirits." He was also surprised by the ethnic and linguistic diversity of the other Africans he met, and astonished by his first sight of the ocean and the great ships lying at anchor.

Although Equiano had never seen Europeans before, contact between southern Europeans and African people was already centuries old. The North

African conquest and occupation of the Iberian Peninsula, beginning in 711, lasted for hundreds of years. For more than seven centuries Africans and Europeans shared this region, with the Africans wielding power. There was regular interaction between the races until the Spaniards pushed these Moors, as they were called, back across the Mediterranean in the eleventh century and finally retook control of the entire peninsula in 1492 with the conquest of the Kingdom of Granada. By that time the region had become what the historian Ronald Sanders called "the most racially varied society in western Europe."[14]

Yet, Iberians were ambivalent on the question of color. The numbers of blacks in the society encouraged both racial tolerance and racial restriction. Although the black population was eventually absorbed into the society, legal prohibitions, such as those that separated burials by race, relegating Africans to a common grave (*"Pocos dos Negros"*), narrowed interracial associations, limited black movement, and lowered African social and political status in the society. Still, it is likely that the region's historical experience made the Spaniards and the Portuguese more aware than the English of the nuances of ethnicity, culture, and skin color among the Africans they encountered in West Africa.[15] Mid-sixteenth-century Spanish traders' and travelers' impressions of Africa evidenced an awareness and an appreciation of the human variety they came in contact with. As the English observed, many Spaniards considered differences in skin color to be "[o]ne of the marveylous thynges that god [*sic*] useth in the composition of man." They were conscious of white and black as the extremes of human skin shades, "utterlye contrary," but they also recognized yellow, tan, brown, and other colors as well.[16] Other Europeans tended to simplify or even ignore cultural differences between Africans and to call them all "black." The English especially, who came to West Africa in the fifteenth and sixteenth centuries, were much more likely to see an indistinguishable African blackness. As the English became increasingly important in the growing Atlantic slave trade, "blackness" gradually imputed to African people the negative characteristics associated with the term in the English language. According to the fifteenth-century *Oxford English Dictionary* "blackness" was evil, sinful, ugly, and unclean, and the English identification of Africans as black marked the African character with these connotations in the English mind.

Contrary to British stereotypes, Africans were ethnically, linguistically, religiously, and culturally varied peoples. In fact, the wide variety of African cultures and histories makes it difficult to tell their story except in the broadest terms. The family was central to African social, economic, and political life. Family lineage was traced through the father in West Africa and through the mother in west central and central Africa. In most regions the lands

Olaudah Equiano,
as shown in the
frontispiece to
*The Interesting
Narrative of the Life
of Olaudah Equiano;
or Gustavus Vassa,
the African.*
Prints and Photographs
Division,
Library of Congress,
Washington, D.C.

were controlled by large extended families. Three families generally collab-
orated in selecting national leaders. The royal family supplied eligible male
candidates, another family selected the leader from among the candidates,
and still another family invested him with the power of office. As in other
traditional societies, individuals were connected to their history through
their family. Africans removed from family, from their ancestors and their land,
were separated from an important part of their identity and were truly lost
and alone. In the months and years after his enslavement, Equiano preserved the memory of his family and traditions as best he could; writing and

publishing his autobiography decades later, in 1789, helped him preserve a part of his identity.

During the days that Equiano was held on the coast, he and his fellow African prisoners learned much about their white captors, and after he found an African with whom he could communicate, he began to understand his situation. He was to be taken far away to the white man's country in one of the great ships. He was relieved once he was convinced that these strange men were not going to eat him, a common fear among those who had never before seen Europeans, and he began to believe that life might be no worse for him than for slaves in his land. Still, what he saw worried him—"the white people looked and acted . . . in so savage a manner, for I had never seen among any people such instances of brutal cruelty." He was terrified not only by the way white men treated the Africans but also—especially—by the way whites treated one another. "One white man in particular I saw . . . flogged so unmercifully with a large rope . . . that he died." The man's body was tossed overboard in a manner unthinkable to an African socialized in a society that held funeral ceremonies sacred.[17]

After several days the ship came that was to carry the Africans from their homeland. They marveled at the ship's arrival under full sail and wondered at the magic that brought this machine and these men to this place. In the next days and weeks, life for these Africans became almost unbearable as they endured the transatlantic voyage that has come to be called the Middle Passage. A cargo of "black people of every description was chained together" below-decks in the hold of the ship for six to eight weeks. As Equiano remembered,

> The stench of the hold while we were on the coast was so intolerably loathsome that it was dangerous to remain there for any time, and some of us had been permitted to stay on the deck for the fresh air; but now that the whole ship's cargo were confined together, and the heat of the climate, added to the number in the ship, which was so crowded that each had scarcely room to turn himself, almost suffocated us.[18]

The passage from the west coast of Africa to America was one of the most agonizing and dangerous parts of the enslavement process for the Africans. As if to testify to Equiano's description, hearings on the slave trade were held by the English Parliament in the 1780s. In these hearings a diagram of a slave ship, the *Brookes*, sailing out of Liverpool, depicted the unbelievably crowded conditions aboard one vessel. Resulting legislation prescribed the space to be provided to each slave aboard. Even if these rules of space allocation had been enforced—and they seldom were—slaves would have had half the room allowed to European immigrants brought to America during the seventeenth

Schematic drawing of the slave ship *Brookes,* used to illustrate British
regulations for the number of humans to be loaded aboard during the
Middle Passage from Africa to the Americas. British law required no more
than 451 slaves to be carried by a ship of that size. Abolitionist member
of Parliament William Wilberforce produced records to show, however,
that this ship had transported as many as 609 slaves on some of its voyages
to North America.

century as indentured servants, or even to prisoners transported to colonies such as British colonial Georgia or Australia. On the slave ships shelves were added to increase the capacity of the hold, dividing the area into two sections. A space six feet by one foot four inches was allotted for each adult man, five feet ten inches by one foot for each adult woman, five feet by one foot two inches for each boy, and four feet six inches by one foot for each girl. Using these calculations, British lawmakers estimated that a ship of the *Brookes's* size could reasonably transport up to 451 slaves, albeit in the most cramped conditions. The full horror of the Middle Passage is barely suggested by the impersonality of reducing human beings to deck-space dimensions. The whole story was even more grotesque, and many in Parliament were shocked to learn from a former crew member's testimony that the *Brookes* had completed the trip several years before carrying over 600 slaves, and they had lost many during the voyage.[19]

Alexander Falconbridge, a British surgeon, made the voyage from West Africa to the West Indies thirty years after Equiano's journey. Dr. Falconbridge's description of the hardships of the trip and the crowded conditions in the hold reveals little improvement. When the doctor ventured belowdecks in an attempt to attend the sick, he was forced to step on chained bodies, as slaves covered the entire floor. He reported that each slave was locked in irons attached to a long chain fixed to the lower deck, binding fifty or sixty men to the ship and to one another. Twice a day, at about eight in the morning and at four in the afternoon, weather permitting, these slaves were allowed abovedecks for food and exercise. As Falconbridge described it, their food consisted "chiefly of horsebeans, boiled to the consistence of a pulp; of boiled yams and rice, and sometimes of a small quantity of beef and pork."[20]

Conditions on board ship made death from disease, malnutrition, mistreatment, or lack of fresh air, frequent. Slaves who resisted their bondage by refusing nourishment were force-fed by the application of special jaw screws to force their mouths open. The whip was liberally employed to discourage protest of any kind. Equiano told of a group of Africans on his ship who elected suicide over slavery, making their way through the deck netting and flinging themselves into the ocean to drown. The crew "rescued" several of them and pulled them back aboard. Those who survived were severely and brutally punished as an object lesson to others who contemplated such action.

While some Africans sought freedom through suicide, others watched for opportunities to escape or to rebel. Slavery's defenders often argued that the dangers of ocean crossings in general accounted for the high death rate among slaves. In reality slave ships were floating prisons that held men and women for weeks under the most inhumane circumstances. The crew members were essentially prison guards, and there was great incentive for these guards to take their work seriously, since all knew the danger of slave rebellions at sea. Capt. Philip Drake, an experienced slave trader, explained to those seeking to enter the business that "the Negroes [fight] like wild beasts" and warned that "slavery is a dangerous business at sea as well as ashore."[21]

Slave ships generally carried more crew members than did other vessels, partly because of their special security needs. Many captains felt it essential to have at least one crewman for every ten slaves, and although this was not always the case, a ratio of one to twelve or fifteen was not uncommon. Some captains increased the security aboard their vessels by keeping male slaves chained belowdecks for the entire trip. This may have helped protect the crew, but it devastated the health of the slaves, killing many more than died during the average voyage.

Life on a slave ship was dangerous and uncomfortable even for the captain and crew. The crew's diet was almost as meager as the slaves', except that they received regular and larger portions of meat and a ration of rum. Disease was far more dangerous belowdecks, but the crew was not immune to the deadly plagues that were common on slave ships. Under these conditions the mortality rate was very high, 15 to 25 percent, reaching 33 percent for the slaves and almost that for the crew. Slave ships attracted a steady escort of sharks because the dead were tossed over the side each morning. Most captains endured the hardships in return for a share in the profit from the sale of the slaves. While profits fluctuated, returns from 100 percent to 150 percent on investments per voyage were usual. Some crew members were paid; others were impressed into service or were convicts offered duty aboard a slave ship as the only alternative to prison. Yet, even under the worst of circumstances, the voyage abovedecks could not be compared to that in the hold. Slaves, of course, had no choice and profited not at all.

African women received somewhat different treatment aboard ship than did the men. They were sometimes confined to a separate section of the hold and were often allowed to remain abovedecks for longer periods of time because they were believed to be less dangerous. Thus they were somewhat less likely to suffer the health hazards and extreme physical hardships of the crowded quarters in the hold. However, because they were abovedecks, the women were at the constant mercy of the crew. Although all women were at risk, young slave women were especially likely to be raped and otherwise abused by the captain and crew while they were at sea. Often the captain depended on the crew's access to the women to quiet dissatisfaction during long difficult voyages.

Although captains generally allowed women and children to remain untethered above deck, many knew better than to underestimate their female captives. As one captain was cautioned, "put not too much confidence in the

Women nor Children least they happen to be Instrumental to your being surprised which may be fatal."[22] Women too were responsible for deadly shipboard rebellions. An unnamed woman played a key role in an abortive escape attempt by three slaves being transported aboard the English ship *Robert* in 1721. Because she was allowed to move about the ship more freely, she was able to carry information from one captive to another and coordinate the attack. The strike killed two of the crew, but it ultimately failed, and the slaves involved were executed. Adding a gruesome touch to the deadly business, the captain forced the three insurgents to eat the heart and liver of one of the dead white crewmen before he killed them. As if to make a special example of the woman, the captain had her hanged by her thumbs, whipped, slashed with knives, and allowed to bleed to death.[23]

Horrifying as these events were, they were not unique. The slave trade was one of the bloodiest, most brutal aspects of African, European, and American history. After Europeans established settlements in America their labor needs increased greatly. The Spaniards in Latin America used native American Indians at first, but they died in such large numbers and at such a rapid rate that they provided an inadequate supply. King Charles II of Spain had prohibited the use of African labor in New Spain, but was persuaded to lift the ban by those who, like Bishop Bartolomeo de Las Casas, advocated the importation of African labor as a "humanitarian effort" to keep the Indian populations from total destruction. Later, after witnessing the brutality of African enslavement, Las Casas reconsidered and opposed the importation of Africans, but by the mid–sixteenth century Africans had become the favored substitute for Indian labor.

The African slave trade, which had progressed at a trickle during the fourteenth and fifteenth centuries, became a torrent during the next four hundred years, as it was redirected from southern Europe to South America, the Caribbean, and to a lesser extent North America. The first slave ships, mainly Spanish, to come directly from Africa to the Western Hemisphere traded in the West Indies as early as 1532, while the Portuguese brought Africans to supply their sugar plantations in Brazil after the mid–sixteenth century. The wealth extracted from the Americas by the Spaniards and the Portuguese was directly connected to the increased demand for sugar, which outpaced the supply from southern Europe. As the number of Europeans who could afford to indulge a taste for sweets grew, the value of sugar increased, and the demand for slaves to cultivate this extremely labor-intensive crop climbed sharply. By the end of the century sugar production in the Caribbean and Brazil was absorbing two thousand African slaves a year. The Africans imported to the Spanish colonies of South America were not all used in sugar production immediately. They replaced Indian laborers in the gold mines of New Spain and suffered comparably high death rates. By the end of the eighteenth century, however, sugarcane had become the Americas' major slave crop.

Other Africans came not as slaves but as sailors or as part of the Spanish military forces. Ancient cultural artifacts found in Latin America suggest to some scholars that Africans may have traveled to the Americas hundreds of years before the arrival of Christopher Columbus, although this hypothesis is not universally accepted.[24] Certainly many came during the age of European exploration. At least one of Columbus's crew is believed to have been of African ancestry, and thirty blacks traveled with the Spanish explorer Vasco Núñez de Balboa when he became the first European to discover the Pacific Ocean in 1513. In 1519 when Hernándo Cortez defeated the Aztecs in what is now Mexico, more than three hundred Africans were there to position his cannon. Other Africans entered the American West with the early Spanish expeditions. They produced the first wheat crop harvested in America, and in 1565 helped to build St. Augustine in Florida, the first city established by Europeans in North America.

Estevanico, a black Spaniard who acted as a guide for Cortez, excited the Spanish imagination by relating the Indian tales of the "Seven Cities of Gold." In 1539, with Estevanico guiding the way and acting as Indian interpreter, Father Marcos de Niza led Spanish troops through the American Southwest (in the areas that are the present-day states of New Mexico and Arizona) in search of the mythic treasure site. Posing as a medicine man, Estevanico enlisted the aid of several Indian villages in the search. The Spaniards hoped to discover these cities, with their limitless supply of gold, but their dream was never realized. Estevanico was killed by Indian forces, and the expedition retreated to the main Spanish settlement in Mexico. Yet the journey had fueled the Spaniards' fantasies of great wealth, and the story of Estevanico encouraged many other expeditions to continue the search. Centuries after Estevanico's death the Zuni Indians of the Southwest still tell of the black man who died searching for the golden city. Although Africans played various roles among the Spaniards in America, they were most likely, by far, to be slaves in South and Central America. It is fair to say that Spain's ascension to economic and military dominance during the fifteenth and sixteenth centuries rested on African and American Indian slave labor.[25]

The Portuguese produced great quantities of sugar in Brazil, using slave labor supplied from its trading posts in the Congo and Angola. Although they gained an early lead through their involvement in the slave trade, the government did not officially sponsor the activity until the late seventeenth century, and Portugal was overshadowed by other European traders who rose to power with the full support of their government. After Holland emerged from Spain's control at the end of the sixteenth century, it established a government-assisted slave trading effort that resulted in the formation of the Dutch West India Company in 1621. This company, which held a monopoly on all slave trading between Africa and the Dutch New World, produced spectacular profits for the nation and company stockholders. Holland translated its economic power into a strong naval force and managed to push Portugal out of its Gold Coast trading posts. Rivalries with neighboring France and, later, England eventually weakened the Dutch hold on the slave trade and allowed other Europeans to participate in the profits, but Holland continued to trade slaves for at least another one hundred years.

As Europeans realized the economic potential of the African trade, more nations established slave-trading centers in West Africa. During the seventeenth century Sweden, Denmark, and the German principality of Brandenburg took part in the lucrative trade.[26] Thus by the eighteenth century the African continent was supplying great wealth and power to Europe and to Europe's emerging American settlements. Meanwhile Africa was being drained of one of its greatest assets—many of its young, strong, healthy people.

England entered the slave trade later than most of its competitors, but it quickly eclipsed the field. The English had traded gold and ivory in Africa for more than a century before Sir John Hawkins became one of the first English traders to bring African slaves, in a ship called *Jesus,* to be sold in New Spain. Initially there was resistance at home to British participation. Queen Elizabeth I was afraid that God would punish her nation for selling human beings, but her fears of a catastrophic event were calmed when Hawkins demonstrated the vast profit to be made. Subsequently she encouraged him to undertake another slave trading voyage and invested her own money in the enterprise. Thus, long before England established its own colonies in America, it profited from the New World through its participation in the slave trade.

Three times during the 1560s Hawkins sailed between Africa and America, and each time the returns were considerable, so much so that several English merchants followed his example. British colonists in America entered the slave trade in 1644 when Boston merchants sponsored their first commercial voyage to Africa. Their ship, the *Rainbow,* brought slaves and other merchandise to British colonies in the Caribbean. In 1655 Britain established plantations in Jamaica and imported slaves to grow sugarcane. The increasing profit from sugar encouraged increased slave importation so that by 1673 there were ten thousand Africans and only eight thousand English settlers in Jamaica. Within fifty years Africans accounted for almost 70 percent of the island's population.

In 1672 the Royal African Company was formed to coordinate the slave trade, by then partly underwritten by the Crown. The company entered the trade just at the point of its most rapid expansion. Clashing with Holland over its move into Dutch-controlled West African areas, England expanded its participation. The trade became so lucrative that even though the Royal Africa Company secured a grant of monopoly from the Crown in 1673, it could not prevent other English dealers from infringing on its trade. Finally, in response to mounting pressure, Parliament rescinded the company's monopoly in 1711 and opened slave trading to all Englishmen. By that time Britain had established colonies in North America and was supplying them with African slaves.

The economic rivalries developing in Europe bore striking similarities to those in existence hundreds of years earlier in West and North Africa. Both centered around the African and European intercontinental trade. On both continents powerful nations had risen to preeminence based on their ability to control and profit from that trade, only to be supplanted by competing nations. Whether Ghana or Portugal, Songhay or Spain, each owed its economic and consequent military power to the profit from that trade. Old World dominance was constructed on traditional commodities, which included gold and slaves. From the eighth to the sixteenth century, most of the western world's gold came from the Sudan, controlled there by African merchant powers. Much of the struggle in the fifteenth and sixteenth centuries focused on Europe's attempt to circumvent that control. Europe's incursion into the Americas was a part of this effort. There, too, gold, and the slaves to extract it, became central to increasing wealth and power. By the mid–sixteenth century, sugar grown in America became ever more significant, overshadowing production in southern Europe. The wealth generated by trade in these commodities underlay the political and military power of Europe, as it had for Africa.

Figures are disputed, but the best recent scholarship estimates the total number of Africans brought to the Americas at something under fifteen million. The vast majority of those taken as slaves were males, a fact only marginally affected by economics. Generally male slaves brought higher prices as labor for the early American sugar plantations and gold mines, but after the late seventeenth century, women were in demand and brought prices comparable to those for men. African merchants, however, were less willing to sell African women. Women were valued at home as the bearers of children and, in most African societies, as the chief agricultural producers. There were also fewer female slaves available to African coastal traders because slaves were likely to be taken in battle, making men most likely to be captured. Very few children were taken because they brought prices too low to make their trade profitable. Only about 10 percent of the slaves who made the Middle Passage were under the age of ten.[27]

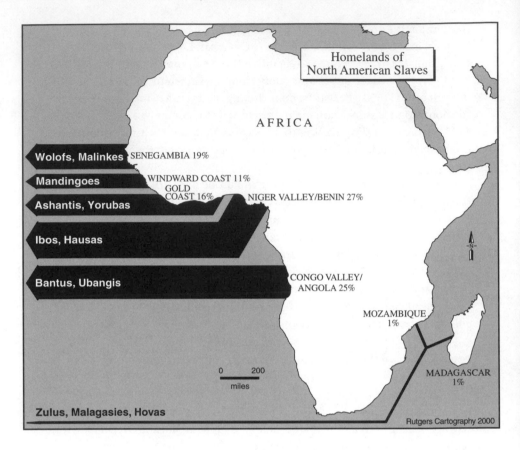

Homelands of
North American Slaves

AFRICA

Wolofs, Malinkes · SENEGAMBIA 19%

Mandingoes · WINDWARD COAST 11%
GOLD
COAST 16% · NIGER VALLEY/BENIN 27%
Ashantis, Yorubas

Ibos, Hausas

Bantus, Ubangis · CONGO VALLEY/
ANGOLA 25%

MOZAMBIQUE
1%

0   200
miles

MADAGASCAR
1%

Zulus, Malagasies, Hovas

Rutgers Cartography 2000

Economics did substantially determine the slaves' destination, however, and since the return on slave labor used in sugarcane fields was great, African slaves brought the highest prices in the sugar-producing regions south of the present-day United States. Ninety percent of all the slaves brought to the Americas were sold to those regions. During the first 350 years of the slave trade to the West (1502–1860), more than 50 percent of the Africans were enslaved in the West Indies by Spanish, French, Dutch, Danish, Swedish, and English sugar planters. Slightly less than 40 percent were bound to the Portuguese in Brazil; only 6 percent of enslaved Africans brought to the Western Hemisphere were held in the British colonies of North America. Initially most of the slaves brought to North America were transported through the large slave markets and plantations in the West Indies. After 1700, however, North American officials, slave importers, and their customers became convinced that West Indian traders sold the strongest and healthiest Africans to the more lucrative Caribbean market and shipped the less able, or sometimes the more rebellious, workers northward. Joseph Dudley, colonial governor of Massachusetts,

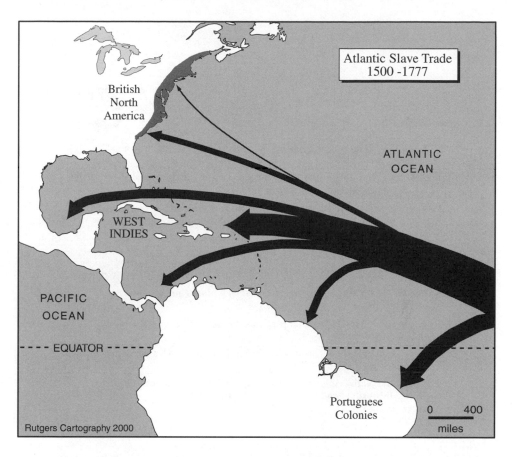

British
North
America

Atlantic Slave Trade
1500 -1777

ATLANTIC
OCEAN

WEST
INDIES

PACIFIC
OCEAN

---- EQUATOR ----

Portuguese
Colonies

0   400

miles

Rutgers Cartography 2000

complained that slaves imported from the West Indies were "usually the worst Servants they have." Many suspected that they were "Criminalls or otherwise of Little worth." By the mid–eighteenth century, traders were bringing an increasing majority of those enslaved in North America directly from Africa.[28]

Fifty years before Equiano was enslaved, the average annual importation of slaves to the Americas had reached more than twenty thousand, and it increased so rapidly that by the 1780s it stood at more than eighty thousand.[29] Perhaps it was this staggering increase in the Atlantic slave trade that fueled the stories Equiano heard about the white men's cannibalism—stories that provided one possible explanation for the Europeans' voracious appetite for African slaves. Equiano was landed in the West Indies in the 1750s and eventually was taken to the colony of Virginia. He spent more than a decade struggling to regain the freedom he had lost. Once free, he raised his voice on behalf of the millions kidnapped from their homelands in Africa and cast into the wilderness of American slavery.

Chapter 2

1607   Founding of Jamestown, Virginia, first permanent English settlement in North America

1619   First Africans brought to British North American colonies landed in Jamestown, Virginia

       Virginia General Assembly, the House of Burgesses, first representative government in colonial British North America

1620   Pilgrims arrive on the *Mayflower* at New Plymouth, Massachusetts

1635   African Anthony Johnson freed

1651   Anthony Johnson receives 250-acre land grant in Northhampton, Virginia

1670   Repeal of Virginia law that had allowed free blacks and indentured servants to vote

1676   Bacon's Rebellion in Virginia; participants include slaves and white indentured servants

1688   Germantown Protest; Quakers in Germantown, Pennsylvania, denounce slavery and the slave trade

1712   Slaves and Native American allies burn sections of New York City. Nine whites killed and twenty-one slaves executed

The Evolution of Slavery in British North America

*I*n Virginia, Olaudah Equiano became one of the tens of thousands of Africans and African descendants who tended the tobacco fields, maintained the households of planter families, and provided the skilled labor to build their homes and establish their settlements. By the time of Equiano's arrival, colonial law in British North America had transformed a loose system of African long-term labor into codified, perpetual, and inherited racial slavery. Virginia was a corporate venture financed by the sale of stock in the Virginia Company of London. The company employees who settled Jamestown in 1607 had not intended to build a society based on African slave labor. Drawing their lessons from Spain's extraction of gold from America, they hoped for riches from a similar enterprise employing American Indian labor. Despite a desperate first decade during which many Indians and many colonists died, the English settlers soon recognized that Virginia held a different sort of promise. With some instruction from the Indian population, farmers hoped to take advantage of the mild climate and fertile soil to supply both food and cash crops to sustain the colony. Tobacco, not gold, was to become the source of Virginia's wealth, and the unexpected arrival of twenty Africans aboard a Dutch trading ship in 1619 presented Virginians with another potential source of the labor to harvest this wealth.

Britain saw great potential for the colony of Virginia. It might provide produce that could not be grown at home and offered a place to transplant the growing numbers of unemployed people who crowded English cities and threatened the peace and stability of British society. Taxes on goods traded from Virginia brought needed revenue to the national treasury, and merchants and Virginia Company stockholders looked forward to reaping great profits. This lucrative potential could not be realized, however, without a stable, reliable labor force. Attempts to force Indians to labor were unsuccessful, as most escaped back to their own people, rebelled against British demands, or died of European diseases. When American Indian labor proved infeasible, the Virginia Company turned to Britain's poor, launching a campaign enticing them with promises of a new start in a place with virtually limitless land and great potential wealth. The land was strewn with gold, they were told, and a man could get rich quickly with little work. Those unable to pay their own passage were allowed to sign indentures, pledging five to seven years of work in return for the cost of the trip. Many believed the company's promises, and these indentured servants provided much of Virginia's work force during the early seventeenth century. But as the British birthrate fell, and wages and the prospects for employment in Britain rose after the 1630s, they became a less reliable labor source. As fewer of the English poor were willing to become indentured servants in Virginia, the company turned to African laborers, and the number of black servants in the colony began to increase steadily.

At the same time British holdings in the West Indies were turning to the cultivation of sugarcane for a reliably profitable crop and importing growing numbers of African slaves to supply the labor. Many slave traders believed that Africans' resistance to enslavement could be broken by the harsh system of gang labor in these sugar plantations. Accordingly, until well into the eighteenth century, many slaves bound for the mainland were taken first to the West Indies for a process called "seasoning." In his short stay in the West Indies, the young Equiano was horrified by the brutality of the life sugar plantation slaves were forced to endure. It was under these conditions that the British developed the customs and laws governing the operation of their slave system, providing the precedents in English law that were applied to mainland colonies. Gradually, over the next hundred years, the British colonies established a uniquely American form of racially based slavery.

North American slavery emerged slowly and unevenly, simultaneously manifesting different stages of development in different locations. The early black laborers in Virginia, not yet slaves but less free than white indentured servants, were sometimes allowed their freedom after a set period of time, almost always serving a longer indenture than white servants. There is evidence that some black servants were already serving for life by the middle of the seventeenth century. This implication can be drawn from the fact that when masters recovered seven escaped servants in Virginia in 1640, all were whipped, branded, and put in chains for a year, but only the whites' terms of service were extended as punishment. No such adjustment was necessary for the African, Emanuel, whose original service was apparently not limited by time. In the same year three other Virginia servants ran away from their master. When they were caught, two of them, a Dutchman and a Scot, received four additional years in servitude but the third, a black servant named John Punch, was ordered to serve for the rest of his life. In some instances blacks and whites of similar circumstance seemed to be treated similarly. When a white man and a black woman were found guilty of fornication in 1650, the church required them both to stand in shame before the congregation, clad only in white sheets, following a customary form of church-administered justice.[1]

Anthony Johnson

In the early 1620s slave traders captured a man in Angola, gave him the name Antonio, and brought him to the Americas, where he was sold to a colonist in Virginia. During these early days in British North America, before the system of slavery was strictly codified, some bound Africans were treated much like indentured servants. Although, unlike European servants, they had no contracts, some Africans were freed after a period of servitude. Perhaps this was how Antonio and his wife, Mary, also African, gained their freedom. Antonio may also have been granted a tract of land as the customary freedom dues for an indentured servant. By 1641 Antonio, a free man known as Anthony Johnson, was the owner of a small farm with livestock on Virginia's eastern shore. By midcentury, the Johnsons' farm had grown to about 250 acres, and the family held servants of their own.

During the formation of slavery, although race was a factor, color did not yet define life chances as comprehensively as it would by the nineteenth century. The Johnsons suffered a setback in 1653 when fire burned many of the buildings on their farm. The colonial court, noting that Johnson and his family were respected members of the community, granted them tax relief. A few years later, however, the Johnsons' white neighbor, Edmund Scarburgh, forged a letter in which Anthony Johnson appeared to acknowledge a debt. Though Johnson clearly was illiterate, the court granted Scarburgh a substantial portion of his land on the strength of that letter. The family purchased more land in Maryland and continued to live on their Virginia land. But when Anthony died in 1670, an ominous court ruling foreshadowed a more precarious future for free blacks. A white planter was allowed to seize the Virginia land because, the court said, as a black man, Anthony Johnson was not a citizen of the colony. His children maintained their hold on enough land to remain independent farmers, but they faced greater racial restrictions. By the turn of the eighteenth century, slavery was defined by laws that restricted the lives of all black people, both free and slave.

By midcentury it was becoming clear, however, that Africans would not be treated like other colonials. In 1652 Virginian John Pott's purchase of ten-year-old Jowan included "her Issue and produce duringe her (or either of them) for their Life tyme. And their Successors forever."[2] African slavery was thereby hereditary and perpetual, a condition recognized in law in 1660 in Virginia and 1663 in Maryland.[3] In 1662 the Virginia assembly reversed the English common law tradition whereby a child took its father's status by declaring that bondage passed to a child if the child's mother was bound. In this way Virginia assured that the offspring of Englishmen and African women remained in service and provided a larger supply of perpetual servants. During the same decade another potential avenue to black freedom was closed when the question of whether an African convert to Christianity could be held as a slave was resolved by a General Assembly ruling that baptism did not protect an African from perpetual bondage.[4] As more Africans served for life, the punitive value of lengthening the time of service was lost, and masters demanded that they be allowed to use corporal punishment against slaves who resisted their control. Virginia authorities agreed, and in 1669 they ruled that masters would not be held liable for such punishment even if the slave were killed, since it was presumed that no person would intentionally destroy his own property.[5]

In Maryland, the Chesapeake colony established by Cecilius Calvert in 1634 as a haven for Catholics, indentured servitude played a greater role in the labor system for a longer period, and British convict labor was imported when voluntary servants became more difficult to find. Many Africans served terms much like white indentured servants, and their similar situations increased the likelihood of interracial cooperation in such ventures as running away. In 1664, in an attempt to help protect slaveholders from the loss of their slaves, Maryland passed legislation aimed at discouraging the most intimate form of interracial association. The law declared that any white woman marrying an African slave could be forced to serve her husband's master for as long as her husband lived. By 1700 heavy penalties were imposed for interracial marriage, Africans commonly served for a lifetime, and slaves' children became slaves. Eighteenth-century advertisements for runaway slaves demonstrate that legislation could not entirely prevent such liaisons. Isaac Cromwell, a forty-year-old mulatto slave, escaped from northern Maryland with Ann Greene, an Englishwoman who was an indentured servant in the same area. They fled on two of Isaac's master's horses, and his master believed they were living together in Philadelphia as husband and wife. When Peggy, a black slave who spoke with a Welsh accent, escaped from slavery, she left with her Portuguese lover, who was an indentured servant.[6]

The status of some blacks in both Chesapeake colonies remained ambiguous until the end of the seventeenth century. There were exceptional experiences like that of Anthony Johnson, who was brought to Virginia in 1622, gained his freedom, and eventually prospered as a middling planter. Freed after a term of service, he married and acquired substantial acreage and a herd of cattle. Johnson held slaves of his own, turned a reasonable profit from his land, and even used the colonial court system to protect his right to the labor of his slave against a claim by a white neighbor. He was one of a few free blacks who moved to the ranks of small planters before 1700. By the eighteenth century Africans constituted 80 percent of the unfree workers in the region, largely

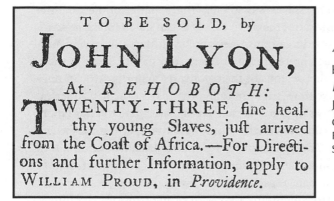

TO BE SOLD, by

JOHN LYON,

At *REHOBOTH:*
TWENTY-THREE fine healthy young Slaves, juſt arrived from the Coaſt of Africa.—For Directions and further Information, apply to WILLIAM PROUD, in *Providence.*

"To Be Sold by John Lyon," *Providence Gazette,* June 11, 1763. Graphics Division, Rhode Island Historical Society, Providence.

replacing the Chesapeake's white indentured servants, and slavery had evolved from an ambiguous form of indenture to a permanent, inherited status. Increasingly whites came to assume that any black person was a slave unless there was explicit evidence to the contrary.[7]

To the south of the Chesapeake the British established the colony of Carolina in 1663. The initial settlers in the southern part of the colony that later became South Carolina produced timber and livestock for the British colonies in the West Indies, but within a generation rice became the chief money crop. Carolina settlers came mainly from the British West Indian colony of Barbados, where African slaves worked in the sugarcane fields. Unlike the Chesapeake, Carolina relied on slavery from the beginning, with slaves first herding livestock and felling the timber to be shipped to Barbados, then cultivating rice. Since Africans had grown rice for hundreds of years in the region south of the Gambia River in West Africa, many were brought to South Carolina as slaves to teach rice culture to their English masters and to grow rice in the lowlands along the Atlantic coast, where tidewater flooded the fields and West African techniques were most successful. Blacks were the vast majority of the population in this region, especially during the summer months, when the danger from malaria drove whites farther inland. They were 90 percent of the population by the mid–eighteenth century in the wealthiest, most established plantation areas near the capital city of Charleston, and more than 60 percent in the entire region. The largest plantations in the British North American colonies were located in tidewater Carolina, where the subtropical heat and humidity in the summer were much like those in the areas from which these Africans had been taken. Those who had spent their childhood in these regions had generally developed some resistance to such diseases as malaria, giving them an advantage over the British, who had a high mortality rate from tropical diseases.[8]

Carolina's demand for slaves was so great that Charleston became the major port of entry for Africans brought to the American mainland from Africa and the Caribbean. By the time of the American Revolution almost one hundred thousand slaves had entered through Charleston harbor, most of them bound for the rice-growing regions of the colony. Its majority African population made it more like the Caribbean than other parts of North America. The great number of blacks in Carolina enabled Africans there to retain more of their languages and cultural practices for longer than perhaps anywhere else in North America. The plantations of Carolina became the home of large African slave communities, with internal social and political structures based on West African models. Especially in the low country of southern Carolina, an amalgam of African cultures shaped an American African culture. In Africa traditional rivalries might have made many of these people deadly enemies, but in Carolina their suffering and shared disadvantage brought them together.

The large number and high proportion of Africans in Carolina created other similarities with slavery in the West Indies—heightened white fears of slave rebellion and harsh measures to control the slave population. Rumors of slave unrest in Charleston in 1711 and 1720 led to death by burning for suspected rebels. White slaveholders' insecurity undoubtedly helps to explain the extremely harsh slave codes enacted in South Carolina in 1696, even harsher than the Barbadian codes on which they were modeled. These codes were so restrictive that some masters complained that they infringed on slaveholders' property rights. Slaves without written permission were restricted to their master's property, and any white person who discovered a slave violating this rule could whip the slave, although the punishment could not exceed twenty lashes. Fines were imposed on any white overseer who discovered an unknown slave on his plantation and did not report and whip the slave. No master could allow his slave to hunt except with a special license, renewed monthly. Masters were required to inspect all slave quarters regularly to ensure that no weapons were available to their slaves. Volumes of regulations detailed punishments ranging from whipping for many offenses, branding for petty theft, cutting off the right ear for the first offense of striking a white person, castration for a fourth escape attempt, and death for rape, attempted murder or murder of a white person. Those who administered punishment were not held liable if death resulted inadvertently. These sanctions were among the most draconian anywhere in the Americas.[9]

Yet even in South Carolina there was occasional evidence of surprising tolerance during the colonial era. One striking example of this was the establishment of a school in Charleston for area slaves. The plan, sponsored by the Society for the Propagation of the Gospel in Foreign Parts, an auxiliary of the

Anglican Church, was to train slaves in the Christian religion and to have them instructed by a slave specially educated to be the schoolmaster. In 1743 the school opened under the direction of Harry, considered a "genius" by some local whites, and the student body quickly rose to sixty. Although some whites were concerned about the experiment, the school continued for more than twenty years until Harry died in 1764. The coexistence of this school with South Carolina's harsh slave codes illustrates the contradictory nature of American slavery.[10]

On the southern border of South Carolina lay the colony of Georgia. Granted by the Crown to James Edward Oglethorpe in 1732, this colony was intended to serve an important military function as a strategic outpost separating British North America from Spanish Florida to its south, standing against the expansionist ambitions of one of England's most powerful rivals. Among its earliest British settlers were the abject poor of English society, many drawn from the nation's debtor's prisons. British liberal reformers saw this new land as an asylum in which these unfortunates of society might be rehabilitated. Their dream was to establish Georgia as a utopian community of independent small farmers. No one person could own more than five hundred acres, and the inheritance of land was restricted. To encourage hard work and civility among the settlers, alcoholic drink was outlawed, and in the interest of public tranquillity slavery was forbidden. Further, since white Georgians feared that Africans might join with the Indians and the Spanish in military action against them, both slaves and free blacks were prohibited from entering the colony.

This commitment to a slave-free colony was not universally accepted among the colonials, and many bent on rapid economic development argued for the necessity of slave labor. These "malcontents," as other Georgians called them, claimed that white laborers could not grow rice as profitably as slaves did in South Carolina. Opponents of slavery, motivated as much by antiblack prejudice as humanitarian sentiment, countered by citing the example of Austrian planters from Salzburg who were successfully growing rice in the small community of Ebenezer, near Savannah. After a decade of debate it became clear that the original vision of Georgia as a utopian community would not be sustained. In 1742 the ban on alcohol was lifted, and eight years later restrictions on slavery and large landholdings were repealed. Thereafter Georgia moved rapidly in the direction of other southern colonies, establishing large plantations where great numbers of slaves supplied the labor on which the wealth of a powerful planter class was based.[11]

North of the Chesapeake there were a few large plantations, but most slaveholdings were much smaller, and blacks accounted for a tiny proportion of the population, especially in New England. Whereas in 1750 slaves constituted

61 percent of the colonial population in South Carolina, 31 percent in Maryland, and 46 percent in Virginia, they were only 2 percent in Pennsylvania, 7 percent in New Jersey, and 14 percent in New York. In New England, except for Rhode Island's 10 percent, no colony's slave population exceeded 3 percent of the total. Although slavery was not the major enterprise in the northern colonies that it was in the South, it was still economically and socially important. Slavery became an issue for debate early in the life of Pennsylvania, a colony established by English Quakers on Maryland's northern border in 1661. In 1682 its founder and governor, William Penn, who had envisioned a refuge for Quakers persecuted in England, proposed to limit slavery in the colony. Two years later 150 Africans were imported to help clear the land. Penn preferred to have Pennsylvanians rely on indentured labor, with African indentures for fourteen years of service, and many blacks received land as their customary freedom dues. But demand for labor in the colony was too great to be satisfied by the supply of indentured servants. Within three years of his original proposal, Penn decided that perpetual slavery was more economical than temporary service, abandoned his plan, and became a slaveholder himself. As the number of white servants declined, Pennsylvania came more and more to rely on African slave labor, and its capital city of Philadelphia became a major slave-trading center.[12]

By the 1760s almost 8 percent of the inhabitants of Philadelphia were of African descent. Estimates of the black population in Pennsylvania vary widely, ranging from 2,500 to 5,000 in 1721 and 2,900 to 11,000 by mid-century. After that time a large and relatively sudden influx of German and Irish indentured servants reduced the demand for slaves and curbed the growth of the colony's black population. Whenever the supply of white servants was disrupted, however, Pennsylvania slaveholders imported more African slaves. Some Pennsylvanians expressed concern about the colony's growing number of slaves. In fact, as early as 1707 and 1722 white laborers complained of competition from slaves. Others expressed fears that the increasing number of Africans would bring a greater danger of slave rebellion. Acting partly on these fears and partly on a desire to generate revenue for the colony, the Pennsylvania Assembly imposed a tax on the importation of slaves. Still, the continuing demand for slave labor made it difficult to control the number of importations effectively. Pennsylvania's taxes were easily circumvented by landing slave cargos in neighboring New Jersey and smuggling them overland into the colony, and smuggling became so common that New Jersey seaside towns such as Perth Amboy and Cape May became major slave ports.[13]

Yet Pennsylvania's Quakers had always been uneasy about slavery, and their discomfort grew with the increasing slave population, while their disquiet moderated the institution. In fact many visitors reported that slavery in Penn's colony was milder by far than in colonies farther south. Many Quakers favored providing opportunities for the colony's blacks, and in the 1750s, Israel Acrelius, a visiting minister, was impressed by the better treatment of Pennsylvania slaves. In 1758 a Philadelphia Quaker educator, Anthony Benezet, established a school for blacks and used the educational achievement of his students as the basis for his arguments against the notion of African intellectual inferiority, calling it "a vulgar prejudice founded on . . . pride and ignorance."[14]

Sometimes the tolerance extended to slaves provided them with opportunities that approached independence. Many slaves were allowed to "hire out" their time, providing most of their earnings to their master but keeping a portion for themselves. Although slave marriages were not legal, there were apparently some efforts to prevent the separation of families when slaves were sold. So long as slaves did not seem dangerous, few restrictions were imposed on their movements, and they associated freely during their nonwork hours with family and friends among other slaves, free blacks, and even white servants. The lax enforcement of slave codes angered some colonists, but by the mid–eighteenth century sentiment against slavery had gained strength in Pennsylvania, and the annual Quaker meetings debated ways to discourage the importation of more African slaves and encourage the manumission of slaves already there. Despite an increase in antislavery sentiment, slave codes still restricted slaves in Pennsylvania. Slaves were clearly distinguished from free people in colonial law and were not guaranteed legal protection. Curfews; restrictions on slave gatherings; pass systems; and harsh penalties including whipping, castration (for attempted rape), and death (for burglary, murder, or rape) were used to control Pennsylvania's slave population, as they were in the southern plantation colonies.

Discussions among the Quakers continued, and by 1693 the Yearly Philadelphia Meeting asserted that no Quaker should buy slaves except as a means of freeing them. More radical Quakers called on all slaveholding members to free their slaves. During the 1730s Benjamin Lay, a Quaker from Barbados who had witnessed large-scale slavery, testified at one annual meeting after another about the horrors of the institution and once even abducted a slaveholder's child to dramatize the pain slavery caused to families. He was expelled from the meeting for this action and for the publication of *All Slave-Keepers That Keep the Innocent in Bondage,* in which he roundly condemned all Quakers who participated in or condoned slavery. Other influential Quakers opposed to slavery included John Woolman from New Jersey, whose writings on antislavery were widely read among Quakers, and Anthony Benezet. By 1758 the work of the Quaker antislavery activists bore fruit—Penn's Yearly

Meeting declared that Quakers who imported, bought, or sold slaves after that year should be expelled from the congregation. Further, it strongly suggested that slaveholding members free their slaves and provide them with Christian training. These were tentative steps, but they marked the start of a conviction among Quakers that spread from Pennsylvania throughout the middle colonies into New England and even into the South, where Quaker settlements became centers of antislavery philosophy.[15]

———

The middle colonies continued to import white servants throughout the pre-Revolutionary period. Interracial relationships developed as black slaves often worked with white laborers and indentured servants in ways not common on the larger southern plantations. These workers associated with one another in iron manufacturing in New Jersey and Pennsylvania, as dock laborers in New York City, and even in the skilled trades of the urban centers. Consequently Africans in the middle colonies were more likely to learn about English culture and to learn the English language faster and better than Africans in the large, insular African communities on southern plantations. Whereas most slaves in the South were required to know only enough English to be able to carry out the work-related orders of masters and overseers, in the middle colonies slaves often lived in the master's household and spent much of the day with European Americans.

Differences in background and experience help to explain the differences in linguistic abilities reflected in newspaper advertisements for runaway slaves. Blacks imported from the West Indies often spoke French and Spanish. One slave named John, who was born in Dominica and ran away soon after coming to Philadelphia in 1745, was described as speaking French well but only a little English. Another fugitive, it was said, spoke Spanish but no English, while a third was fluent in English, French, and Spanish. One runaway from Pennsylvania spoke both English and "Swede," and a New Jersey runaway, Claus, spoke "Dutch and good English." Blacks in the region that had been controlled by the Dutch frequently spoke both English and Dutch. When Toney left his master in Philadelphia, he was well-dressed in a "Striped Linsey Woolsy Jacket," a "Tow shirt," matching pants, and a felt hat. His distinguishing characteristics included his being "a likely lusty" twenty-four-year-old who spoke English and "High Dutch" (actually, proper German).[16]

Because the British colony of New York began as the Dutch corporate colony of New Netherland, slavery there had a slightly different foundation. Although the first eleven slaves were landed in New Netherland in 1626, slave labor was never an important part of the colony's economy. African slaves worked the Dutch West India Company's great Hudson River Valley estates as they did the plantations of the South, but most slaves were employed on smaller farms or were part of the Dutch military forces that defended the colony against the Indians during the early 1640s. The Dutch intended their reliance on slave labor to be temporary, but white workers moved quickly from agricultural work to trades, leaving the colony with too few farmhands and an unstable labor supply. By the 1640s the Dutch regularly imported African slaves to fill their labor needs.

The Dutch West India Company employed a flexible style of bondage called "half freedom." Africans were allowed to live independently in exchange for their agreement to pay a yearly tax and provide labor to the company when needed. Under these circumstances slaves' daily lives were much like those of free persons. Married slaves lived in family units and supported their own families. Despite the fact that the children of slaves bound under the system owed their labor to the company for life, it was still one of the mildest forms of slavery practiced in North America. If they were freed, blacks were accorded the same rights as whites in the colony. They could own property, pursue trades, and even intermarry with whites. Race was a factor in that being black carried with it the probability of being enslaved, but blacks were treated as free people so long as their white neighbors knew that they were free.[17]

In the 1660s England went to war against Holland, attempting to eliminate Dutch trade competition and to gain control of the Hudson River fur-trading region. When the British took over the colony in 1664, they gradually made slavery there conform to the system in their other American colonies, and slaves lost the advantages of the half-freedom arrangement. As the number of slaves increased, rising colonial anxieties encouraged harsh restrictions. In 1682 flogging was prescribed for any four or more slaves caught meeting together without white supervision. A sunset curfew was imposed on all adult slaves in New York City, but when that arrangement proved inconvenient for masters, the provision was changed, and slaves were required to carry lighted lanterns when they moved about the city after dark. A slave-regulating act was passed in 1702, in 1708 whipping became mandatory for minor infractions, and after 1710 colonial courts rejected several cases brought against masters by slaves claiming wages for unpaid labor. By the early eighteenth century virtually all that remained of New York's Dutch past were a few large estates in the Hudson Valley, Dutch cultural festivals and traditions, and the Dutch language spoken by many blacks and whites.[18]

Under the British during the first half of the eighteenth century, New York became the major slaveholding colony north of Maryland, with more than ten thousand slaves, constituting about 15 percent of the population by 1750. With continued growth, there were more than nineteen thousand slaves in New York on the eve of the Revolution. Slaves were provided with

Venture Smith, an African, Tells of His Capture and Enslavement

I was born at Dukandarra, in Guinea, about the year 1729. My father's name was Saungm Furro, Prince of the tribe of Dukandarra. My father had three wives. Polygamy was not uncommon in that country, especially among the rich, as every man was allowed to keep as many wives as he could maintain. . . . I descended from a very large, tall and stout race of beings, much larger than the generality of people in other parts of the globe, being commonly considerable above six feet in height, and every way well proportioned. . . .

[At word of a planned attack by an army supplied and incited by whites] my father and his family set off about the break of day. The king and his two younger wives went in one company, and my mother and her children in another. We left our dwellings in succession, and my father's company went on first. We directed our course for a large shrub plain, some distance off, where we intended to conceal ourselves from the approaching enemy, until we could refresh ourselves a little. But we presently found that our retreat was not secure. For having struck up a little fire for the purpose of cooking victuals, the enemy, who happened to be encamped a little distance off, had sent out a scouting party who discovered us by the smoke of the fire, just as we were extinguishing it and about to eat. As soon as we had finished eating, my father discovered the party and immediately began to discharge arrows at them. This was what I first saw, and it alarmed both me and the women, who, being unable to make any resistance immediately betook ourselves to the tall, thick reeds not far off, and left the old king to fight alone. For some time I beheld him from the reeds defending himself with great courage and firmness, till at last he was obliged to surrender himself into their hands.

They then came to us in the reeds, and the very first salute I had from them was a violent blow on the head with the fore part of a gun, and at the same time a grasp around the neck. I then had a rope put about my neck, as all the women in the thicket with me, and were immediately led to my father, who was likewise pinioned and haltered for leading . . . my father was closely interrogated respecting his money. . . . But as he gave them no account of it, he was instantly cut and pounded on his body with great inhumanity. . . . All this availed not in the least to make him give up his money . . . until the continued exercise and increase of torment obliged him to sink and expire. . . . I saw him while he was thus tortured to death. The shocking scene is to this day fresh in my memory. . . .

The army of the enemy was large, I should suppose consisting of about six thousand men. . . . After destroying the old prince, they decamped and

(continued)

immediately marched towards the sea, lying to the west, taking with them myself and the women prisoners. . . . The enemy had remarkable success in destroying the country wherever they went. For as far as they had penetrated they laid the habitations waste and captured the people. The distance they had now brought me was about four hundred miles. All the march I had very hard tasks imposed on me, which I must perform on pain of punishment, I was obliged to carry on my head a large flat stone used for grinding our corn, weighing, as I should suppose, as much as twenty-five pounds; besides victuals, mat and cooking utensils. Though I was pretty large and stout of my age, yet these burdens were very grievous to me, being only six years and a half old. . . .

[At the end of the long march and more slave-raiding battles, in a coastal settlement called Anamaboo] the enemy's provisions were then almost spent, as well as their strength. The inhabitants, knowing what conduct they had pursued, and what were their present intentions, improved the favorable opportunity, attacked them, and took enemy, prisoners, flocks and all their effects. I was then taken a second time. All of us were then put into the castle and kept for market. On a certain time, I and other prisoners were put on board a canoe, under our master, and rowed away to a vessel belonging to Rhode Island, commanded by Captain Collingwood, and the mate, Thomas Mumford. While we were going to the vessel, our master told us to appear to the best possible advantage for sale. I was bought on board by one Robertson Mumford, a steward of said vessel, for four gallons of rum and a piece of calico, and called VENTURE on account of his having purchased me with his own private venture. Thus I came by my name. All the slaves that were bought for that vessel's cargo were two hundred and sixty.

After all the business was ended on the coast of Africa, the ship sailed from thence to Barbadoes. After an ordinary passage, except great mortality by the small pox, which broke out on board, we arrived at the island of Barbadoes; but when we reached it, there were found, out of the two hundred and sixty that sailed from Africa, not more than two hundred alive. These were all sold, except myself and three more, to the planters there.

The vessel then sailed for Rhode Island, and arrived there after a comfortable passage. Here my master sent me to live with one of his sisters until he could carry me to Fisher's Island, the place of his residence. I had then completed my eighth year. After staying with his sister some time, I was taken to my master's place to live.

Venture Smith, *A Narrative of the Life and Adventures of Venture, A Native of Africa, But Resident Above Sixty Years in the United States of America. Related by Himself* (1798; reprint, Middletown, Conn.: J. S. Stewart, Printer and Bookbinder, 1897), 4–10.

virtually no legal protection, and no slave could testify against a free person in court. As in other northern colonies, slavery was not the basis of New York's economy, but slaves did provide an important part of the labor supply, and there were many slaveholders in the colony. In the rural areas outside New York City, slaves accounted for between one-fifth and one-third of the population. The estates on Long Island and in the Hudson River Valley, as well as those in the tobacco-growing areas of the Narragansett region of Rhode Island, continued to use large numbers of slaves throughout the eighteenth century, functioning more like the plantations of South Carolina than did most other regions in the North. New York City was the major urban slaveholding center. Only Charleston surpassed it in slave ownership, and although the proportion of slaveholders in New York City's population declined as the century progressed, the actual number of slaves in the city increased, so that by the mid–eighteenth century slaves were a common sight. In the early 1770s one foreign visitor to New York was surprised by slavery's visibility, remarking, "It rather hurts the European eye to see so many negro slaves upon the streets."[19]

There were fewer blacks in New England than in the Middle Colonies, but even there slavery was a familiar aspect of colonial life. From 1624, when Samuel Maverick became the region's first slaveholder, New Englanders imported small numbers of Africans, mainly from the British West Indies. The slave population increased slowly—only a few arrived each year before 1700, and only a few dozen each year during the first part of the eighteenth century. By 1700 there were barely one thousand Africans in all of New England; about half of those were in Massachusetts.

The Puritans of New England seem to have struggled more with the morality of slavery than did the planters of the Chesapeake or Carolina, though somewhat more legalistically than the Quakers in Pennsylvania. In the Massachusetts Body of Liberties of 1641, colonial authorities justified slavery only for those who sold themselves or who were taken captive in "just wars." Previously, in 1637, the colony's need for labor had encouraged a tortured interpretation of this principle, allowing several hundred Indian men captured during the Pequot wars to be taken to the West Indies and traded there for Africans who were then brought to New England as slaves. Pequot women and children captured during the wars remained in Massachusetts and were treated as servants. This interpretation hardly satisfied the spirit of the colony's principles, but it provided justification enough given the rising expense of white labor.[20] The Massachusetts General Court clarified this issue with a ruling in 1645 that the importation of slaves was legal so long as the purchase was made from "legitimate" slave traders. By 1670 the question of the status of children born to slave women and white men was resolved by following the precedent, set in Virginia, that such offspring took the status of their mother. Massachusetts set the example for other New England colonies, and by the early 1700s slavery was legal and well-established in the region. Economic pressures had overcome theological and philosophical reservations to allow slaveholding in the region, but the number of slaves remained very small. Massachusetts was the largest slaveholding colony in New England, but even in Boston, where slaves were concentrated, there were only 150 Africans by 1690 and fewer than 500 in 1710. The average slaveholder held only two slaves, and only about 12 percent of Boston's white population owned even a single slave.

With such small slaveholdings, slaves were as integrated into the colonial household and society in New England as they were in the Middle Colonies. This situation not only facilitated their learning English but often provided them with other advantages. The experiences of the slaves in the household of a physician in Plymouth, Massachusetts, provide examples of the potential benefits from this form of slavery. The slaves Pompey; Phyllis, his wife; Quasho; and Prince, the household cook, lived in two rooms above the kitchen in the home of Dr. LeBaron, a widower with many children. LeBaron exercised authority over his slaves, but he also allowed them privileges not generally granted to southern slaves. Phyllis controlled her own money and successfully invested in the business ventures available in the busy commercial port. With part of the profit she made for her share in the cargoes of a schooner, she bought a set of "Guinea-gold beads" that she wore along with her "portentous turban" to express her own African sense of beauty and style.[21]

When disagreements arose between a northern master and the slaves who lived in his household, compromises were likely to be reached, or the slaves might even be able to impose their own wills. When Dr. LeBaron decided to extend the classical allusions in his household by adding "Julius Caesar" to the Pompey already there, he suggested that Quasho accept that name. The slave refused, saying that his mother in Africa had called him by the name of Quasho Quando, and he did not intend to take another. LeBaron attempted unsuccessfully to change Quasho's mind with punishments ranging from the deprivation of food to whipping. He then tried bribery but finally dropped the matter.[22]

Although colonies in New England had fewer slaves, and they were less likely to be strictly controlled than in the South, African slaves were an integral part of New England's labor system. They worked mainly on small farms or as domestic servants, unskilled workers, or even skilled artisans in the cities.

> *Newport, July* 6, 1764.
> Juſt imported in the Sloop *Elizabeth*, from *Africa*, and to be ſold, by
> # John Miller,
> At his Houſe, or Store ;
> # A Number of healthy
> Negro Boys and Girls.
> Likewiſe to be ſold,—*Tillock's* and *Kippen's* Snuff, by the Caſk or Dozen.

"Just imported in the Sloop *Elizabeth,* from Africa," *Providence Gazette,* July 6, 1764.

Graphics Division, Rhode Island Historical Society, Providence.

Most whites in Massachusetts agreed with colonial Governor John Winthrop that the colony could not survive without "a stock of slaves sufficient to dow [*sic*] all our business."[23] Except perhaps in the areas with large estates, the economic importance of slavery in New England and New York was more a matter of slave trading than of slaveholding. New England sea captains often commanded the slave-trading vessels, merchants from New England and New York often financed the ventures, goods produced in these regions served as items traded for slaves, and vessels built in New England moved the trade across the ocean. Slaveholding was important to the trade, since African workers in New England provided labor for the distilling industry that turned West Indian sugar into rum. The New England ships that brought sugar to North America, finished goods and rum to Africa, and Africans to American slavery were built with slave labor.[24]

Although much of the colonial economy rested on slave labor, and many whites believed that slavery was the only suitable institution for controlling Africans, not all Africans were slaves. As slavery evolved and the number of slaves increased, especially in the plantation South, and legal measures for the protection of slaveholders' property rights were established, free blacks were increasingly seen as a threat to those rights. It became more difficult for slaves to gain their freedom, as a few had before the mid–seventeenth century. Thus, the development of slavery was closely tied to a deterioration of the rights of free blacks, and prosperous former slaves like the Anthony Johnson family of seventeenth-century Virginia became increasingly rare. In 1691 Virginia's General Court declared that no slave might be set free unless that freedom was accompanied by enough money to transport the freed slave out of the colony within six months of emancipation. In 1723 the judgment was strengthened by a declaration that a slave could only be manumitted for some "meritorious service" certified by colonial officials. Those blacks who did acquire their freedom were not truly free; their rights were severely restricted by special regulations devised to control them. In Virginia free blacks had no right to vote or to a jury trial, and they could be sold into slavery for minor infractions.

Since the free black population in Maryland was smaller than that in Virginia, it was less threatening, and there were fewer restrictions on the manumission of slaves. An attempt to prohibit emancipation failed to pass the colonial legislature in 1715, but by midcentury the requirement of special written freedom forms issued by the colonial authorities made freeing a slave more difficult. Concerns that freed slaves might become public charges prompted other regulations, requiring that a manumitted slave be healthy, capable of self-support, and not over fifty years of age. As in Virginia many of the restrictions placed on the movement of slaves also applied to free blacks, and these restrictions made it extremely difficult for them to find employment outside of indentured servitude.

A series of slave rebellions in Barbados from 1639 to the 1690s made South Carolina planters, many of whom came from that island, uneasy about their growing black population. They were especially concerned about the potentially disruptive influence of free blacks on their slaves and took measures to discourage the growth of the free black population. In 1715 the colony passed a regulation preventing the emancipation of any runaway or rebellious slave, although a master could free a slave for loyal and faithful service. Once freed, however, just as in Virginia, a black person was required to leave the colony within six months. In what might seem an unnecessary addition, a 1721 colonial statute limited the right to vote to "free white men."[25] Planters' apprehension intensified after a major slave uprising at the Stono River in South Carolina in 1739, and with the expanding number of African arrivals in the colony.[26] Between 1735 and 1740, slave traders brought twelve thousand Africans to work the South Carolina rice fields. In 1741 this prompted futile efforts on the part of colonial officials to control the size of the colony's black population by levying a tariff on further importations. Although the number of free blacks remained relatively small, the slave population soared. Within a decade Africans and their descendants accounted for almost two-thirds of South Carolina's population. Controls on slaves and free blacks were tightened, and a new law prohibited freeing any slave except for some exceptionally honorable service, and with official approval. Even such loyal slaves could only remain in the colony for six months after gaining their freedom.[27]

Despite the restrictions the number of free blacks increased all over the South, and a few even prospered. Some free blacks became landowners, a few grew wealthy, and a small number became slaveholders themselves. In North Carolina those few who could meet the property requirement became eligible to vote after 1737 when the king lifted the colony's prohibition against voting by blacks and Indians.[28] It is surprising that Carolina slaveholders tolerated even their small free black population in the eighteenth century, but some were tied by blood to the most powerful planters, who saw them as trusted allies, a protective buffer against slave rebellion. Though this trust was sometimes misplaced, as when free blacks were implicated in slave conspiracies, free blacks could often use it to their advantage.[29] Still, their lives and freedom were precarious, and restrictive and exclusionary laws could be enforced whenever the white minority felt threatened.

There were more free blacks south of Maryland and Virginia, but a larger percentage of the total black population was free in the Middle Colonies and in New England. Many factors encouraged the growth of a free black population in these areas—many blacks gained their freedom after serving their terms as indentured servants; Quaker opposition to, and Puritan reservations about, slavery led to fewer restrictions on manumissions. Philosophical and moral reservations also seemed more persuasive in regions where slavery was not the dominant labor system and where there were relatively few Africans.

Especially where there were small slaveholdings, the lives of free blacks and slaves were intertwined, and often they were members of the same family. Marriages involving slaves were not generally recognized in the colonies, and even under the best circumstances, they were maintained only at the master's convenience. The tenuous existence of slave families is illustrated by the advertisement in a New England newspaper offering for sale a "likely negro woman about 19 years and a child of about six months of age to be sold together or apart."[30] One way for free black people to protect slave members of their families was to secure their freedom, and free blacks often spent years working and saving to purchase the freedom of family members. Laws restricting free blacks often made it more difficult to gain the freedom of family members in the southern colonies. On occasion, because newly freed blacks could not legally remain in a colony, it was more efficient for a free black person to purchase a family member and hold that person as a slave. Such ownership would be a legal convenience allowing the newly purchased slave to remain with the family. Many of the slaves listed as the property of free blacks in South Carolina, Virginia, and elsewhere in the South were "owned" under these circumstances.

Dealing with the problem of enslaved family members was only one of many problems faced by free blacks. Even the most fortunate were not truly free to take advantage of opportunities open to whites. In New England, Lucy and Abijah Prince were well off by the standards of the day, though both had been slaves in Deerfield, Massachusetts. Lucy had been kidnapped into slavery at the age of five in her native Africa. She was known in Deerfield for her narrative poem describing the Indian attack she witnessed on the village in 1746. Abijah Prince gained his freedom through his master's will, which also gave him a sizable plot of land. This land provided the funds to buy Lucy's freedom and to give the couple a comfortable start when they married in 1756. The Princes acquired additional land in nearby Vermont, where they raised their six children and settled into a life as respectable members of the community. Despite their exemplary lives, when their oldest son, Caesar, reached college age, he was refused permission to enroll at Williams College in western Massachusetts. Not easily discouraged, Lucy set their case before the college trustees, presenting a three-hour argument drawing on the law and the Bible, but to no avail. The college held fast to its policy that no black person, no matter how qualified, could attend Williams.[31]

If the financially stable, determined Prince family faced obstacles to its advancement in New England, one of the most tolerant regions in the colonies, it is not surprising that less well-situated free blacks in less tolerant surroundings fared poorly. North or South, they were discriminated against, restricted, and generally despised. Free blacks were often limited to the least desirable sections of a town for their residences or to the least productive land in the countryside for their farms. In most public places they were segregated, and regardless of the weather they were relegated to the outside of carriages, the outside decks of ships, and the unsheltered decks of ferries. If they were allowed to attend white churches at all they were often limited to seats in the rear or in out-of-the-way areas, and they were barred from or segregated in places of public entertainment. More important economically, free blacks also faced occupational restrictions and were often unable to take up even the trades they had practiced in slavery. As early as 1717 the Connecticut colony required that blacks get special permission from colonial officials before they could open any business. Under such conditions it is not surprising that most free black people were poor, and they faced all the hardships of poor people as well as some problems peculiar to blacks. Many New England towns, for example, could simply order transient poor whites deemed undesirable, and any free blacks presumed to be undesirable, out of town.

The sea offered one of the few areas of employment open to free black men, and a great many worked as sailors throughout the eighteenth century. Unlike life ashore, life at sea was generally unsegregated, partly because of the limitations of the ships' quarters and partly because conditions for everyone were so harsh that any attempt at fine differentiation would have been futile. The sea offered some of the best opportunities for black men during the period, even though blacks were generally relegated to the lower ranks and the least desirable, most dangerous jobs and often got a smaller share of the profits from the voyage. For free black women, there were few desirable alternatives to domestic service, and black women provided the domestic labor for many rural and urban colonial households. In the South almost all of these women were slaves, but in the North both slaves and free women were in the domestic workforce. On occasion a skilled black woman might be employed as a seamstress or a weaver, among the most desirable jobs available to blacks in any region.

There was no clear place for free blacks in the society of the colonies. Yet they were not the only marginalized peoples in British North America—they shared this position with American Indians. Most of the Native Americans who had survived the wars with the English and exposure to European diseases lived on the fringes of colonial society, trading and occasionally working for the colonists, their presence on the frontier a constant source of conflict and concern. When officials were slow to act, frontier settlers—who continually demanded that colonial authorities protect them from local tribesmen—were sometimes willing to take matters into their own hands. Often the informal colonial forces that defended frontier settlements or attacked Native American neighbors included blacks as well as whites.

In 1676 Nathaniel Bacon, a white frontier planter, led an interracial army of poor whites, servants, and slaves against the Native Americans of western Virginia. Incensed when colonial authorities condemned his actions, Bacon turned his interracial force against the governing elites. The colonial governor declared Bacon and his men outlaws and moved against them with a substantial force. Bacon died and his army was defeated, but among those who held out longest were eighty blacks and twenty whites. This incident alerted Virginia's elites to the dangers of interracial alliances among the lower classes. In fact many laws were designed to control the perceived threat to the public order, and to slavery, represented by such relationships. In Virginia the first racially based laws prohibited interracial marriages. In 1705 Massachusetts also prohibited such relationships, providing that black men and women in interracial relationships be whipped and sold into slavery outside the colony. White men would be whipped, fined, and held responsible for any children resulting from the relationship, and white women would be whipped and bound into a period of indenture. A 1726 Pennsylvania law declared that any free black person who married a white person could be sold into slavery.[32]

Bacon's Rebellion also illustrates the complex, shifting interracial alliances that emerged during the eighteenth century. British colonials found both enemies and allies against rival Europeans among American Indians. Blacks often found common cause with Native Americans against white colonists, but even in the areas of greatest slaveholding, they sometimes helped defend the colonies against European or Native American enemies. In 1747, for example, South Carolina expressed formal appreciation to the black militiamen who "in times of war, behaved themselves with great faithfulness and courage, in repelling the attacks of his Majesty's enemies."[33] Both free blacks and Indians, however, were generally viewed with suspicion by white settlers. Indeed, the fact that they occupied similar statuses sometimes brought blacks and American Indians together in political and personal alliances. On occasion they were allied in military action, as in 1657, when a combined force attacked and burned part of Hartford, Connecticut; or in 1727, when blacks and Indians terrorized Virginia settlements. Fearful whites responded to such incidents with restrictive regulations. In 1690 several Connecticut settlements set a 9 P.M. curfew for both Indians and blacks. Boston officials prohibited blacks and Native Americans from carrying canes or sticks that might be used as weapons. In order to discourage slaves' attempts to escape to the Indians or to the French in Canada New Yorkers enacted harsh laws calling for the execution of any slave caught traveling forty miles north of Albany.[34]

Blacks and American Indians frequently developed close personal relationships as well. Large numbers of Native American men had been killed or exiled from New England in the wars in the seventeenth century, leaving a society with a gender imbalance heavily favoring women. The preference for importing male slave labor, on the other hand, resulted in a higher proportion of men in the area's black population during the late seventeenth and early eighteenth centuries. Colonial records document the significant number of American Indian–African marriages that resulted partly from these complementary imbalances. The customary practice of treating the offspring of these marriages as black was made official in 1719 in South Carolina by the colonial governor's proclamation that all those "not entirely Indian" would be counted as black. The records of colonial New Jersey indicate that that colony also listed those of Indian and African parentage as black. Under this provision Cyrus Bustill, Jr., the son of a black baker and a Delaware Indian woman, was listed on official documents as "negro." As an adult Bustill was a successful Quaker businessman, an advocate of antislavery, and a powerful spokesman for the black community.[35]

Some people of American Indian and African heritage functioned as members of both groups. Paul Cuffe of Massachusetts was born to a Native American mother and an African father. Although Paul spent most of his life outside Indian society, he claimed his Indian heritage and signed separate political petitions representing both Indian and African interests. Several of his siblings lived alternately in Indian and non-Indian settlements in Massachusetts.

His older brother, John, married an American Indian woman and remained with the Indians.[36] Intermarriage between blacks and American Indians was so common that treaties struck between colonial authorities and several Indian nations to prevent their sheltering fugitive slaves commonly threatened to separate families. Such treaties were generally ineffective, and cooperation between Africans and American Indians was always a potential source of instability for colonial slaveholding societies.[37]

By the middle of the eighteenth century, colonial British America had developed the beginnings of a distinctly American culture, a culture shaped by the influence of Africans and American Indians and by the limitations and possibilities of the New World. Black celebrations through the eighteenth and well into the nineteenth century illustrate one aspect of this cultural evolution. Negro elections or black coronation festivals were popular seasonal celebrations generally held in the spring or early summer. Especially in the northern colonies, but also in the Chesapeake region, slaves selected a ceremonial king or governor and celebrated with several days of merrymaking. In New Amsterdam (capital of New Netherland), Africans participated in a two-day observance of Paas (or Easter), vying for the honor of having baked the best Paas cake and competing in traditional Paas cake-throwing. The Dutch celebration of Pinkster, or Pentecost, in New Amsterdam and, later, New York and New Jersey, was eventually dominated by Africans and their traditions. Blacks celebrated all these festivals in similar ways, often electing "kings," sometimes from among families known to be from the ruling class in Africa. Celebrations combining African and European traditions and resembling those in the West Indies and Latin America featured parades with high stepping and baton twirling, athletic competitions, great feasts, and abundant music and dancing. Whites were often fascinated by the performances of African celebrants. One white observer in Albany, New York, reported that at one festival the slave king, a "Guinea man" dressed in an elaborate costume and wearing a yellow lace hat, led a long parade sitting astride one of the finest horses in the region provided for the occasion by his master. Later he led the "Guinea dance," an "original Congo dance as danced in [the slaves'] native Africa." Dancers were accompanied by music provided by musicians playing traditional African instruments including banjos, violins, and drums.[38]

What was less apparent to European observers of these celebrations was their connection to West African theology and religious practice and their function as a form of cultural resistance. Equiano observed the centrality of dance and music among his people not only for secular purposes but as sacred ritual. Singing, drumming, and dancing were part of the worship of African ancestors and gods. These were ancient expressions of spirituality. "So essential [were] music and dance to West African religious expression," the historian Albert J. Raboteau observed, "that it is no exaggeration to call them 'danced religions.'" These rituals helped form the connection between worlds. For the African enslaved in a foreign place, the music and dance of these African American celebrations provided outward expression of the African cultural traditions and familiar practices of worship passed down over generations of American slavery. Preserving these traditions provided links with African cultural homelands, helping African Americans resist slavery's attempt to define their identity. During the seventeenth and eighteenth centuries, African religions were more important than Christianity in the spiritual lives of the vast majority of American blacks. African religions were especially strong among the large African American populations of the lower South, where traditional African religious beliefs and forms of worship remained well into the nineteenth century.[39]

In the American colonies religion was just one aspect of many of these multilayered black celebrations. Some whites, especially indentured servants, attended and even participated in these celebrations, as a poem composed in 1760 made clear. According to the poet, the merrymakers were "of black and white, and every sort." Colonial officials were not comfortable with such associations of white and black servants. According to a white observer from Lynn, Massachusetts, "black celebrations" included so many of "the lower class of . . . our own complexion" that it alarmed the elite, who feared they might lead to dangerous political alliances among the "mean" classes against the "better" classes of the colonies. The eighteenth-century poet echoed these apprehensions, describing the revelers as "a motley crew of Whites and Blacks and Indians too."[40] Colonial elites also attended the festivals, perhaps to oversee such associations but also to enjoy the merriment—merriment undoubtedly made especially attractive by what these staid white European Americans perceived as African abandon. Children of the upper class were sometimes taken to the celebrations by black servants. Years later James Eights remembered a Pinkster celebration he attended as a boy with a household servant and his wonderment at the music, the baskets, and the other wares being sold by Native American families, and the exotic animals, including a lion and tiger, on display.[41]

Each group in the colonies contributed to the amalgam shaping American culture. Africans provided their knowledge of agriculture to make the rice culture of South Carolina profitable, and African techniques for inland river navigation greatly enhanced the ability of planters to move their goods to market.[42] Both African and American Indian medicine, though sometimes discounted by Europeans as superstition, were widely used and incorporated into eighteenth- and nineteenth-century American medical practice, especially in the southern colonies. Planters called on African doctors to treat their slaves

Slave cabins in Savannah, Georgia, reflecting traditional West African design.
Photographs and Prints Division, Library of Congress, Washington, D.C.

and their own families. In South Carolina a slave named Caesar was granted freedom and a cash reward for developing antidotes for several poisons based on African herbal cures. In Massachusetts, the Puritan minister Cotton Mather learned the principle of inoculation as a defense against smallpox from his black servant. Mather reported interviewing several Africans, who explained that the practice of inserting a small amount of material from an active smallpox pustule into a small cut on the arm of a healthy person was used with great success to prevent death from the disease in West Africa. Although the patients did become mildly ill they never developed smallpox. Africans used this rudimentary inoculation technique for protection against several diseases in other colonies in North America and in the West Indies. African medical knowledge, including the use of barks and herbs to treat everything from headaches to syphilis, eventually blended with European medical practices and a host of American Indian medicines to form early American medical practice.[43]

Though Americans of European origin probably owed the greatest part of their culture to their European roots, much of what they came to consider American had African roots. Before the end of the eighteenth century African music changed white Americans' musical sense. African foods like okra, collard greens, and yams became the foundation of American southern-style cooking and the American greeting "Howdy" was blended from the English "How do ye" and the African American "How de" or the Afro–West Indian "Hodi."[44] An emergent multiracial and multicultural America was apparent in the British colonies. This culture developed in the context of the important political and social changes facilitated by colonization. The lines of social status among whites that were so fundamental in England underwent a gradual erosion, a process already noticeable by the eve of the Revolution. The availability of cheap land dampened Europeans' willingness to accept extended indentures or to work for wages any longer than was necessary to become landholders. This propensity for personal independence encouraged a political commitment to individuality that by the late eighteenth century came to be known as the republican ideal. Ironically this passion for personal independence grew simultaneously with a reliance on a system of racially defined slave labor that became the very antithesis of freedom. The presence of an enslaved African people provided the contrast by which white Americans defined liberty. Black Americans, however, refused to accept a definition of liberty that excluded them, and they remained determined to claim freedom for themselves.

Chapter 3

1739   Slave rebellion in Stono, South Carolina

1741   Suspicious fires in New York City result in execution of thirty-one blacks and five whites convicted of slave conspiracy

1758   Pennsylvania Quakers demand that their members not hold or trade slaves; Quakers elsewhere follow over the next few decades

1765   British Parliament passes the Stamp Act; blacks participate in anti–Stamp Act protests

1770   African American population of British North America is 459,822 (more than 21 percent of the total population); 89 percent of blacks live in the southern colonies

Boston Massacre, five men killed, including escaped Massachusetts slave Crispus Attucks

1775–1783   American Revolution

1775   African Americans, led by Prince Hall, organize African Masonic Lodge No. 1 in Boston

Pennsylvania Abolition Society established in Philadelphia, first in nation; Benjamin Franklin becomes its president in 1787

1777   Vermont constitution abolishes slavery

Slavery and Freedom in the Age of Revolution

*J*ust before 10 A.M. on a Sunday morning in September 1739, William Bull, the lieutenant governor of South Carolina, and his four companions confronted their worst nightmare on the road near Charles Town (later called Charleston). Suddenly the horrified party faced an army of armed slaves, hesitated for a moment, and then wheeled their horses around and rode for their lives.[1] The slaves' military action had begun in the early morning hours, when twenty black men, captives from the Kingdom of Kongo, met at the Stono River about twenty miles west of Charles Town.[2] Led by an African named Jemmy, these former warriors hoped to take advantage of the distraction provided by the war being waged between Spain and Britain to fight their way to freedom.

Colonial Spanish Florida, bordering Georgia, was barely 150 miles south of South Carolina. Hoping to disrupt the British plantation economy, in 1693 the Spanish Crown granted freedom to slaves who ran away from the British colonies. Thereafter many South Carolina fugitives escaped to Fort Mose, near St. Augustine; and in 1738 the Spanish governor of Florida granted these blacks homesteading lands where they founded Gracia Real de Santa Teresa de Mose. Fiercely loyal to the Spanish Crown, this first free black settlement in colonial North America became an asylum for fugitives, who formed a sizable military force to man its garrison. The Spanish Fort Mose discouraged the British raids that endangered settlements in the St. Augustine area throughout the early eighteenth century.[3]

Hoping ultimately to make their way to Florida and the protection of the Spaniards, the South Carolina rebels near the Stono first broke into a store to acquire guns and ammunition and killed two shopkeepers in the process. As they marched south they stopped at plantations, and other slaves joined them. By midmorning at least fifty boldly marched down the road "with Colours displayed, and two Drums beating."[4] Their banners were "like the unit flags that African armies flew in their campaigns."[5] By afternoon they numbered more than a hundred. Those of the original rebels who had been soldiers in their Kongo homeland provided the battle strategy. They were skilled with firearms and conversant with Kongolese military rituals, and they joined in the traditional battle dance that in Africa served as a military drill in preparation for meeting the colonial militia that had formed during the day. Most of the large slave army that engaged the militia, however, were agricultural workers without military training. The initial battle took place in an open area, leaving the Kongo men, who traditionally fought in a skirmish style, without cover against a force of superior arms. Forty blacks fell in the initial engagement. As they were driven from the field, military men withdrew to regroup, but many untrained fighters fell away, hoping to return to their masters with their rebellion undiscovered. The military men marched thirty miles toward Florida before they were overtaken by the militia. Most of the rebels were killed, but some escaped to the swamp and the woods. A year later, colonial authorities were still pursuing members of the fugitive band, and one rebel eluded capture for more than three years.[6]

The rebellion at the Stono River reinforced fears among planters of both the possibility of slave rebellion and the threat of Spanish invasion. Within a year James Oglethorpe led the South Carolina and Georgia militia in a land and sea attack on Fort Mose and drove the black forces out of the settlement to the safety of nearby St. Augustine. Spanish blacks rebuilt the fort, but British raids continued intermittently throughout the next two decades. In 1742 South Carolina was again shaken by word that a Spanish force, with at least one black battalion, threatened an invasion. These uncertain times prompted colonial authorities to place greater restrictions on slaves and free blacks. Instability may also have prompted some efforts to forestall rebellion, perhaps explaining the 1740 regulation that provided fines for slaveholders who failed to give slaves sufficient food or clothing or to allow them the customary Sundays off from work.[7]

The threat of slave uprising and the growing size of the colony's black majority made most South Carolina slave masters intolerant of any perceived challenge to their control over slaves. When, during this period, evangelical missionaries moved into the colony seeking to convert not only whites but blacks as well, planter reaction was decidedly cool. Hugh and Jonathan Bryan were at first persuaded by Methodist preacher George Whitefield that their slaves ought to be brought to Christianity. When planters in the vicinity suspected that the slaves were drawn mainly by what they took to be an evangelical antislavery message, however, the experiment was brought to an abrupt conclusion. Still, elsewhere in the colonies evangelical missionaries were successful in converting thousands of whites and many blacks.[8]

A religious fervor called the First Great Awakening emerged in England during the 1720s and brought a new spirit of equality and democracy to the American colonies in the 1740s and 1750s. Revivals swept in with plainspoken, emotion-laden preaching, a contempt for formal church hierarchy, and a greater emphasis on believers' ability to communicate directly with God. The new sects formed under this movement, the Methodists and the extremely decentralized Baptists, converted thousands in the British North American colonies. Their appeal was especially strong for ordinary white people, and they even made converts among less isolated African Americans in northern colonies and in the Chesapeake region. The strength of African cultures in the large slave communities of the Lower South, however, hampered conversions there.[9] Evangelical revival services of prayer, song, and testimonials, often held in tent encampments, created a far different atmosphere from the more staid services of established churches. Some of the difference was attributable to the democratic nature of participation; congregations included blacks and Native Americans as well as whites; slaves as well as free people; and men, women, and children. Some of the difference was due to the influence of African music and styles of worship. Much as whites were drawn to African performances in the celebrations of Pinkster and governors' elections, evangelicals found that the style of worship practiced by Africans and African Americans was a great attraction to white yeoman farmers, servants, and the nonelites. Some preachers relied on the participation of blacks to help "bring down the spirit," allowing whites in the congregation to throw off their inhibitions, commit themselves fully to the religious spirit, and accept the call to God's salvation.[10]

Informal evangelical worship practices allowed interracial gatherings to incorporate many aspects of African spirituality and worship styles, such as call-and-response singing, and this form and context gave the message of Christianity greater appeal to the slaves. Particularly in the Upper South, evangelical religion became a mixture of African and European practices, providing another arena for interracial interaction. Massive numbers of white people were attracted to the simple, more democratic theology and the more emotional worship style, which might include both music and dancing. Fearing such associations and disapproving of such practices, many of the churchgoing colonial elite vehemently objected to this brand of worship.

An especially dangerous aspect of evangelical religions in the eyes of the elites was that virtually anyone seemed to be able to assume a position of leadership. One Boston reporter was upset by the fact that "there are among the exhorters . . . young persons, sometimes lads, or rather boys; nay women and girls; yea, Negroes, have taken upon them to do the business of preachers." From the perspective of the established clergy and other colonial authorities, this was the unmistakable sign of their diminishing control over potentially dangerous elements of society, as "private persons of no education and but low attainments in knowledge" were allowed to preach the gospel.[11] The stand that many evangelical preachers took against slavery, even in the South, provided sure proof of the dangers. For those already uncomfortable with the work of educating slave children and adults, being conducted by the Anglican Church's Society for the Propagation of the Gospel in Foreign Parts, the antislavery language of the evangelicals was especially disconcerting.

The interaction of blacks and whites, especially poor servants and slaves, in religious gatherings, festivals, and cooperative political actions, was so prevalent in the North during the colonial period that authorities passed legislation to block such alliances, much as they had done to curb black and Native American interaction. An ordinance adopted in Rhode Island in 1708 forbade any free person, white or black, from entertaining a slave except in the presence of the slave's master, but such regulations did not keep evangelical reformers from their ministry among servants and slaves. Sarah Osborn of Newport, Rhode Island, was one who opened her home to the poor of all stations and conditions. She conducted a school during the week and held educational religious services on Sunday evenings. An average of seventy African Americans attended her Sunday evening gatherings by the 1760s. From these meetings sprang a small religious community of free blacks and slaves, many of whom became prominent in the religious life and the antislavery struggle of the revolutionary period. Newport Gardner, a slave who later gained his freedom and opened a music school for black and white students, regularly attended Osborn's religious meetings. Also a part of this group was a young African-born woman named Obour Tanner, who occasionally held her own services. Tanner's preaching deeply affected Phillis Wheatley, a Boston slave who was also a well-known poet, and the evangelical message often appeared in her poetry. This evangelicalism brought blacks and whites together in religious worship in a manner that allowed them near equality in their participation. The potential social disruption of evangelical practice was exacerbated by the nature of the evangelical message itself: a theological equality that became part of the foundation of early antislavery thought.

There is little doubt that colonial authorities feared the potential disruptiveness of interracial associations, although moralistic arguments often obscured their political concerns. In New York officials claimed that such socializing was "destructive to the morals of servants and slaves." The influential editors of the *New York Weekly Journal* described these associations as "the principal bane and pest of the city."[12] Elite concerns were well founded, since there were many occasions when interracial actions challenged colonial authority. In New York City two white saloon keepers, John Romme and John Hughson, operated theft rings that included a number of slaves and free blacks. Romme and Hughson made arrangements to sell the stolen goods supplied to them by their associates. By the 1740s each man's tavern served as a criminal headquarters catering to an interracial clientele that included street gangs. Hughson's pub was especially popular with New York slaves, and on their Sundays off many spent the afternoon after church services enjoying the special dinner served there. Blacks and whites partook of goose and mutton served with freshly baked bread, rum, cider, and punch. There were music, dancing, and conversations about unjust masters and inconsiderate bosses, all reinforcing the commonalities of their social and economic status.[13]

These commonalities were said to have shaped the discussions at Hughson's tavern into a major "slave plot" to burn New York City and kill many of its white inhabitants in 1741. Mary Burton, who lived at the tavern, informed the authorities of the plot, which she insisted she had overheard being discussed by three black Spanish sailors. A major investigation concluded that this plot was indeed being planned, and 150 blacks and 25 whites were prosecuted for their alleged roles in the conspiracy. Although the evidence presented at the trial was circumstantial at best, 32 blacks and 4 whites (including Hughson and his wife) were executed. Historians disagree about whether there was actually a plot or whether it was an exaggeration of a scheme to cover criminal activity and made believable by the general fear of such plots. There may well have been some New Yorkers old enough to remember the attack on the city in 1712, when slaves and Indians set fires, killing 9 whites and wounding several others. The proven existence of the 1712 slave plot lent credibility to testimony about the 1741 plot. Real or not, anxiety about interracial joint action was strong enough to create near panic among the white citizens of New York: strong enough to lead to the execution of thirty-six people.[14]

Attacks by the resentful poor became an increasing threat to authorities during the mid–eighteenth century as wealth and power became more concentrated in the hands of those at the top of colonial society, a trend reflected in the tax rolls, and an increasing display of wealth. The economic disparity was most apparent in the South, but after midcentury it was clear everywhere that the poor were less likely to rise above poverty than they had been before. In the cities growing relief roles testified to the relative permanence of poverty—three times as many people received relief in Philadelphia in 1765 as had in 1750.[15] The consolidation of wealth was accompanied by a concentration of power, and economic and political advantages were reflected in the application of the law, as colonial courts were likely to favor those of higher rank over those of lesser status.[16] In 1767, for example, the court refused to render a judgment against a military officer and governor designate on behalf of a "yeoman." The court justified its refusal on the grounds that a "[g]entleman by office" might "abate [such a] writ." Gentlemen also seem to have been immune from certain punishments routinely prescribed for crimes. Although whipping was a common sentence for those found guilty of even petty offenses in New York, and gentlemen were occasionally found guilty of such offenses, no gentleman was ever whipped in colonial New York City.[17]

The increasing distance between rich and poor did not go unnoticed by those at the bottom of colonial society, and officials were concerned about a "general murmuring against the government and the rich people." The problem was evident as early as the 1730s, when unemployment and inflation worked a special hardship on the poor in some cities, while yeomen farmers in the surrounding countryside received decreasing prices for their produce from urban merchants. Poor people from Boston tried to solve this problem by bypassing local merchants, traveling into the farm areas, and buying directly from producers, but by the end of the decade evidence of the merchants' continued price manipulation provoked them to mob action. Like those who gathered in Romme's tavern in New York, according to contemporary accounts, these poor urbanites who eventually forced price reforms were "young People, Servants and Negroes."[18]

Another important issue that prompted interracial action was British impressment, the practice of drafting young men into British naval service in a summary fashion that amounted to virtual kidnapping. British "press gangs" roamed rural areas and towns, taking young men whenever naval personnel needs required it. Men were taken immediately and without warning, fathers forced to leave their work in the fields, sons forced from their dinner tables. Taverns and other places where the common people gathered were the favored sources of manpower, and poor people of all races were vulnerable. Public reaction to impressment was strong and often violent. In the 1740s Bostonians battled press gangs in the streets in what one inquiry called a "riotous, tumultuous assembly of foreign seamen, servants, Negroes and other persons of mean and vile condition." At one point in the melee several thousand people attacked the governor's house. Local authorities expressed sympathy for those unfairly impressed, but they vigorously condemned this interracial, lower-class mob violence.[19] In the 1760s impressment attempts provoked riots in Maine, New York, Maryland, and Virginia. Five hundred "seamen, boys and Negroes" resisted the press gangs in Newport, Rhode Island, in the summer of 1765. Clearly this was an issue that galvanized popular opinion into concerted action. While the revolutionary cry of "No taxation without representation!" might have rallied those in the middle and upper ranks of colonial society in the 1770s, in the eyes of the poor impressment was the most serious sign of English disregard for American freedom. For the poor impressment was at least as devastating as the taxes imposed by Britain.

Developments in the colonies by the 1770s had created some divergence of interests between groups of colonists, according to their place in the
economy. Poor people reacted most strongly to colonial policies that inflated
prices, threatened jobs, and deprived them of their liberty. All colonials were
concerned with these issues, but the elites were not generally sympathetic to
the freedom demanded by slaves and servants. They were determined to
wrest additional political power from England and to establish control over
trade policies. In the years after the mid–eighteenth century the growing numbers of middling Americans, not at the bottom but below the elite, were less
likely to protest impressment than they were to react when the crown tightened controls on the American economy and threatened what they saw as the
"rights of Englishmen." Nevertheless they often joined the poor in mass
action, especially on economic issues.

In 1765, when Parliament passed the Stamp Act in an attempt to force the
colonies to reimburse the Crown for expenses incurred during the French and
Indian War (1754–1763), colonials claimed that Britain had no right to levy
a tax designed to raise revenue rather than to regulate trade. The regulation
required that fees be collected in the colonies, as they were in Britain, for stamps
to be affixed to newspapers, wills, contracts, marriage licenses, and other legal
documents. This had the effect of raising the cost of doing business and was
especially burdensome for merchants and lawyers. Although poor people were
seldom involved in such transactions, colonial leaders fostered their opposition by drawing a parallel between the Stamp Act and impressment, arguing that in both cases Britain ignored the rights of Americans. The resulting
mob actions that erupted all over the colonies included a far more diverse group
of protesters than had many earlier actions, bringing together black and
white, poor and nonpoor. In New York City mob leaders, who were beginning
to be thought of as revolutionaries, gathered at the Queen's Head Tavern to
lay plans and discuss strategy. Owned and operated by "Black Sam" Fraunces,
a West Indian mulatto, the tavern became notorious as the revolutionaries'
headquarters during the 1760s and 1770s. From the Queen's Head, New
Yorkers launched their equivalent of the Boston Tea Party in 1774.[20]

As the political debate between the colonies and the mother country over
economic control continued, colonial leaders called on the mobs with increasing frequency. Mob actions supported the cause of well-to-do colonials, but
mob participants often had their own interests, and mobs always presented
the troubling prospect of uncontrolled popular excess. Samuel Adams and other
members of the "better" classes who had ties to the lower ranks attempted
to direct the mob but occasionally lost control, as in 1770 when sailors,
dock workers, and the unemployed attacked British soldiers in Boston. This
particular revolutionary mob was reacting to the specific grievances of its

ers, and its leader was not controlled or trusted by the colonial elites. was Crispus Attucks, a former slave in his late forties who had escaped from his master outside Boston in 1750 and had remained free for twenty years. In an ad placed by his master in the *Boston Gazette and Weekly Journal* the year he escaped, he was described as a "well set" mulatto, twenty-seven years old, six feet two inches tall, with short curly hair and "knees nearer together than common." Attucks was part African and part Nantucket Indian, and during the years of his freedom he worked as a seaman on whalers sailing out of Boston and in a rope factory in the city's North End.[21]

As a seaman Crispus Attucks faced the danger of impressment, the economic pain of inflation at the end of the French and Indian War in 1763, and the uncertainty of irregular employment. When Britain redoubled its efforts to regulate colonial trade under the Navigation Acts and other tax legislation, it dispatched soldiers to American ports. In Boston, as elsewhere, British troops were a constant reminder of the authority of the Crown and the power of the Parliament over daily life in the colonies. For ordinary working people the soldiers were also competitors in the job market. With full-time employment to satisfy most of their needs, soldiers could afford to accept part-time work below the customary wages. This competition for jobs lowered the wages that employers were willing to pay and imposed great hardships on the colonial work force. This was an important aspect of workers' resentment of British soldiers and contributed greatly to the tensions between the two groups. In Boston during the winter of 1770, seamen and laborers instigated sporadic attacks on the British troops.

These were the issues that dominated the conversation of the seamen and laborers who gathered to drink in a Boston pub on the afternoon of March 5, 1770. Tempers flared when an unsuspecting newly arrived British soldier entered the pub, ordered a drink, and inquired about part-time employment in the city. The crowd became hostile; one seaman suggested that the soldier clean his outhouse, another made similarly insulting propositions. Confronted by such anger, the young soldier left the pub. For the rest of the afternoon and into the early evening, the men continued drinking, and their talk became bolder. Finally the club-wielding crowd of twenty or thirty "saucy boys, negroes and mulattoes, Irish teagues and outlandish jack-tarrs," led by the former slave Crispus Attucks, spilled into the street and snaked its way to the Customs House on King Street. There they confronted the British soldiers standing guard. Attucks took the lead in harassing the sentries, poking one of them with a stick and calling him a "lobster," an allusion to the British soldiers' red coats. Some threw snowballs, then chunks of ice, and finally stones. The situation escalated rapidly— "the multitude shouting and huzzaing, threatening life, the bell ringing, the mob whistling and screaming like an Indian yell,

Eighteenth-century romanticized sketch of the Boston Massacre of 1770.
Prints and Photographs Division, Library of Congress, Washington, D.C.

the people from all quarters throwing every species of rubbish they could pick up in the street." "The way to get rid of these soldiers is to attack the main-guard," Attucks shouted. "[S]trike at the root: this is the nest."[22]

Deadly violence swiftly followed. As word of the Customs House con-frontation spread, crowds gathered in other parts of the city to challenge British soldiers, and in one skirmish a soldier stabbed a young boy with his bayonet. At the Customs House Attucks and his compatriots grew still bolder until finally a British officer, fearing the mounting danger to his troops, gave the order to fire into the crowd. When the order was ignored it was given again, but once more the soldiers failed to react. The people in the crowd assumed the troops would retreat, not fire, but they were wrong. A third order rang out: "Damn you, fire, be the consequence what it will." This time soldiers responded with a volley; three in the crowd were killed, and two others were wounded. Attucks was hit twice and died instantly, the first casualty in what became the revolutionary cause of American independence.[23]

The events of March 5, 1770, became known as the Boston Massacre, mythologized not as the reckless actions of a few intoxicated seamen and labor-ers, but as the symbol of American colonists' willingness to stand up to armed troops to oppose British tyranny. Attucks's role was central to the event and is crucial for the understanding of the social and political relations in the late eighteenth century. When Massachusetts held a trial, the British soldiers were defended by Boston attorney John Adams, a future revolutionary leader. Adams was troubled by the Crown's disregard for the rights of the colonials as English citizens, but he was even more disturbed by the increasingly frequent "mob violence." He denounced the mob's taunts and rock throwing, and condemned Attucks for having "undertaken to be the hero of the night," but he expressed no surprise that the mob was interracial or that its leader was an African American.[24] Nor were racial distinctions made during the funeral services held for those who died at the Boston Massacre. Despite Adams's condemnation the fallen were treated as patriots. Their funeral procession was a "vast multitude of people, walking, six deep, and a long train of carriages belonging to the principal gentry of the town." Their bodies were given a place of honor in one of the city's most prestigious cemeteries. The ceremony, it was said, attracted "the greatest concourse which had then ever assembled upon one occasion in America." Crispus Attucks was buried along with the three other fallen patriots.[25]

John Adams later acknowledged that the Boston Massacre opened the rift with England that became American independence. The presence of the British army continued to be an irritant; as Sam Adams put it, a standing army was "always dangerous to the liberties of the people." During the 1770s even those who feared the excesses of the mob came to accept them as useful to building the revolution. In his diary John Adams recorded a letter to the royal governor of Massachusetts, Thomas Hutchinson, signed with the name "Crispus Attucks." Holding Hutchinson responsible for the troops under his authority, and arguing that his crimes against "the people in general" were "chargeable before God and man, with our blood," the letter was dated 1773, three years after Attucks was killed. Thus it is likely that Adams wrote the letter and signed Attucks's name recognizing the former slave as a revolutionary symbol and acknowledging the important role blacks played in the cause of American freedom.[26]

As the rhetoric of revolution escalated, whites concerned about the loss of their freedom used the word "slavery" to describe the relationship with Britain they wished to avoid. African Americans pointed out the hypocrisy inherent in the use by slaveholders of the rhetoric of slavery and freedom.[27] In 1773 and 1774 Massachusetts slaves confronted colonial authorities with the question of their freedom. "We expect great things from men who have made such a noble stand against the designs of their fellow men to enslave them," they declared. Their demands were not revolutionary, simply that slaves be allowed one day a week to labor for their own benefit so they might accumulate funds to purchase their own freedom. This petition was refused, but

Petition for Freedom by Massachusetts Slaves

Boston, April 20th, 1773

Sir, The efforts made by the legislative of this province in their last sessions to free themselves from slavery, gave us, who are in that deplorable state, a high degree of satisfaction. We expect great things from men who have made such a noble stand against the designs of their *fellow-men* to enslave them. We cannot but wish and hope, Sir, that you will have the same grand object, we mean civil and religious liberty, in view in your next session. The divine spirit of *freedom,* seems to fire every humane breast on this continent, except such as are bribed to assist in executing the execrable plan.

We are very sensible that it would be highly detrimental to our present masters, if we were allowed to demand all that of *right* belongs to us for past services; this we disclaim. Even the *Spaniards,* who have not those sublime ideas of freedom that English men have, are conscious that they have no right to all the services of their fellow-men, we mean the *Africans,* whom they have purchased with their money; therefore they allow them one day in a week to work for themselves, to enable them to earn money to purchase the residue of their time, which they have a right to demand in such portions as they are able to pay for (a due appraizement of their services being first made, which always stands at the purchase money). We do not pretend to dictate to you Sir, or to the Honorable Assembly, of which you are a member. We acknowledge our obligations to you for what you have already done, but as the people of this province seem to be actuated by the principles of equity and justice, we cannot but expect your house will again take our deplorable case into serious consideration, and give us that ample relief which, *as men,* we have a natural right to.

But since the wise and righteous governor of the universe, has permitted our fellow men to make us slaves, we bow in submission to him, and determine to behave in such a manner as that we may have reason to expect the divine approbation of, and assistance in, our peaceable and lawful attempts to gain our freedom.

We are willing to submit to such regulations and laws, as may be made relative to us, until we leave the province, which we determine to do as soon as we can, from our joynt labours procure money to transport ourselves to some part of the Coast of *Africa,* where we propose a settlement. We are very desirous that you should have instructions relative to us, from your town, therefore we pray you to communicate this letter to them, and ask this favor for us.

(continued)

(continued)

In behalf of our fellow slaves in this province, and by order of their Committee.

Peter Bestes,
Sambo Freeman,
Felix Holbrook,
Chester Joie.

For the Representative of the town of Thompson

Herbert Aptheker, ed., *A Documentary History of the Negro People in the United States* (New York: Citadel Press, 1951), vol. 1, 7–8.

others followed, each carefully worded to highlight the parallels between their cause and the colonists' desire for a "free and Christian country."[28]

Colonials organized Committees of Correspondence to protest Britain's denial of their rights as Englishmen, while Africans in Massachusetts called on the Enlightenment ideal of the natural rights of man to petition for an end to their enslavement. Some colonial leaders had made the connection between their desire for freedom from English tyranny and the slaves' longing for liberty. When James Otis asserted in 1765 that all those born in the colonies were "British subjects" entitled to civil rights, he concluded that all blacks as well as whites were "by the law of nature free born" and argued therefore that slavery must be ended. Abigail Adams pointed forcefully to the incongruity in a letter to her husband in 1774: "It always seemed a most iniquitous scheme to me to fight ourselves for what we are daily robbing and plundering from those who have as good a right to freedom as we have."[29]

African Americans found themselves in a complex situation at the start of the Revolution. They had grievances against both the British and the Americans. When Parliament closed down the Port of Boston as a punishment for the Boston Tea Party, black seamen and dock laborers suffered the consequences just as their white counterparts did. Both blacks and whites were endangered by impressment and angered by the passage of the punitive "Intolerable Acts" forced on the colonies in 1774. Despite their shared circumstances, however, most American patriots seemed willing to pursue freedom from England without acting against slavery at home. Black protests created fears among some southern patriots. After "some Negroes had mimicked their betters in crying Liberty," as Henry Laurens of South Carolina put it, their focus shifted from the threat of British tyranny to the more pressing prospect of slave insurrection at home.[30]

Phillis Wheatley

In the summer of 1761, a young African girl no more than seven or eight years old arrived in Boston on the ship *Phillis*. Slave traders had captured her in the Gambia River region of West Africa in the Fulani nation. In Boston, John and Susanna Wheatley bought her and called her by the name of the ship that brought her to the colonies. Phillis was extraordinarily bright, and the Wheatleys allowed her to learn to read and write. Within sixteen months she was proficient in English, and within three years was literate in Latin. In 1767 Phillis published a poem in Rhode Island's *Newport Mercury*, and by the mid-1770s published several others, many about freedom. She joined Boston's Old South Church, where the Wheatleys were members. The church served as a forum for patriotic meetings during the 1770s, although John and Susanna Wheatley remained loyal to Britain. In 1772 Phillis accompanied her owners to England, where she met the British abolitionist Granville Sharp and Benjamin Franklin, who was in London at the time. Franklin was impressed by her talent, and the Londoners helped her publish a book, *Poems on Various Subjects, Religious and Moral,* in 1773. Phillis returned to Boston as America's first black published author, and that fall, the Wheatleys granted her freedom.

Then in her early twenties, Phillis Wheatley strongly supported the American Revolution. Her poem dedicated to George Washington drew an enthusiastic reception from the commander of the Continental forces and an invitation to visit him at his headquarters. Her views on freedom may have influenced Washington's personal struggle over slavery. In 1778 Phillis Wheatley married John Peters, a free black man. The couple struggled financially while Phillis worked on an ambitious three-hundred-page manuscript, a project she did not live to publish. She died in childbirth in Boston in 1784. One of her last poems, written in honor of the Treaty of Paris, ending the Revolution, was entitled "Liberty and Peace." As manumission societies were formed at the end of the eighteenth century, Phillis Wheatley came to symbolize the Africans' longing for freedom and became a reminder of talents to which the slave system generally denied expression.

Frontispiece from a book of poems written by Phillis Wheatley in 1773. Prints and Photographs Division, Library of Congress, Washington, D.C.

The ambivalence many blacks felt toward the American cause continued as political protest became a war for independence. Africans and African descendants took up arms along with their fellow Americans when the British marched through Lexington, Massachusetts, on their way to capture American arms in the nearby town of Concord. Some were Minutemen who served with the special militia, while others volunteered as the British army approached. Massachusetts black men, like Peter Salem of Framingham, Samuel Craft of Newton, and Cato Wood and Cuff Whittemore of Arlington, stood their ground in Lexington and Concord with their white compatriots when the "shot heard around the world" was fired, signaling the beginning of the Revolutionary War. "Prince the Negro" was wounded in the battle that followed. Titus Coburn, Salem Poor, Grant Cooper, and Peter Salem, who eventually served seven years in the Continental army, were among those who held out against the British at the Battle of Bunker Hill, near Boston. Several blacks who participated in the battle were commended for bravery, and Peter Salem's hometown later erected a monument to his courage as a Revolutionary soldier.[31]

Despite blacks' participation in initial Revolutionary military actions, their presence in the Continental forces was questioned. On July 9, 1775, just five days after he was appointed commander of the American troops, George Washington, a slaveholder from Virginia, ordered that although those already on active duty might remain, no new black recruits should be enlisted. Black participation was heatedly debated by the Continental Congress. Representatives from southern areas struggling to control their large slave population were keenly aware of the danger of arming blacks. At the same time they contended that blacks were too servile and timid by nature to make good soldiers and asserted that white southern military men could not be induced to serve beside black soldiers. Edward Rutledge, the delegate from South Carolina, led southerners in demanding that all slaves and free blacks be removed from the army. Northerners, less fearful of slave revolt, were more likely to see the benefits of black enlistment and argued that blacks had proved their worth in early battles. The attempt to remove blacks failed, and Washington's compromise stood as a recognition of the courage of the African Americans who had already served. The strength of southern fears is apparent in light of the fact that blacks had already served in all the colonial wars, including King William's War (1690–1697), Queen Anne's War (1702–1713), King George's War (1744–1748), and the French and Indian War (1755–1763). In 1747 South Carolina had officially thanked black troops for helping defend the colony. Further, Africans had formed the major body of the Spanish army in the American Southwest as early as the sixteenth century, had served the Dutch in New Netherland before British occupation, and were used by the British in Barbados. Given this evidence it seems likely that it was the fear of arming slaves, not skepticism over their fitness for military service, that was at issue.

White southerners had good reason to be concerned about arming slaves and to fear the specter of interracial uprisings. There were many rumors about servant and slave conspiracies planning to provide military service to the British and to strike against southern plantations. According to one southerner many believed that the "malicious and imprudent speeches of some among the lower classes of whites . . . induced [the slaves] to believe that their freedom depended on the success of the King's troops."[32] In South Carolina, newspapers reported that large bands of "the most infamous banditti and horse thieves [which included] a corps of Indians, with negro and white savages disguised like them," were raiding settlements and "stealing slaves" throughout the region. These banditti were groups of fugitive slaves, indentured servants, Cherokee, poor farmers, and backcountry Tories who worked independently and with British forces and were commanded by men like "Captain" Jones, "Colored Power Man," or the mulatto William Hunt. These guerrilla bands burned and looted plantations, stole horses, and attacked Continental forces in many regions. In New Jersey, a band under the leadership of Tye, "a Negro who [bore] the title of colonel," attacked American fortifications and a number of large slaveholding estates, freeing slaves and indentured servants. Guerrilla fighters continued to operate even after the end of the war. For more than half a century bands of blacks calling themselves the King of England Soldiers harassed southern plantations and freed slaves when possible. Ironically the persistence of these bands bore testimony to the power of the revolutionary message of liberty.[33]

Many patriots argued that the only way to discourage black participation in loyalist groups like the banditti was to enroll them in the American cause. It was the colonial governor of Virginia, Lord Dunmore, however, whose actions quickly forced the Americans to reconsider their policy on black enlistment. In November he struck at the heart of the colonials' contradiction with a strategy designed to infuriate and humiliate them, especially the slaveholders. Dunmore promised freedom to all slaves and indentured servants who escaped from their rebellious masters and fought on the side of the British.

In light of the ruling in the *Somerset* case a few years before, slaves were inclined to believe the British offer of freedom. James Somerset was a slave who had run away from his master in England in the early 1770s. When he was recaptured and his master threatened to ship him to Jamaica to be sold, abolitionist Granville Sharp persuaded the court to take up his case. In a carefully worded decision the British court ruled that no slave could be forcibly taken from England. Some American slaves acted on the promise of the Somerset ruling directly, as their masters attested when they advertised for their return. One Virginia slave, a master speculated, would probably "board a vessel for Great Britain . . . from the knowledge he has of the late Determination of the Somerset Case." Another master believed his runaway slave couple was on the way to Britain, "where they imagine they will be free," adding, "a Notion now too prevalent among the Negroes." Drawing the implication from the court ruling that slavery was incompatible with the rights granted by English common law gave the hope of freedom to slaves in England and in the colonies and gave credence to Dunmore's promise of freedom in return for military service.[34]

The promise of "liberty to slaves," as the insignia on the uniforms of Dunmore's Ethiopian Regiment proclaimed, was wildly successful. In a few months three hundred blacks served in the regiment, and by the end of the war eight hundred blacks had served, constituting more than half of Dunmore's troops. Other effects of the proclamation were to provide the British with support troops and to deprive many slaveholders of their labor supply. Wherever the British went, nearby slaves sought sanctuary with them, though only the approximately one thousand slaves who fought in the army were promised freedom. Estimates are that the Americans lost as many as one hundred thousand of their approximately five hundred thousand slaves to the British during the war. The disruption of wartime itself, of course, also provided opportunities for slaves who did not need the motivation of British promises to escape from bondage. By 1778 Thomas Jefferson reported that thirty thousand Virginia slaves had run away to the British; others have estimated that South Carolina lost at least twenty-five thousand and that Georgia lost more than twelve thousand of its fifteen thousand slaves before the war's end.[35]

Lord Dunmore's strategy forced the patriots to compete for the loyalties of African Americans and reconsider their policy against enlisting blacks. The threat of conspiracies and guerrilla actions by allied white loyalists and slaves became reality in many communities and was rumored in many others. In a letter to one of his officers, Washington worried that Dunmore's black troops would draw more and more slaves to the British lines. Indeed Washington predicted that the use of black troops would make Dunmore "the most dangerous man in America," and that ultimately "success [would] depend on who [could] arm the Negroes the faster." Under these circumstances he saw little recourse but to reverse his policy on black recruitment. Recruiting blacks into the Continental forces would also help address the problem of a growing troop shortage. White soldiers were reluctant to serve for longer than short three-month enlistments or to serve great distances from their homes, and the availability of black troops might ease this situation. On January 6, 1776, Congress acted on Washington's recommendation and set into motion a series of orders that eventually opened the Continental ranks to African Americans. Eventually all the states except South Carolina and Georgia enlisted black soldiers. The dwindling white enlistments as the war continued created economic hardships and reinforced the argument for recruiting blacks. In the end most states matched Dunmore's promise of freedom for slaves who served in the army.[36]

Some states allowed the enlistment of slaves as replacements for whites unwilling or unable to serve the American cause. This proved a boon to many slave masters, who sent their slaves to service in their stead. Nathan Dibble and his son Eli, both of Connecticut, avoided military service by sending their slave, Jack Anthony, to serve in their places. After a term of service that lasted until the end of the war Anthony was granted his freedom. London Hazard, a Rhode Island slave, served for several members of his master's family in order to secure his freedom, and Cezar Negro, who had been born at sea during his mother's crossing from Africa, won his freedom after serving in place of his master's son. James Armistead served as a spy for General Lafayette and was granted his freedom by the Virginia legislature in 1786. Blacks served with Francis Marion, "the Swamp Fox," and his guerrilla band in South Carolina. Thousands of slaves gained their freedom by helping to win freedom for the United States, many serving in place of their masters or members of their masters' families. In doing so these blacks generally served for long periods, often two to three years longer than white soldiers. Prince Hazeltine served in the Second Massachusetts Regiment for six years and was not discharged until the end of the war. He received two badges of merit for his heroism at Worcester, where he rescued several of his fellows from an explosion and fire that cost many lives. He was so badly injured in the process that for the rest of his life he was unable to work regularly.[37]

Not all who fought were slaves fighting for their own freedom; free blacks also served in the Continental army. Since few free blacks could afford to pay for a substitute, and because most believed that their lives might be better in an independent United States, a great many served. Abijah Prince served with the Green Mountain Boys of Vermont, under the command of Ethan Allen. As a part of the French allied contingent, five hundred freemen from Haiti also took their places among the American forces. Henri Christophe, who later became the King of Haiti, was one of them. The official count of black revolutionary soldiers and seamen was five thousand, but many more served as spies, guides, laborers, and musicians. Unknown numbers of black women served the Continental forces as nurses and cooks, and a few may have disguised themselves as men and served as regular soldiers. Many blacks served as merchant seamen and military sailors in both the American and the British navies. Even whites who objected to arming slaves on land were generally willing to allow slaves and free blacks to serve on warships. Blacks served either in integrated units or in a few all-black regiments.[38]

After the British took the capital city of Newport, destroyed many farms, and occupied two-thirds of the state, Rhode Island raised its own black unit.

Portrait of
Lemuel Haynes,
former Revolutionary
War soldier and
African American
minister to a white
congregation in
eighteenth-century
Vermont.

Photographs and Prints
Division, Schomburg
Center for Research
in Black Culture,
The New York Public
Library, Astor, Lenox,
and Tilden Foundations.

Most of its troops came from the Narragansett region, an area with some of
the few large slaveholding estates in the North. As in the South the large
planters in Rhode Island objected to arming slaves and were successful in ending slave enlistments, but were too late to stop the black unit from going into
action. The First Rhode Island Battalion, as it was called, was commanded by
Col. Christopher Greene, a white Quaker who violated the pacifist tenets of
his religion to join the war effort. The battalion served in its home state and
in Virginia and New York. Greene had led a unit of four hundred black troops
in Delaware before taking charge of the Rhode Island unit, and other black
units were formed in Connecticut and Massachusetts. New York, New Jersey,
and New Hampshire enlisted blacks in the ranks of its general military units.
In Maryland the state legislature rejected the idea of raising an all-black regiment and integrated slaves and free blacks into its regular state militia. Virginia allowed free blacks to join its militia but refused to arm slaves, although
some slaveholders enrolled slaves in their stead by claiming that the slaves
were free. No amount of persuasion could break the resolve of Georgians and
South Carolinians not to allow black troops to be raised within their borders,
however. Several plans were proposed, one supported by Alexander Hamil-

ton of New York, that would have provided three thousand blacks to assist Georgia and South Carolina in filling their quota of troops, but they were soundly rejected. As one South Carolinian wrote, "We are much disgusted here at the Congress recommending us to arm our Slaves, it was received with great resentment, as a very dangerous and impolitic step."[39] A counterargument was advanced that by enlisting slaves in common cause with slave masters, slave uprisings might actually be averted, but it was to no avail, even when it appeared that South Carolina and Georgia would fall to British forces. White Georgians tolerated having black troops from the French West Indies defend the port city of Savannah, but fear of the consequences of arming slaves prevented them from making any further concessions. Georgia fell to the British in early 1779, and Charleston, South Carolina, was taken in the summer of 1780, but still no black troops were enlisted.[40]

Yet black soldiers fought in every theater of the war, even in the South. They saw action in the Green Mountains of Vermont and in the Blue Ridge Mountains of North Carolina. They endured the snow and freezing temperatures alongside the white troops at places like Valley Forge, Pennsylvania. Cato Cuff was frostbitten so badly there that he could never work outdoors in cold weather again. At the Battle of Lake Champlain in New York, Samuel Coombs, though wounded himself, tended the wounds of other injured men. Prince Whipple and Oliver Cromwell were among those who manned the oars of the boat carrying George Washington across the Delaware River to the battle at Trenton, and blacks like African-born Prince Bent of the Rhode Island regiment were serving with Washington when Cornwallis surrendered.[41]

The Revolution brought independence to the new American nation and freedom to thousands of African American slaves, but not all blacks who were promised freedom were freed even after they had completed military service. Many substitution agreements between masters and slaves consisted only of a verbal promise, which masters easily denied at war's end. Some slaves successfully brought suit against these masters, but the national government did little to ensure that masters abided by state legislation freeing slaves who had served. Although many were properly freed and some freed themselves by simply walking away from slavery during the postwar disruption, many others remained in slavery.[42]

The last British contingent, which surrendered New York in November 1783, took four thousand blacks with them. More than fourteen thousand blacks departed that fall, and most of those who had not served with the British forces but had simply escaped to British lines remained in slavery. Some went to Canada with Loyalists or to England with the troops. Others ended up on sugar plantations in Jamaica or some other British West Indian colony, where life was unspeakably harsh for slaves. The British granted some people a choice of destination; Phyllis Thomas, "a free black woman," was granted passage to the West Indies or "elsewhere at her option." Other free blacks traveled to Britain, Europe, Canada, or parts of Latin America. Some found opportunities abroad that they would probably not have had in the United States. Bill Richmond, a slave of the duke of Northumberland on New York's Staten Island, went to London with his master when the duke withdrew from the United States. There Richmond was educated, became a boxer, and by 1800 was billed as "the Black Terror," a bare-knuckle contender for the national championship. Although Richmond lost to champion Tom Cribb in a brutal one-and-one-half-hour contest for the title, his fame enabled him to retire from the ring and establish the Horse and Dolphin Inn and his own boxing academy at the Royal Tennis Court; he trained many well-known British personalities, including Lord Byron, who attended regularly.[43]

Hundreds of blacks who went to Canada settled in Nova Scotia, accounting for at least 10 percent of those who settled the Halifax area during the early 1780s. Many were families like Charles and Dolly and their five children, who had been slaves in New York and settled in Port Roseway, Nova Scotia. There Charles found work as a carpenter with the British army engineers, they survived the harsh winters, and the family built a life in freedom. Others who settled in Canada were not so fortunate, and with increasing urgency the new black Canadians reported that land and employment were difficult to secure, racial intolerance was increasing as the black population grew, and life was generally hard. Even though these blacks valued their new freedom, neither Canada nor England offered most blacks the opportunities they sought for progress and self-determination, and many migrated elsewhere. A few went to other countries in Europe, but by 1790 many American-born blacks were among the settlers of the British West African colony of Sierra Leone.[44]

In the new United States, antislavery forces continued their agitation during the war, arguing that slavery was inconsistent with both Christianity and the values of the Revolution. Many colonies—even including Virginia, North Carolina, and Georgia—had temporarily outlawed the slave trade during 1774 and 1775. In 1775 the first antislavery society in the world was established in Philadelphia, calling itself the Society for the Relief of Free Negroes Unlawfully Held in Bondage. Two years later Vermont became the first state in the nation to abolish slavery within its borders, adopting a state constitutional provision that declared, "All men are born equally free and independent." Local abolitionists attacked slavery everywhere but in the Deep South.[45] In 1779 a group of slaves petitioned the legislature in New Hampshire for their freedom. They argued that their being kidnapped from their native Africa and held in the United States against their will was plainly against all natural law, since the "God of nature gave them life and freedom, upon the terms of most perfect equality with other men." But New Hampshire officials were deaf to the slaves' plea, though the 1783 state constitution seemed to deny slavery's ligitimacy. Although slavery waned in the state, and the number of slaves dwindled to practically zero before the nineteenth century (eight slaves were recorded in the state in 1800), the institution was not officially abolished there until 1857.[46]

The antislavery arguments of slaves and their abolitionist allies were more directly successful in other northern states. Most of these states abolished slavery through strategies of gradual emancipation that were less economically and socially disruptive than immediate emancipation, at least from the perspective of the white society. In Connecticut a combination of economic depression and antislavery pressure encouraged the legislature to institute a plan that freed the children of slaves when they reached the age of twenty-five. In Pennsylvania any slave born after 1780 was to be set free at twenty-eight, being treated as an indentured servant until that time. New York and New Jersey enacted gradual emancipation plans in 1799 and 1804. Massachusetts answered the revolutionary rhetoric in a slave petition with immediate emancipation, after the state supreme court ruled in 1783 that slavery was incompatible with the state constitution of 1780. By 1800 slavery was abolished or in the process of being gradually abolished throughout the North.[47]

The ideals and the rhetoric of the Revolution made arguments for emancipation difficult to ignore, but other factors also contributed to the demise of slavery in the North. Urban white workers, wanting to limit both employment competition and the number of blacks in the local population, pressured officials to abolish slavery. Northern employers found free labor sufficient for their needs and thus a financially viable alternative to slavery. The relatively small number of slaves in most northern states, and the fact that northern economies were generally not built on slavery, meant that there were few powerful voices in favor of the institution. All these circumstances created the conditions under which the arguments of those working for emancipation could be successful.

In the Lower South, where planters held the political and economic power, the impact of Revolutionary idealism was negligible. As South Carolina and Georgia had resisted enlisting slaves in their militia during the war, so they stood fast against the winds of abolition drifting across the northern states. Maryland, Virginia, and North Carolina retained slavery too but far less adamantly. There, for a generation or more, state regulations allowed and even encouraged the voluntary manumission of slaves. As a result the free black population in those Upper South states grew substantially during the late eighteenth century and the first two decades of the nineteenth. By 1810 more than 107,000 free blacks, almost 58 percent of the nation's total free black population of 186,000, lived in the southern states. The rate of growth of the southern free black population declined after the 1820s as fewer southern slaves were freed. The numbers of slaves grew substantially, to 1.5 million by 1820 and to more than double that number by midcentury. Thus slavery became more significant in the South as it was gradually abolished in the North, and the social and political distance between North and South increased steadily.[48]

The divergence between the North and the South regarding slavery created new dangers for northern slaves. When it seemed clear that slavery would be abolished in the North, many slaveholders rushed to sell their slaves farther south before freedom prevented them from doing so. Even after the passage of emancipation laws, children and young adults particularly faced this risk. Under gradual emancipation, young slaves might be held as servants only until they reached their mid-twenties. Although the practice was illegal, handsome prices for young slaves in the plantation South provided an incentive for northern masters to sell their slaves to the South before they reached the age of manumission. In Connecticut in 1792 one slaveholder was charged with attempting to circumvent state law by "exporting" two slave children.[49] The closer northern slaves lived to the South, the greater the danger of their being transferred into southern slavery, and many traveling slave traders roamed the southern regions of the North in search of good buys. Some masters tricked slaves, sending them into the South for temporary employment and selling them once they were there. Eighteen-year-old Harvey had only a few more years to serve when he was persuaded to travel from Middlesex County, New Jersey, to Louisiana to work "temporarily." He was enslaved there for the rest of his life.[50] In this way many young slaves never gained their promised freedom, and the tragedies of slavery continued for them long after official emancipation in the North. Isabella, a slave with a strong Dutch accent who lived in New York State, understood the dangers as well as anyone. She looked forward to freedom for herself and her children under New York's emancipation law, but before freedom came her youngest son was given as a wedding present to her master's daughter who was leaving New York for Alabama. When a distraught Isabella confronted her mistress, the white women refused to take her concerns seriously. "A fine fuss to make about a little nigger! Why, haven't you as many of 'em left as you can see to?" Many parents carried such painful memories into freedom as slavery came to an end in the North. Isabella was eventually able to recover her son, but the incident contributed to her determination to fight against slavery and for the rights of women. In that fight she took the name Sojourner Truth.[51]

With the prolonged process of gradual emancipation in most of the North, many African Americans throughout the country continued to suffer the hardships of slavery after the Revolution. Even those who were freed faced hard times in the postwar period, as all Americans were confronted by economic uncertainty and an unstable currency. The situation was especially difficult for the poor, including ex-slaves and indentured servants, and those who had gained their freedom by fighting in the war often carried additional burdens. Cato Howe, freed from bondage in return for his years of service for Massachusetts, returned to his wife and farmwork. The Howes settled in a section of Plymouth, Massachusetts, known as New Guinea or Parting Ways, with the families of three other black war veterans—Plato Turner, Quamony Quash, and Prince Goodwin. The depression of 1784 meant that the farmers received low prices for their produce. When Howe developed rheumatism from his war wounds he had trouble working around the farm and his life became even harder. Recognizing the hardships suffered by these veterans, in 1792 the town of Plymouth granted the men the rights to 106 acres of the land where they were living in return for the labor it would take to clear it. Despite this aid, the support and friendship of his comrades, and the pension to which his wartime service entitled him, Cato Howe was forced to rely on public assistance in his old age.[52]

For African Americans the Revolution brought an incomplete freedom and a precarious status in the United States. In Georgia and South Carolina nearly all the slaves who did not escape to the British lines remained in slavery. In the Chesapeake region, slavery remained as an institution, but the conditions under which masters could free their slaves were liberalized so that the number of free blacks increased. In the North slavery was ending, but freedom brought limited benefits to former slaves. The lingering revolutionary spirit held promise, but the future of black people in the United States was even more uncertain than the future of the new nation.

Chapter 4

1787   Adoption of the United States Constitution

Northwest Ordinance outlaws slavery in the territory northwest of the Ohio River

British found Sierra Leone as West African colony for freed slaves

1789   George Washington elected as the first president of the United States

Olaudah Equiano publishes his *Narrative*

1790   First United States Census records nearly 4 million residents, more than 750,000 (19 percent) of whom are black

1791   Benjamin Banneker assists in surveying area to become District of Columbia

Slaves revolt in French Haiti

1793   Eli Whitney invents the cotton gin

Congress passes the first federal Fugitive Slave Law

1800   U.S. population 5,308,483; black population 1,002,037 (19 percent)

Gabriel's massive slave revolt in Virginia is betrayed

Thomas Jefferson elected president, the first president to reside in Washington, D.C.

1803   Louisiana Purchase more than doubles the land area of the United States

1804   Haiti achieves independence from France

1808   United States prohibits the African slave trade

1809   Thomas Paul organizes the Abyssinian Baptist Church in New York City

1812–1814   War between the United States and Great Britain

1815   Andrew Jackson commands U.S. troops, including a large force of African Americans, in the Battle of New Orleans

1816   American Colonization Society established

1820   West African colony of Liberia founded by colonization society for settlement of freed slaves

Missouri Compromise maintains balance of slave and free states (twelve each); Missouri admitted as slave state and Maine as free

The Early Republic and the Rise of the Cotton Kingdom

*J*ames Forten returned from the Revolution to a Philadelphia that was the new nation's largest city and its financial, intellectual, and scientific center. This commercial hub had more than thirty-two thousand residents and a rapidly growing black population of more than eleven hundred, which would double in the next decade. The fourteen-year-old Forten, born free in Philadelphia, had served aboard the colonial ship *Royal Louis* and been captured by the British and held for seven months on a prison ship before finally returning to his family in his home city. Forten learned the trade of sailmaking and was so talented at the work that by the age of twenty he was foreman of a shop owned by white sailmaker Robert Bridges. He became a prominent member of the city's free black community, which by the mid-1780s accounted for almost 90 percent of the African Americans in Philadelphia. The small slave population continued to dwindle in the city and in the state, but the nation remained largely committed to the institution, no matter how it contradicted the national purpose.[1]

The United States was beginning to work out the meaning of citizenship for its people; and African Americans, having sacrificed to make independence possible, were determined to gain both liberty and full citizenship. Especially in urban areas the establishment or expansion of free black communities provided crucial economic and social support. The willingness of reformers to aid the newly free with services like education was a hopeful sign, as was the emergence of antislavery organizations. The debate over slavery was critical to the future of the United States as the new nation contemplated the construction of its government. The documents of the Revolution were filled with the language of equality, arguing for the right to liberty and self-determination. These sentiments had contributed to the decisions to abolish slavery in nearly all the northern states, and African Americans now called upon the nation to live up to its principles. Indeed historian Gary Nash has called the 1770s and 1780s the "opportune time for abolishing slavery" in the country. According to Nash the new nation could have outlawed slavery at that time because antislavery sentiment was strong; the Lower South, where slavery was dominant, was too weak to stand alone; a belief in innate black inferiority was not yet widespread; and western lands might have been used to compensate slaveholders for freeing their slaves or for black colonization.[2] Post-Revolutionary leaders, however, having rebelled against a strong colonial power, were acutely aware of the dangers of governmental centralization, and wartime disagreements had exposed the divergent interests of the new states. Thus they limited the power of the federal government to impose its will on the states by establishing a relatively weak, decentralized system of government under the Articles of Confederation, leaving the issue of slavery to the separate states.

The turbulent decade of the 1780s exposed the vulnerability of a limited federal government. In the years after the Revolution, economic pressure increased as returning soldiers faced deteriorating conditions. The Continental scrip with which they were paid was practically worthless, their debts had accumulated, and the prospects for financial improvement seemed remote. Britain had been the major market for colonial goods before the war, and the loss of that market, combined with England's restrictions on American trade with the British West Indies, fueled a depression, further demoralizing urban workers and small farmers. In western Massachusetts debt-ridden farmers led by Daniel Shays, a Revolutionary War hero and prominent landholder, revolted against the increasing number of farm foreclosures. From August 1786 to March 1787, under Shays's leadership, thousands of armed farmers closed the local courts and prevented authorities from foreclosing on their property. One of Shays's inner circle was Moses Sash, a free black laborer from Massachusetts who had also served in the war. Sash had received land as part of the payment for his service—land he too was struggling to retain. For those in authority concerned with political and economic stability, Shays's Rebellion was especially distressing. Congress had neither the funds nor the authority to raise troops to put down the revolt. Black war veteran Prince Hall offered to take a force of seven hundred Boston area African American volunteers to quell the rebellion, but Massachusetts preferred to raise a force of white troops paid by wealthy Boston merchants. By the spring of 1787 the privately financed militia had routed Shays and his followers, many of whom then turned to state politics to redress their grievances. Boston blacks were greatly offended by the rejection of their offer of service to the new republic. Three months after Shays's Rebellion ended, Prince Hall and more than seventy others petitioned the Massachusetts General Court for funds to transport all blacks who wanted to go to Africa.[3]

At the same time representatives were meeting in Philadelphia in a constitutional convention to consider broad new powers for the federal government. As the founding fathers sat in hot, humid, summertime Philadelphia arguing, compromising, and finally composing the Constitution, slavery was a major point of contention, a point on which the Lower South especially

Portrait of Prince Hall, founder of the Colored Fraternity
of Free and Accepted Masons, Boston, Massachusetts.

Photographs and Prints Division, Schomburg Center for Research in Black Culture,
The New York Public Library, Astor, Lenox, and Tilden Foundations.

resisted compromise. Northern states were already moving toward the abolition of slavery, and delegates like Pennsylvania's Benjamin Franklin and New York's Alexander Hamilton had expressed the expectation that the new nation would follow their example. Virginia delegates George Washington, Thomas Jefferson, and Patrick Henry and others had assumed that an end to slavery would have to be negotiated at the Constitutional Convention. Yet northern delegates did not press the South, especially resistant South Carolina and Georgia. Perhaps feeling their weakness as part of a fledgling nation faced with continuing European designs on its territory and resources, the framers of the Constitution avoided a confrontation on the contentious issue. The harmony purchased at the cost of leaving the slavery question unresolved allowed the convention to construct a Constitution that provided a strong tripartite central government with access to financial resources and increased control over a military that might be called on to meet foreign threats or contain popular unrest. As it was finally written the Constitution never referred to slavery directly but did accommodate slavery in three respects. First it protected property rights in slaves by providing slaveholders with the assurance that runaway slaves would be returned even if they crossed state lines. Second it allowed the African slave trade to continue for a period of twenty years (and to reopen in places like South Carolina, where it had been closed), protecting it until 1808. Finally it provided additional representation, and thereby greater political power, in the federal House of Representatives to slave states by allowing three-fifths of the slaves to be counted in determining the basis for a state's representation. The Constitutional Convention did not define the requirements for citizenship, in effect reaffirming the traditional political system that gave citizenship rights to propertied white males. Although the Bill of Rights, the first ten amendments to the Constitution, seemed to offer the possibility of some legal protection for African Americans, the position of free black people remained unclear. The general term "person," occasionally with the qualifier "free," was used to refer to American citizens, while the term "other" delineated slaves, to whom no constitutional rights were guaranteed.

Although the silence of the Constitution on slavery left the existence and regulation of this institution to each state, the new Congress did concern itself with slavery in the territories directly under federal control. In 1787 Congress passed the Northwest Ordinance, governing territories north of the Ohio River that were not yet ready to gain admission to the Union as states. This ordinance outlawed slavery in these northwestern territories, but by not mentioning the southwestern territories gave tacit approval for the introduction of slavery there. As a concession to slave owners, slaves already in the northwestern territories, including those brought in by the French before British settlement, could remain in slavery. Strong proslavery feeling in the portion of the territory that later became the states of Indiana and Illinois led to continual attempts by officials to circumvent the ordinance.[4] As each new state was admitted to the union, the issue of black status was debated by state constitutional conventions. During the next two generations, western and southern territories applying for admission either protected slavery or outlawed slavery and restricted black migration. In Kentucky in 1792 antislavery elements raised religious and philosophical objections, but strong proslavery forces made Kentucky the first new slave state admitted to the Union. Four years later Tennessee, with more than ten thousand slaves, applied and was admitted as another slave state. In areas covered by the Northwest Ordinance, new states tried to limit the size of their black population. Indiana, Michigan, Wisconsin, and Iowa prohibited black immigration, and Illinois threatened bondage for blacks who attempted to settle there permanently. Ohio passed a series of "black laws" requiring that free blacks post a five-hundred-dollar bond of good conduct and denying blacks the right to vote in most areas, to hold public office, or to testify against a white person in court. Free blacks were prevented from serving on juries and testifying against white people in many states. Restrictive laws were irregularly enforced, however, and the free black population continued to grow, especially in areas bordering the South.[5]

Discouraged about their prospects for equality in America, members of African societies in Newport and Providence, Rhode Island; and in Boston and Philadelphia expressed cautious interest in the British colony of Sierra Leone in West Africa during the late 1700s. They were especially encouraged for a time in 1787 when the English committee for Sierra Leone hired the African Olaudah Equiano, then known as Gustavus Vassa, as the clerk in charge of outfitting and loading the ship bound for the colony. In his long route from his capture in Africa as a boy to this responsible position, Equiano had indeed been fortunate under adverse circumstances. He had spent only a few weeks in Barbados in 1756; as no one purchased him for plantation work there, the traders took him to Virginia, where they sold him to a tobacco planter who named him Jacob. He spent a month of terrible isolation. He could not speak English, and no one spoke his language. While working around the master's house and yard, he caught the eye of a visiting sea captain, who purchased him, took him to England, and named him Gustavus Vassa. When this new owner received an appointment as a naval officer in 1756 during the French and Indian War, Equiano embarked on a dangerous life. During his five years at sea, he had a fair amount of freedom for a slave, learning to read; accumulating some clothing, books, and cash; and sharing the perils and camaraderie of ships at war. At the end of the war, however, he was stripped of his possessions, sold to the West Indies, and resold in Montserrat to a Quaker man from Philadelphia. Equiano's fortunes changed again as his new master allowed him to work for wages and to purchase his freedom in the summer of 1766. For the next two decades the free African sailed the Caribbean and traveled in various parts of Europe, returning to London several times and working there for extended periods. In 1785 he visited the United States, spending time in Philadelphia. By this time Equiano had become a part of the antislavery movement, and within a year he was a major figure, appointed by Britain to supervise efforts to supply the Sierra Leone colony.[6]

In 1789 readers of English in Britain, the United States, and Europe were captivated by an extraordinary new autobiography. Published in London, this two-volume account was the work of an African of indisputable intelligence, imagination, talent, and humanity. *The Interesting Narrative of the Life of Olaudah Equiano; or Gustavus Vassa* was Equiano's powerful first-hand account of his life in Africa, his capture and enslavement, and his life under the British-American slave system. It was so popular that at least eight editions were sold in the first five years of its printing. Equiano's writing provided a glimpse of what Europeans and Americans saw as the exotic society in his African home, but it was also a morality tale that condemned Christians' complicity in slavery's destruction of African lives and families and unequivocally blamed the avarice of Christian slave masters and their accomplices

At Salem, " *Cæfar Pratt*, a black man, aged 65—remarkable for his inftinctive facility in numbers, by which he was able to make, in an inftant, calculations which would require in common perfons the aid of many figures; his memory was alfo the regifter of every perfon's age of which he had ever been informed, and which he was fure to remind them of as the anniverfary of their birth came round; and in other refpects he was a convenient chronologift."

"Eulogy for Caesar Pratt," *Providence Gazette,* May 19, 1804.
Graphics Division, Rhode Island Historical Society.

Benjamin Banneker

The scientist, mathematician, and astronomer Benjamin Banneker was born free near Baltimore, Maryland, in 1731. His father came to North America from Guinea, West Africa, as a slave and was later freed. His mother was also free, the child of an English indentured servant and an African who had gained his freedom before she was born. Benjamin's white grandmother taught him to read, and he became an avid reader with a natural aptitude for mathematics. He once constructed a mechanical clock on mathematical principles alone, having never seen one. Banneker farmed until rheumatism made it impossible, but retirement at middle age allowed him to take up mathematics and astronomy in earnest. In 1791 the presidentially appointed surveyor, Andrew Ellicott, asked Banneker to help him survey the area for the new national capital of Washington, D.C. For three months Banneker made the astronomic calculations each night that Ellicott used for his surveying the following day. Returning to Baltimore, Banneker organized his calculations, and in 1792, published them as the first of several almanacs.

Banneker was more than a man of science. He was also a man of keen political understanding, who used his learning and accomplishments to argue for racial equality. Ellicott and other scientists familiar with his work were impressed, but some were unwilling to acknowledge his obvious talent. Learning of Thomas Jefferson's doubts about the intelligence of African Americans, Banneker sent Jefferson copies of his calculations. Jefferson returned a polite reply but privately expressed doubt that a black man could have produced such intricate work. Curiously Jefferson, one of the most intellectually inquisitive men in America, never tested his doubts and never invited Banneker to demonstrate his skill.

Banneker's almanac sold widely in the United States and Great Britain, and at least twenty-eight editions were published before his death in 1806. Benjamin Banneker died in his sleep at his home in Baltimore, just one month short of seventy-five years of age. In 1980 the U.S. Postal Service issued a postage stamp in his honor.

Benjamin Banneker, astronomer and mathematician who assisted in the surveying of Washington, D.C. Prints and Photographs Division, Library of Congress, Washington, D.C.

for the horrors of the slave trade. Equiano's literary skill created a powerful argument for antislavery forces, which used it to refute notions of African inferiority.[7]

In the face of post-Revolutionary antislavery sentiments in much of the United States, and the growing international interest in abolition, slavery became more firmly entrenched in the American South during the last decade of the eighteenth century. Thomas Jefferson had published his suspicions of black inferiority in his *Notes on Virginia* in 1787. Although he was troubled by slavery, his reflections later formed the core of a powerful proslavery argument. In his writing Jefferson ignored the accomplishments of such prominent blacks as Equiano, the impressive poetry of Boston slave Phillis Wheatley, or Benjamin Banneker's sophisticated mathematical computations and observations in his scientific almanac. Jefferson was anxious that his reflections not be taken by his fellow slaveholders as an attack on slavery. Southern slave states were deeply affected by events on the French-held island of St. Domingue in the Caribbean. The spirit of the revolution spread from France in 1789 to St. Domingue as slaves there determined to secure freedom for themselves. In the late summer of 1791, slaves rebelled against their masters with such fury that the French government sent troops to the colony to subdue them. By the time the French forces arrived, blacks had organized themselves under the leadership of a former slave carriage driver named Toussaint L'Ouverture. In 1793 slaves and free blacks defeated the French army stationed in the capital and captured the city. Whites fled in ships bound for the United States, and on their arrival American newspapers were filled with their accounts of the horrors of the rebellion, stories that terrified southern slaveholders.[8]

Meanwhile, in St. Domingue, full-scale war frustrated Napoleon's plans for American expansion. Finally, in 1800, he resolved to end the resistance and sent a force of 25,000 men. The French offered to negotiate a peace with the rebels, but when L'Ouverture arrived for the talks, he was captured, shackled, and taken to Paris. Nevertheless, the revolt continued, and on the first day of January 1804 Jean-Jacques Dessalines, its new leader, proclaimed Haiti's independence, the first independent black nation in the Western Hemisphere. France's defeat ended Napoleon's dreams of a New World empire and encouraged him to dispose of his American lands while some profit could still be derived from them. In 1803, in exchange for fifteen million dollars, approximately four cents an acre, France sold the United States a huge tract of land. The Louisiana Purchase, as it was called, amounted to 828,000 square miles, stretching from the Gulf of Mexico northward to the Canadian border, and from the Mississippi River on the eastern boundary to the Rocky Mountains in the west. President Thomas Jefferson's acquisition of this new

Benjamin Banneker's letter to Thomas Jefferson

Maryland, Baltimore County.

Near Ellicott's Lower Mills August 19th. 1791

Thomas Jefferson Secretary of State.

Sir, I am fully sensible of the greatness of that freedom which I take with you on the present occasion; a liberty which Seemed to me Scarcely allowable, when I reflected on that distinguished, and dignifyed station in which you Stand; and the almost general prejudice and prepossession which is so previlent [*sic*] in the world against those of my complexion.

I suppose it is a truth too well attested to you, to need proof here, that we are a race of Beings who have long laboured under the abuse and censure of the world, that we have long been looked upon with an eye of contempt, and that we have long been considered rather as brutish than human, and Scarcely capable of mental endowments.

Sir, I hope I may Safely admit, in consequence of that report which hath reached me, that you are a man far less inflexible in Sentiments of this nature, than many others, that you are measurably friendly and well dis-posed towards us, and that you are willing and ready to Lend your aid and assistance to our relief from those many distresses and numberous calami-ties to which we are reduced.

Now, Sir, if this is founded in truth, I apprehend you will readily embrace every opportunity to eradicate that train of absurd and false ideas and oppinions [*sic*] which so generally prevail with respect to us, and that your Sentiments are concurrent with mine, which are that one universal Father hath given being to us all, and that he hath not only made us all of one flesh, but that he hath also without partiality afforded us all the Same Sensations, and endued [*sic*] us all with the same faculties, and that how-ever variable we may be in Society or religion, however diversified in Situation or colour, we are all of the Same Family, and Stand in the Same relation to him. . . .

Sir, Suffer me to recall to your mind that time in which the Arms and tyranny of the British Crown were exerted with every powerful effort, in order to reduce you to a State of Servitude; look back I intreat you on the variety of dangers to which you were exposed. . . .

This, Sir, was a time in which you clearly saw into the injustice of a State of Slavery, and in which you had Just apprehensions of the horrors of its condition, it was now Sir, that your abhorrence thereof was so excited, that you publickly held forth this true and invaluable doctrine, which is worthy to be recorded and remembered in all Succeeding ages. "We hold

(continued)

(continued)

these truths to be Self evident, that all men are created equal, and that they are endowed by their creator with certain inalienable rights, that amongst these are life, liberty, and the persuit [*sic*] of happiness."

Here, Sir, was a time in which your tender feelings for your selves engaged you thus to declare, you were then impressed with proper ideals of the great valuation of liberty, and the free possession of those blessings to which you were entitled by nature; but Sir how pitiable is it to reflect, that altho you were so fully convinced of the benevolence of the Father of mankind, and of his equal and impartial distribution of those rights and privileges which he had conferred upon them, that you should at the Same time counteract his mercies, in detaining by fraud and violence so numerous a part of my brethren under groaning captivity and cruel oppression, that you should at the Same time be found guilty of that most criminal act, which you professedly detested in others, with respect to yourselves. . . .

This calculation [his almanac sent as a present], Sir, is the production of my arduous study . . . altho you may have the opportunity of perusing it after its publication, yet I chose to send it to you in manuscript previous thereto, that thereby you might not only have an earlier inspection, but that you might also view it in my own hand writing.

And now Sir, I Shall conclude and Subscribe my Self with the most profound respect,

Your most Obedient humble Servant

Benjamin Banneker

Sidney Kaplan, *The Black Presence in the Era of the American Revolution, 1770–1800* (Greenwich, Conn.: New York Graphic Society Ltd. / Smithsonian Institution Press, 1973), 118–121.

territory doubled the size of the United States, and slaveholders saw the promise of a vast new area open to slavery.

Although most of the estimated ten thousand French slaveholders who fled the Haitian revolution for the United States settled in the South, some brought their slaves to northern cities such as Philadelphia and New York. In 1792 they petitioned Pennsylvania for the right to keep their slaves, noting that congressmen who brought their own slaves to the national capital at Philadelphia when Congress was in session were exempt from the abolition laws. In answer to their petition, authorities reaffirmed Pennsylvania's constitutional commitment to freedom and recommended that the legislature immediately and totally abolish slavery in the state. Between 1787 and 1810, of the 508 French slaves freed in Pennsylvania, 45 were granted immediate freedom, 2 purchased their own freedom, and the rest were indentured in accordance with the gradual emancipation law.[9] The French slaves' association with the Haitian revolution, their extreme poverty, their tendency to settle together in the least desirable part of the city, and their practice of the island-developed voodoo religion all aroused white fears of disorder. These fears were confirmed in New York City in 1801, when twenty people tried to prevent a white Haitian immigrant from selling her slaves out of the state, threatening to "burn the house, murder all the white people in it, and take away a number of the black slaves." The incendiary potential became even clearer when hundreds of blacks congregated at the house that evening and clashed with fifty watchmen attempting to keep order. The authorities prevailed, the slaves were not freed, and twenty-three rioters were jailed.[10]

The Haitian revolution itself aroused the fears of southern Americans. White nightmares of the spread of slave revolts seemed to be coming true in 1800 when a slave plot was unearthed just outside of Richmond, Virginia. As was typical in the Upper South, Richmond area slaves enjoyed a good deal of geographic mobility. They were often able to hire out their time to planters who needed extra help. Most of their pay was claimed by their masters, but they were generally able to retain a portion of it. Some saved to purchase their freedom or that of family members. While working on William Young's plantation just a few miles northeast of Richmond, Ben Woolfolk, a slave hired during the summer of 1800, was approached by one of Young's slaves and asked to take part in a slave uprising. As the details of the plan became known over the next few months, it became clear that only slaves on the Young plantation and several slaves from Richmond were involved. Three brothers—Martin, Solomon and Gabriel—all skilled blacksmiths who were slaves on a plantation in Henrico County, near Richmond, belonging to Thomas Prosser, were involved at the beginning of the plot; and Gabriel eventually became the leader. The number of recruits grew as black boatmen and other "traveling" slaves carried the word from plantation to plantation and into the cities of the region. The plan was to attack Richmond, take Governor (and future President of the United States) James Monroe prisoner, and use the victory to encourage a general slave revolution in Virginia. These plans took shape in the context of a bitter dispute between the two major political parties in the United States, the Federalists and the Republicans, during the election year of 1800, and growing tensions between the United States and France. There were general fears that the election of 1800 would result in armed hostilities between Federalists and Republicans. Gabriel and his followers planned to take advantage of any disruption that might occur.

Gabriel attempted to enlist the cooperation of local whites, apparently believing his attack on slavery could become the foundation for a larger inter-racial class-based revolt against the privileged. He sought the cooperation of a Frenchman who might aid in devising military strategy, and hoped that white artisans in Richmond, angered by the merchants' use of skilled slaves to curb wages, might join as the revolt progressed or at least might not take up arms against it.[11]

The initial strike was planned for August 30, but it was postponed because of a fierce rainstorm. The delay proved fatal to the revolt's success, as the plan was revealed to whites by slave informants. Word soon reached the governor, state forces were assembled, and within a few days scores of slaves were arrested. A white seaman's efforts to help Gabriel escape failed when two slave seamen informed officials of his hiding place. At the trial, testimony revealed the extent of the conspiracy—apparently thousands of slaves were ready to join the revolt once it began. Gabriel was one of twenty-seven slaves convicted and hanged for their participation. For years after Gabriel's defeat other slaves in other parts of Virginia remained ready to revolt, and authorities un-covered a number of conspiracies, one reportedly involving hundreds of slaves in at least eight counties in southern Virginia and northeastern North Carolina. Other plots were uncovered in South Carolina, though it is unclear how many of these were slaveholders overreacting to the Haitian Revolution and Gabriel's plot. Real or not, fears of slave uprisings led to the execution of twenty-five more blacks in Virginia in 1802 and to the passage of laws in Virginia, North Carolina, and South Carolina regulating slaves and free blacks. Laws established slave patrols, restricted the movements of free blacks and slaves, limited the emancipation of slaves, and mandated the removal of free blacks from the state of their manumission. By the middle of the first decade of the nineteenth century, the South had tightened its grip on slav-ery, reversing the trend toward a more flexible system of bondage and a less restrictive policy of manumission that had been most prominent in the Upper South.[12]

Southerners urged Congress to bar blacks from Haiti or elsewhere in the French West Indies from entering the United States lest they infect Ameri-can slaves with a rebellious spirit. Congress responded in 1803 with regu-lations restricting West Indian immigration. It had also restricted mail carrying to whites in 1802, since black post riders had helped to spread the word of rebellion among slaves in Virginia. The government also feared that, as U.S. Postmaster General Gideon Granger said, carrying the mail allowed blacks to learn of their human rights and disseminate that knowledge. As a further safeguard some in the South called for the removal from the country of all free blacks and troublesome slaves. At James Monroe's suggestion, President Thomas Jefferson considered the American West as a place to establish a colony for this purpose, but Jefferson decided that eventual American expansion into the West should not be blocked by a black colony. He considered the West Indies, particularly Haiti, as a place where unwanted black Americans might be shipped. The South, however, feared any arrangement that might enlarge the population of the black West Indian revolutionary forces. There was a brief flirtation with a plan to ship unruly slaves to the British African colony of Sierra Leone, but many were concerned that this would reward rebels with freedom, thus the idea was at least temporarily abandoned. Finally the purchase of Louisiana from France and the opening of the southern regions of that area to slavery partially solved the problem of the disposal of unwanted slaves. In 1812 Louisiana was admitted to the United States as the first slave state carved from the new territory. Of the thirteen states formed in the territory, four—Louisiana, Alabama, Missouri, and Arkansas—allowed slavery.

Initially the heart of Louisiana's economy was sugar. Cane could not be grown as easily as in the West Indies, and yields were not as great, but cultivation of the crop required slaves, and rising prices encouraged masters in the Upper South to sell any extra hands into the new western South. Since the gang labor of sugar plantations called for a largely male workforce, Louisiana quickly acquired a slave population of relatively young males who outnumbered whites in many of the large plantation areas.

A shift to cotton production in the western South dramatically increased the demand for slaves in that region. Cotton had been grown in limited quantities in a few coastal areas of the eastern South since the seventeenth century, but South Carolina planters generally preferred to concentrate on rice cultivation. A few small planters grew cotton, and slaves made their clothing from cotton they grew in small gardens. During the Revolution a boycott of English cloth encouraged home production, but the most desirable long-staple cotton could be grown only near the coast. The short-staple cotton could be grown inland, but the tedium involved in removing the seeds from the fiber of this type of cotton made its production difficult and costly. The invention in 1793 of a simple device called the cotton gin by Eli Whitney, a Yale-educated teacher who traveled to South Carolina to tutor planters' children, made it economically feasible to expand the production of this crop. Using this new machine, essentially a box containing a rotating cylinder with protruding nails, a worker could remove seeds fifty times faster than by hand. The Louisiana Purchase provided fertile land, treaties and skirmishes subdued the Creek, Chickasaw, Choctaw, and Cherokee Indians who lived there, and Whitney's new technology made it possible to create a new "Cotton Kingdom" in the western area known as the Deep South. The new states of Mississippi, Alabama, and Arkansas joined western Georgia to become the prime cotton-growing region of the nation. Its rich black soil (hence the area's designation as the Black Belt) produced the crop that became the foundation of the nineteenth-century southern economy and plantation culture. The Black Belt's demand for slaves increased just after Congress ended the African slave trade in 1808, and this reduction in the supply increased the value of the slaves in the Upper South who might be sold to the Deep South. The average price of a prime field hand grew fitfully during the first half of the nineteenth century from about six hundred dollars in 1802 to as much as eighteen hundred dollars by 1860. Over the same period the number of slaves in the nation increased dramatically from about seven hundred thousand to nearly four million.[13] Although cotton prices fluctuated, they generally increased during the early decades of the century, and production rose dramatically in response. By 1815 cotton, the chief slave crop in the United States, was also fast becoming the country's single most valuable export, supplying the raw material for the textile mills of Britain and France. It continued its growth throughout the antebellum years, representing one-third of the value of all American exports by 1820, more than half by 1840, and almost 60 percent by the time of the Civil War. Mississippi alone produced ten million pounds of cotton in 1821, thirty million pounds in 1826, and eighty million pounds by 1834.[14]

In Louisiana sugar was also an important slave crop and like cotton its cultivation exacted a terrible toll. In 1830 a New Orleans newspaper estimated that there was a death rate of at least 25 percent among slaves transported from the Upper South to work in the cane fields, and one contemporary observer speculated that the life expectancy of a slave in the cane fields was no more than seven years. Historian Charles Duncan Rice described sugar-producing Louisiana's reputation as "the most terrifying of all the various hells of the Deep South to which blacks from the older slave economies of the tidewater states could be sold."[15] Sugar profits generally grew throughout the antebellum years and soared after midcentury, as the demands of this crop absorbed the labor and the lives of thousands of slaves. Yet cotton remained king even in Louisiana, and the steady increase in its economic value ensured its political power. Whatever the crop, especially after 1830, slavery was the dominant labor system in the South. Its centrality to the economy of that region, and thereby to the nation, made its abolition unlikely, especially where it was most concentrated.[16]

The development of the Deep South expanded the internal slave trade, and as the trade became more profitable, the major cities of the eastern and

Upper South became primary trading centers. During the late summer and early fall, traders in Washington, D.C., and Alexandria and Richmond, Virginia, bid on likely workers to be sold in New Orleans, Louisiana, and Mobile, Alabama, in December and January, when planters had marketed their summer crop and could afford cash payment. It was also in winter that planters returned to the Deep South from their retreats to more healthful climates where they routinely sought escape from summer's malaria and yellow fever. Then too, newly-arrived slaves had time to become acclimatized before the onset of summer heat and humidity. Traders generally auctioned slaves in urban slave markets, but they traveled around to local plantations selling individual slaves when market sales were slow. In the Black Belt, slaves generally found the work harder, the hours longer, the climate nearly unbearable, and the treatment more brutal. Since many planters were absentee owners during the heavy growing season, overseers with no personal financial investment in slaves to safeguard were left to handle the day-to-day operation of the large plantations.

A slave's life expectancy was diminished by severe conditions in the Deep South. The hot, humid climate so good for growing sugarcane in Louisiana was also ideal for breeding malaria-carrying mosquitoes. Cane cultivation in Louisiana was more intense and physically demanding than in the West Indies, where the growing season was slightly longer. Even after the worst summer heat was over, the work was hard. During the sixteen- to eighteen-hour days between mid-October and late December, when the crop was harvested, slaves worked at an exhausting pace, and masters increased the amount of cane each slave was expected to harvest as new agricultural techniques and new varieties of sugarcane increased the yield per acre. On the expansive cotton plantations of Mississippi and Alabama, established during the first three decades of the nineteenth century, slaves not only cultivated and harvested the crop but also did the backbreaking labor of clearing the land during the early years of settlement. Lewis Clarke, a slave from Kentucky, reported that slaves knew that being taken to the Deep South was a horrible fate because they were "driven very hard there, and worked to death in a few years." Even the threat of being "put in the master's pocket" (that is, traded South for money the master could put in his pocket) was enough to cause rebellion, flight, or even suicide. James Williams, an Alabama slave, knew of some slaves who, when they learned that they were to be sold South, died "of grief, and others [who committed] suicide on account of it." One made himself unfit to be sold South by cutting off the fingers of his left hand with an ax. Another drowned herself, and a third cut her own throat with a razor. All were terrified of labor in the Deep South, a fate some regarded as worse than death. Masters often used this fear to control their slaves.[17]

The burgeoning internal slave trade increased the splintering of slave families in the Upper South. Prior to 1820 a southern planter or a planter's son was likely to move west with many of the slaves from his eastern plantation, but the opening of the Deep South changed this pattern. By 1820, 70 percent of the slaves who were taken South were moved by slave traders who realized great profits from the relatively high prices brought by young male slaves in the markets of the Black Belt. Between 1820 and 1830 a quarter of a million slaves were traded south, with a devastating impact on slave families and communities. In New Orleans, Natchez, Montgomery, and elsewhere in the western South, male slaves between the ages of ten and thirty were considered "prime hands" bringing the best prices. About 10 percent of all Upper South slaves in their teens and 9 percent of slaves in their twenties were sold south during the 1820s. One recent study has estimated that after 1815, about one-third of all adults were sold south before they were forty years old. High transportation costs discouraged conveying small children or other family members so that generally only the most valuable were taken. A major route for transporting slaves was the Mississippi River, and so great was the likelihood that a family might lose a member, especially a son or a young father, to this internal slave trade that a new phrase, being "sold down the river," was added to the American lexicon and came to describe the disastrous consequences of these sales. Statistics on slave families tell the story of the trade's impact and the harsh conditions in the Deep South. Ann Patton Malone found that just over half (57 percent) of the slaves in the rural Louisiana parishes she studied were able to establish two-parent or couple households. Most of the young male slaves brought from Kentucky to work on Walter Bashear's plantation in Louisiana, for example, never married. Messages exchanged with their families in Kentucky made clear that old relationships were not ended by their forced migration. "If you see Daddy," "poor little Hannah" instructed her mistress, "give my love to him." The opening of the Deep South may have brought great economic opportunity for the planter class, but it increased the misery of their slaves.[18]

During this same period, as slavery ended in the North, black families there were reunited or established. Expanding trade with Europe and economic prosperity attracted many free African Americans to the eastern port cities in search of work and the relative security provided by a black community. Even during the colonial era, free blacks had been largely city dwellers, and most had congregated in the Atlantic seaport towns and cities where work was available and new black communities were beginning to take shape. This trend continued during the late eighteenth and early nineteenth centuries with the black population of the major northeastern coast cities growing in actual numbers

Free African American Population

City	1790	1800	Percentage of Increase 1790–1800	1830	Percentage of Increase 1790–1830
Boston	761	1,174	54	1,875	146
New York	1,078	3,499	225	13,960	1,195
Philadelphia	1,420	4,210	197	9,795	590

Sources: *Negro Population in the U.S., 1790–1915*, 55; Leonard P. Curry, *The Free Black in Urban America, 1800–1850* (Chicago: University of Chicago Press, 1981), 250.

and as a proportion of the city's population. Free blacks were, in fact, the most urban group in America.[19]

Paul Cuffe, living in coastal Massachusetts, was one of the free blacks who profited from the growing post–Revolutionary War trade. By the time the Revolution was over, Cuffe was a mature man of twenty-five with many years of experience as a sailor fishing the waters around Nantucket and in the North Atlantic and whaling off Mexico and the West Indies. He had grown up in relative security with close ties to his many siblings and his mother's people in the Indian community at Chilmark on Martha's Vineyard. When his father, the African freedman Cuffe Slocum, died before the war, he left Paul's mother, Ruth, and her ten children settled on their 116-acre farm in Dartmouth, Massachusetts. After the war Paul Cuffe married an Indian woman, Alice Pequit, and established a partnership with his brother-in-law Michael Wainer. By the early 1790s Cuffe and Wainer had two schooners fishing and whaling off the coast of Newfoundland, the beginning of a successful, lifelong business partnership.[20]

As the urban free black population increased, black families formed the basis for more stable, expanded, and diverse community institutions. Among the first institutions were mutual-aid societies, cooperative organizations formed to provide funds for burials and aid to members' widows, the sick, and the unemployed. Racial prejudice and often, ironically, their desperate poverty frequently disqualified blacks from the sources of aid available to most whites. Early charitable institutions were loath to aid those they did not consider to be a local responsibility or those whose extreme poverty, poor character, or bad habits, they believed, did not make them good candidates for reform. Thus African Americans were likely to be forced to rely on the resources of their own communities. This necessity, a traditional African communal ethic, and the African religious significance of a proper burial all contributed to a proliferation of mutual-aid societies among free blacks. There was a general increase in associations in American society after the Revolution, but their

Paul Cuffe,
sea captain,
shipbuilder, and
merchant, with an
engraving of his ship,
Traveller, 1812.

Photographs and Prints
Division, Schomburg
Center for Research
in Black Culture,
The New York Public
Library, Astor, Lenox,
and Tilden Foundations.

growth among blacks also drew on the African traditions still vivid in the memories of thousands of African-born Americans. In many African societies an
individual's identity was derived from the family, an individual's primary
responsibility was to the family, and the community was simply an extension
of the family. This communalism became the basis for social organization in
the black communities established in the West Indies and North America.
"What is mine goes," instructed one African proverb, but "what is ours
abides." One of the earliest mutual-aid groups, the African Union Society, was
organized in Newport, Rhode Island, in 1780. The Free African Society was
formed in Philadelphia in 1787 by free blacks in cooperation with white antislavery Quakers, and blacks in Boston organized the African Society in 1796.
Through these organizations, people contributed to the support of the spouses
and orphans of deceased members and to disabled, unemployed or destitute
members and their families. The Philadelphia organization, with two prominent community leaders, Richard Allen and Absalom Jones, among its
founders, also provided aid to ex-slaves. Both Allen and Jones had been

slaves, and each had bought his own freedom shortly before establishing the Free African Society.[21]

Another early African American community organization was the Masons. Even before the Revolution, a small black Masonic group was organized in Boston by Prince Hall, a native of Barbados and the son of a free mulatto mother and a British father. After he arrived in Massachusetts, Hall had become a soapmaker and eventually a Methodist lay preacher. Under his leadership the black men applied to the white Masonic order in Boston for an official license as a lodge, but the Boston Masons refused to recognize an organization of black Masons. Hall then turned to the British order, through an Irish military regiment stationed in Boston, and they accepted his application. In 1775, just before the British troops were expelled from the city by American forces, fifteen African Americans were initiated into the British lodge, and they continued to meet during the Revolution. After the war Hall, who had served six years with the American troops, again applied to the American Masonic order for recognition, and again was refused. Finally he turned to the Grand Lodge of England, which officially granted permission in 1784 for the formation of the African Lodge Number One of Boston. Formally established in 1787 and renumbered Lodge 459, it was the first black Masonic lodge in the United States. It became a center for community mutual aid, political action, and a catalyst for other black Masonic organizations in Providence and Philadelphia. By the turn of the nineteenth century, there were several black Masonic lodges, some initiated with the support of the Boston group. Philadelphia was rapidly becoming an important center of Masonic activity; one of its lodges was established by black sailors with the aid of the Grand Lodge of Germany in 1798. The proliferation of lodges throughout the North established regular lines of communication among many black communities, facilitating political organization in the nineteenth century. Like other African American associations, Masonic organizations were multipurpose mutual aid, religious, and political action groups.

By the turn of the nineteenth century, African Americans had formed hundreds of mutual aid societies, fraternal organizations, and community service groups boasting thousands of members throughout the North. Often these groups included both males and females, although some—like the African Masonic lodges in many cities or the Female Benevolent Society of St. Thomas in Philadelphia—were restricted. Membership dues provided the funds for the operation of these groups and the benefits they provided. Membership in the African Benevolent Society of Newport, Rhode Island, required a fifty-cent initiation fee, and the African Marine Fund in New York City required an initiation fee of one dollar. Additional monthly dues ranged from twelve and a half to fifty cents. Boston's African Society, for example, charged twenty-five cents to enter the society and another twenty-five cents for monthly dues. These were considerable fees for a generally poor people, but these organizations provided essential services in a manner congruent with African Americans' values, and a great many people joined. Various contemporaneous studies of the benevolent societies in Philadelphia provide some measure of the growth and importance of such organizations. In 1830 there were almost fifty societies, sixty by 1836 and one hundred by 1838, paying out approximately six, nine, and fourteen thousand dollars in annual benefits, respectively. Though there was undoubtedly an overlapping membership, the nearly 7,500 members in 1838 represented a remarkable level of organization in the city's black community of 10,507 people.[22]

Early black organizations concerned themselves not only with the financial and social needs of community members but also with their spiritual and political needs. Free African Societies often provided religious services, and some were the forerunners of African American churches. Philadelphia's Bethel Church, founded by Richard Allen, and the African Church (later called the African Episcopal Church of St. Thomas), founded by Absalom Jones, both grew from the membership of the Free African Society. In Boston the African Baptist church grew out of the African Society of that city and drew its original membership from that organization. As in traditional African life, the distinctions between secular and sacred institutions were never great in African American society. Black churches—the communities' most important public institutions—served as social centers where community drama groups, bands, youth organizations, men's and women's clubs, and debating societies met. They often hosted community educational facilities and served as political forums and convention halls. The first black school in Boston met originally in the basement of the African Meeting House, the home of the African Baptist Church. The building also provided space for William Bassett's music classes for black children, for community band concerts, and for the rehearsals of the Social Harmonic Society, a popular local choir. Similar activities found rooms in the churches of Philadelphia and New York City. In almost all African American communities across the North, whenever community meetings were held, most were held in the black churches.[23]

As the political center of most black communities, the church was also a training ground for black leaders. In white society a young man aspiring to political prominence might enter law, run for minor local office, or work for a politician. In black society the most common route to community leadership was through the church. Black ministers were both the guardians of the spiritual life of the community and its political leaders. Their activities might range from leading worship services, ministering to the sick, and feeding the hungry to hiding fugitive slaves escaping from bondage.[24]

It was much more difficult for free blacks to establish organizations in the South, since southern slaveholders were greatly suspicious of free blacks not under their direct control. Laws prohibiting black gatherings without white supervision limited the movements of all African Americans. Restrictions grew stronger and were enforced more rigorously during periods when rumored or actual slave revolt made slaveholders more apprehensive. Still, southern free blacks formed societies to meet the spiritual and practical needs of their communities. Although some societies managed to meet secretly, public gatherings required white sponsorship. Typically a white clergyman was responsible for the oversight of a black church and its many related organizations. Despite white obstructions African American communities in major southern cities with sizable black populations, such as Charleston, Richmond, Baltimore, and Washington, D.C., were nearly as well organized as those in the North. By 1836 Baltimore blacks, for example, had about forty fraternal, literary, religious, and temperance associations, many attached to churches.[25] One type of free black organization in the South, the oldest of which was the Brown Fellowship Society formed in 1790 in Charleston, South Carolina, seemed to pose little threat to the slave system. Some of the membership was drawn from mulattoes who fled the Haitian Revolution after siding with the French colonials against the black revolutionaries. The color consciousness of these light-skinned Haitians found expression in groups like the Brown Fellowship, groups of economically and socially privileged African Americans whom whites judged less threatening to white supremacy. These mixed-race people were often related to prominent local white families, and many slaveholders hoped they would provide information about the slave population, warning of unrest and conspiracies.

The position of southern free blacks was complex. Since they were unable to depend on southern law for protection, patronage from powerful southern whites was the only buffer between them and the systematic injustice they were liable to suffer in the slave South. Indeed, some slave conspiracies were betrayed by other African Americans, both slave and free. But even elite black groups were involved in the common political issues of central concern to all African Americans: the opposition to slavery and the protection of fugitive slaves. Northern groups were the most visible proponents of black freedom, since even the limited white southern tolerance for antislavery expression had disappeared by 1830. The abolition of slavery, the most serious and immediate problem, was but one of many political concerns for blacks in America. As the new nation defined the rights of citizens through the passage of state constitutions, the rights of free blacks were increasingly limited.[26]

Discrimination and an uncertain future in America continued to spark interest in emigration, especially among African-born blacks. Capt. Paul

Cuffe, with an African father and a Native American mother, was one of those interested in African colonization. In 1810 he set sail in his ship, *Traveller,* with his nephew Thomas Wainer as first mate and an all-black crew, to explore the prospects for settlement in and trade with Sierra Leone. Cuffe was impressed by the settlement he found and hopeful that he could eventually demonstrate that a profitable trade not including slaves could be established between Africa and the United States. Among the 3,500 settlers were former American slaves who had come to the British colony by way of England or Canada, where they had gone with withdrawing British forces after the Revolution. There were also local Africans, blacks from the British West Indies, and people rescued from slave trading ships off the African coast. A handful of Europeans, approximately 1 percent of the colony's population, controlled almost two-thirds of the property in Sierra Leone. Recognizing that initial support for any trading venture would have to come from the British merchants who financed the European property holders, Cuffe sailed for England.

By April 1812, when Cuffe and Wainer returned to the United States, continuing tensions with Britain had escalated, and the United States had instituted a trade embargo. Since the *Traveller* had been in England, U.S. customs authorities confiscated Cuffe's cargo when he entered port in Rhode Island, an inauspicious beginning to his African trading venture. Through his connections with wealthy Quaker merchants, Cuffe was able to meet with President James Madison and Secretary of the Treasury Albert Gallatin, who helped him gain the release of his ship and cargo. But his standing in the business community did not protect him from the indignities of discrimination in public lodging and on public transportation, discrimination that increased his commitment to African settlement. In New York, Philadelphia, and Baltimore, Cuffe met with black leaders, reporting on the promise of Sierra Leone and encouraging them to establish organizations to promote Sierra Leone and organize potential settlers.

The trading ventures of merchants and captains like Paul Cuffe were deferred by the growing hostility between Britain and the United States. Many common sailors suffered more directly, losing work and wages as trade diminished. Americans complained that Britain acted with intolerable arrogance, not respecting the new nation's shipping rights, violating its territory, and impressing its citizens. Contrary to the peace agreements ending the Revolutionary War, British troops remained in western forts, and Britain seized neutral American ships to prevent them from trading with its enemy, France. English impressment gangs roamed European ports and boarded American ships at sea, forcibly taking the most likely sailors to serve aboard British vessels. Many blacks were among the American sailors British naval authorities abducted.[27]

During the spring of 1812 relations between England and the United States deteriorated further, and in June, President James Madison issued a formal declaration of war. Despite the Revolutionary War service of African Americans, American authorities again heatedly debated the question of black participation in the military. For southerners the prospect of arming their enormous, generally enslaved black population again evoked the terrifying specter of the Haitian Revolution. Meanwhile the British once again promised freedom to American slaves who joined their forces. Thousands of slaves escaped to the British army lines, some volunteering for military service. One alarmed southerner reported that blacks were "flocking to the enemy from all quarters."[28] African Americans served aboard British vessels in battles in the Great Lakes and Chesapeake Bay, and when British troops attacked Baltimore and invaded and burned the capital city of Washington in 1814, newly freed slaves were among them. When the United States offered to free slaves in return for military service, many volunteered, even when the terms were unattractive and discriminatory. New York slaves had to serve for three years before they were freed, and the cash payment normally provided to soldiers was generally paid instead to their masters. As in the Revolution, slaves fought for both Britain and the United States, joining whichever forces promised liberty.

Many free African Americans, motivated by patriotism or local loyalties, served with American forces on sea and land. They formed separate units in New York, Philadelphia, and other cities along the Atlantic coast. One New York "Citizen of Color" argued that it was the "duty of every colored man resident in this city to volunteer" when British forces threatened the coast. He argued that white Americans would see this as a "test of patriotism."[29] The spirit and unity of the builders of New York's fortifications were reflected in a popular song called "The Patriotic Diggers." "To Protect our rights / Gainst your flints and triggers," the lyrics challenged, "See on Brooklyn Heights / Our patriotic diggers," claiming, "Men of every age, / Color, rank, profession."[30]

In New England strong antiwar sentiment discouraged residents from participating in the war, and African Americans there were also less likely to join the American army. Black sailors from New England, however, were prominent participants. Cmmdr. Isaac Chauncey, who engaged the British on the Great Lakes, counted the fifty blacks under his command as "among [his] best men." At first Capt. Oliver H. Perry was uncomfortable with his integrated crew, one quarter of whom were black, but after defeating the British fleet in 1813, he praised the action of his black sailors and singled out several for special commendation.[31] Likewise Capt. Nathan Shaler lauded his black sailors, telling of one who after "a twenty-four pound shot struck him in the hip, and took away all the lower part of his body," urged his shipmates on, saying, "Fire away boys!—No haul a color down." Captain Shaler asserted that "while America has such tars, she has little to fear from the tyrants of Europe."[32]

Many American sailors were captured and spent time as prisoners of war in British jails, and some black sailors who had been impressed into British service chose to go to prison rather than fight for England when the war broke out. As many as eleven hundred black and five thousand white Americans were confined in England's Dartmoor prison by 1814. At first the British housed the Americans together, but as the population grew, they eventually segregated the prison barracks by race. Still, visiting between barracks and continual interaction among the prisoners gave Dartmoor an interracial cultural life. The black barracks became an important center of prison life, where interracial casts performed Shakespearean plays, interracial audiences enjoyed African music and dance, and regular church services were held by a black minister. Boxing classes were conducted by Richard Seaver, a black sailor from Salem, Massachusetts. Classes in reading and writing were taught by inmates of the black barracks. Dartmoor was no interracial utopia—it was a prison filled with sailors where racial tensions occasionally erupted into conflict, but it also had a lively interracial political, economic, and social life. Although the prison was segregated, shipboard habits, identifications, and friendships carried over to prison life. One black prisoner from Newburyport, Massachusetts, for example, made a point of sharing his card-game winnings of "a two penny loaf and a pint of coffee" with his white mates from his hometown.[33]

In December 1814 Britain and the United States negotiated an end to their hostilities with the Treaty of Ghent. Napoleon had abdicated as emperor of France, ending the war in Europe and removing the issue of neutrality rights for American shipping. The issue of impressment was not resolved, but the war's end reduced England's need for sailors. Britain did drop its demands for territorial concessions and for American recognition of an independent Indian state and finally withdrew from the western boundaries of the United States. Ironically, the battle of New Orleans, the best-known battle of the war, was actually fought after the war was over, and it involved blacks as combatants on both sides. In New Orleans, Gen. Andrew Jackson, future president of the United States, faced a British invasion. Jackson commanded a force of frontier militiamen which included at least six hundred mulattoes and free blacks. He was uncertain of blacks' willingness to engage the English in battle and so made plans to move them to the rear rather than risk their joining the British troops. In a desperate effort to secure the loyalty of the city's people of color as British forces approached, Jackson promised black troops the same pay, equipment, food, and 160-acre land grants as white troops. Years later Jackson confided to President James Monroe that he had been uncomfortable recruiting black troops but had employed them largely to prevent the British from using them against the city.[34]

Contrary to Jackson's fears black Americans and white Americans successfully defended New Orleans, inflicting heavy casualties on the invaders and providing the United States with an important victory. Jackson kept his promise to the free blacks and rewarded them for their service, but the slaves who fought with him were not so fortunate. James Roberts, born a slave on the eastern shore of Maryland, was twice unlucky. He had earned his freedom for service in the Continental forces during the Revolutionary War, but his master sold him to a slaveholder in New Orleans for fifteen hundred dollars instead. Decades later, when the call went out for slaves to defend the city against the British invasion, Roberts volunteered, hoping to gain his freedom. After the battle Jackson extolled the bravery and skill of the blacks who had stood with him but insisted he was powerless to interfere with masters' rights over their slave property. Roberts returned to slavery a bitter man, feeling he had once again been "duped by the white man."[35] Many of the slaves who escaped to the British fared little better and were sold to the West Indies by British officers who made considerable profit from this illegal trade. In response to persistent complaints by New Orleans slaveholders, England finally agreed to pay more than one million dollars in 1826 to compensate them for the loss of slaves who escaped during the battle.[36]

Winning the war reinforced the developing American identity and heightened nationalism especially for whites, but some blacks continued to contemplate emigration to Africa. Less than a year after the peace had been signed, Paul Cuffe set sail for Sierra Leone on the *Traveller*, carrying goods for trading and fifty-eight African American passengers. Cuffe settled his people on the land he purchased in the colony and by the spring of 1817 returned to the United States to promote colonization. He soon found powerful allies among a number of white men who had formed a group in 1816 to promote the colonization of blacks in West Africa. Hoping for congressional financing, and calling their organization the American Colonization Society, they included some of the era's most prominent men. Virginian Charles Fenton Mercer, New Jersey minister Robert Finley, and Francis Scott Key, composer of the present-day national anthem, the "Star-Spangled Banner," were among the society's founders. Members included powerful political figures such as Henry Clay, the U.S. representative from Tennessee, Daniel Webster, U.S. senator from Massachusetts, future president John Tyler, Supreme Court Justice Bushred Washington, and Gen. Andrew Jackson. The fact that this distinguished group was composed mainly of slaveholders aroused black suspicions, but Paul Cuffe's commitment to promoting African settlement and trade led him to an association with some of the society's members. Cuffe's knowledge of shipping, of West Africa, and of Sierra Leone were extremely useful to the colonizationists. He was able to persuade several black leaders in New York and Philadelphia to consider the organization's project, but most rank-and-file black community members in northern cities rejected any association with the American Colonization Society. The black masses of Philadelphia remained unconvinced even though many of the city's important leaders, James Forten and Richard Allen among them, originally supported colonization. Cuffe's African Institutions provided organizational support, prominent white leaders addressed large crowds promoting the society, and Cuffe himself spoke in black churches extolling the wonders of Africa and the opportunities opened by colonization.

In 1820, with financial help from the federal government, the society founded its own colony and called it Liberia. Daniel Coker, one of the country's most prominent black ministers, led eighty-six African American settlers who set sail on the *Mayflower of Liberia* for a new life in the West African colony. There was significant black support for the American Colonization Society in the states of Virginia and Maryland in the Upper South. There opportunities for free blacks were extremely limited, and some masters were willing to free slaves who agreed to emigrate. Several blacks from Richmond, Virginia, were members of another group, which set off in 1821. Lott Cary, a former slave who bought his own freedom, was one of them. His emigration was sponsored by Richmond's First Baptist Church, an interracial congregation who sent him as a missionary to the African people. Like many settlers Cary had many reasons for emigrating. "I am an African," he declared, explaining that he wanted to regain his heritage and hoped to develop his talents without the restrictions burdening black people in America. For black Americans born in Africa, colonization offered the opportunity to rejoin the friends and family they had been forced to leave behind many years before. African-born Boston Crummel, originally from the region of Sierra Leone and enslaved in New York for many years, was anxious to go home, but Crummel's wife, who had been born on Long Island in New York, was far more skeptical about emigration and about the colonization society. During the years before the Civil War the colony of Liberia survived, but it drew only small numbers of emigrants from the United States.

The establishment of the colonization society was directly connected to the growing importance of cotton, slavery, and the planter class. Even though slavery became increasingly isolated in the South as northern states abolished the institution during the early years of the nineteenth century, the national power of slaveholders grew. Slaveholders such as James Monroe, Andrew Jackson, Henry Clay, and John C. Calhoun held the highest political offices in the nation. New York bankers financed southern cotton production, and

Massachusetts textile mills depended on a steady supply of raw cotton. The American Colonization Society provided a convenient vehicle for whites uneasy about slavery but unwilling to confront the power of cotton and its slave system directly. The society allowed the discomfited to subscribe to somewhat contradictory aims. They could advocate removing free blacks to Africa, thereby placating slaveholders seeking a more secure slave system without the danger posed by free blacks, they could reassure the northern white workers who were becoming increasingly concerned about competition from black labor, and they could use the language of freedom and opportunity in campaigns to recruit blacks for colonization. The multiplicity of goals accommodated by the American Colonization Society's program help to explain both its popularity with whites and its failure to attract most northern blacks. Remembering blacks who had participated in the Revolutionary struggles and defended the new nation in the War of 1812, many African Americans were insulted and offended by colonization schemes sponsored by slaveholders.

As black people struggled to define their place in the United States after the war, there were confusing signals from white authorities. Northern states abolished slavery, but many restricted African Americans' civil rights. Colonization seemed to provide incentives for slaveholders to free their slaves and allow them to emigrate, but the increasing power of the Cotton Kingdom promised an entrenched slave system in the South. As regional tensions between slave and nonslave states grew, Congress became the arena for the struggle to maintain their balance of power. When the Missouri Territory applied for admittance to the Union early in 1819, northern congressmen tried to exact the gradual release of its ten thousand slaves and a restriction on the further introduction of slaves in return for Missouri's becoming a state. The southern congressmen argued that this was unconstitutional, but a crisis was avoided by a compromise providing for the simultaneous admission of Missouri as a slave state and Maine as a free state, and an agreement that Missouri's southern border would be the northern limit of slavery. The Missouri Compromise of 1820, as it was called, was one of a succession of confrontations between the slaveholding and nonslaveholding states, increasing in seriousness and marking the country's widening sectional rift. Years later black abolitionist Frederick Douglass identified the Missouri Compromise as the first of those "shocking development[s] of that moral weakness in high places which [attended] the conflict between the spirit of liberty and the spirit of slavery."[37]

Chapter 5

1821 Ira F. Aldridge, black Shakespearean actor, joins the company of the African Theater in New York City

1822 Denmark Vesey's slave revolt thwarted in South Carolina

1823 Alexander Lucius Twilight graduates from Middlebury College, the first black college graduate in the United States

1825 Erie Canal across New York State opens

1827 John Russwurm and Samuel Cornish begin publishing *Freedom's Journal,* the first black newspaper

1828 Andrew Jackson elected president

White entertainer Thomas Rice performs the first blackface minstrel show in Louisville, Kentucky

1831 Nat Turner leads slave revolt in Virginia

Slavery and the Slave Community

During the eighteenth century, when Equiano was captured and enslaved, slavery was a profitable but still relatively small institution in British North America. By the nineteenth century slavery had grown, filling a large part of the labor needs of the new nation and following the westward expansion of the plantation South. The number of slaves had increased from fewer than seven hundred thousand in 1790 to more than one million by 1810. Even after the constitutional ban on the African slave trade went into effect in 1808, the institution of slavery continued to grow. Illegal imports combined with natural increase to result in a population of nearly four million slaves by 1860. As the northern states completed their abolition of slavery during the first decades of the nineteenth century, nearly all of slavery's growth occurred in the southern states, especially in the western South. These developments increased sectional differences and exacerbated tensions growing from the diverging interests of North and South.[1] The great increase in the slave population was especially notable in light of the fact that the number of slaves imported directly from Africa had actually declined during the last half of the eighteenth century. The experience of many slaves in the nineteenth century was very different from Equiano's in the previous one. All Africans were separated from their families and homelands; with the opening of the western South, even slaves born in America faced the danger of being separated from their families as members were sold to the large plantations in places such as Mississippi and Louisiana. The voracious appetite of this labor system for new workers increased the danger for free blacks even in northern states. In the 1840s musician Solomon Northup, a freeborn man in his early thirties, lived in New York State with his wife and three children. One day while his wife was out of town, he was enticed by the promise of a job playing his fiddle and traveled first to New York City and then to Washington, D.C., where he was kidnapped into slavery. He was taken through Virginia to the auction block in New Orleans. On the way he encountered two other free men who had also been kidnapped, one from Cincinnati, Ohio, and the other from Norfolk, Virginia. Northup labored twelve years as a slave on the sugarcane and cotton plantations of Louisiana before he could get word to his family in New York and gain his freedom.[2]

Abd al-Rahman Ibrahima
(1762–1829)

Abduhl Rahahman (Abd al-Rahman Ibrahima), West African prince, son of the King of Timbo, enslaved in America for almost forty years. Prints and Photographs Division, Library of Congress, Washington, D.C.

Abd al-Rahman Ibrahima was the son of the ruler of the warlike Muslim Fulbe people from the West African interior, traders of ivory, livestock, gold, and slaves to coastal settlements. Ibrahima received a traditional Islamic education and pursued advanced studies in Macina and Timbuktu, more than a thousand miles from home. At seventeen he returned home and joined the army; by the time he was twenty-six, he was a husband, father, experienced horseman, and army commander. After a battle in 1788, he was ambushed, taken prisoner, and sold to slave traders, along with fifty warriors.

Eight months, six thousand miles, and a series of sales brought Abd al-Rahman, or Abduhl Rahahman, to Natchez in Spanish-controlled territory. Tobacco planter Thomas Foster, a man of little learning, bought him and another African on credit for $930. The striking, six-foot-tall Rahahman, with shoulder-length hair and a dignified, intelligent appearance explained to his owner, probably through a Mandinka translator, that his father would pay a king's ransom in gold for his return. Foster responded by naming him Prince.

Six years later Foster bought Isabella, an American-born Christian woman, and soon Ibrahima and Isabella were married. Rahahman endured the rigors of slavery while maintaining his religion and some Arabic literacy. His integrity gained his owner's trust, and on weekends he was able to take produce to the Natchez market where occasionally newly imported Africans gave him news from home. In 1807 he encountered John Cox, a man who had known him and his father in Africa. Cox tried to arrange Rahahman's freedom, but Foster refused to sell him. Cox publicized the story, Rahahman became a celebrity, and eventually Secretary of State Henry Clay and President John Quincy Adams became his advocates. Foster agreed to sell him, but only if he agreed to go to Africa. Aided by the African Colonization Society and a one-year fund-raising tour, Ibrahima and Isabella sailed for Africa in 1829. During forty years of slavery Rahahman had continued to hope for freedom and to return home, but he died in Africa before he could get home. Two of his nine children and five of his grandchildren joined Isabella in freedom in Liberia the following year.

During the nineteenth century an increasing proportion of North American slaves had been born in the United States, and the changing character of the slave population had important consequences. African-born slaves suffered the torment of lost liberty and forced labor and the anguish of separation from their cultural homes and extended families. The many languages people from West and Central Africa spoke were often so distinct that communication between Africans was initially difficult. Over time, however, multiple tongues mingled on the plantations in British North America and combined to form a language not native to any but that made communication between Africans possible. The longer slaves lived in the United States, the more familiar they became with the English language and with the society of their captors. African linguistic styles continued to influence the English spoken by even those Africans who had lived in the country for an extended period or had been born there, and in areas with many blacks they influenced white speech as well. Following African speech patterns, African Americans sometimes dropped the unstressed syllables of English words or eliminated the verb in an English sentence, as in "Henry, he in field."[3] Although African- and American-born slaves suffered equally under the slave labor system, the African Americans' greater knowledge of European ways, their more sophisticated understanding of the slave structure, and wider support system better equipped them to cope with their situation. Their greater facility with English and the Creole languages developed by these American-born blacks made it possible for them to communicate with whites beyond simple work related matters. This also allowed them greater access to information, an important tool in their struggle to deal with the power of slaveholders and the white society.

African-born slaves—reputedly more difficult to control, more likely to run away, and more likely to risk their lives in resistance or escape—were also more likely to fail in their attempts and to be recaptured or killed. They lacked experience dealing with masters and overseers and were unfamiliar with the countryside. The defiant stance or bold action of proud Africans that has provided material for heroic historical drama could mean death for slaves. In the early nineteenth century, when a night patrol with dogs barking at their heels galloped around the Virginia countryside to discover blacks lingering in revelry past their curfew, most slaves could have been expected to disappear safely into the darkness. Instead Robert, "an athletic, powerful slave, who had been but a short time from his 'father land' [and] whose spirit the cowardly overseer had labored in vain to quell" sent the women to a nearby cabin and rallied the men to stand their ground. He stationed two men just inside the door of a darkened cabin with orders to rush out and chase off the patrol's horses when they broke in. In the violent encounter that ensued, two whites

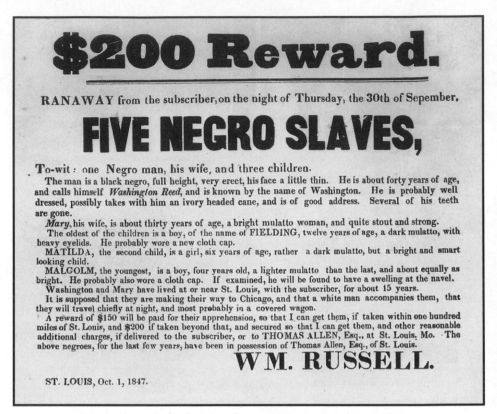

$200 Reward.

RANAWAY from the subscriber, on the night of Thursday, the 30th of Sepember,

FIVE NEGRO SLAVES,

To-wit : one Negro man, his wife, and three children.

The man is a black negro, full height, very erect, his face a little thin. He is about forty years of age, and calls himself *Washington Reed*, and is known by the name of Washington. He is probably well dressed, possibly takes with him an ivory headed cane, and is of good address. Several of his teeth are gone.

Mary, his wife, is about thirty years of age, a bright mulatto woman, and quite stout and strong.

The oldest of the children is a boy, of the name of FIELDING, twelve years of age, a dark mulatto, with heavy eyelids. He probably wore a new cloth cap.

MATILDA, the second child, is a girl, six years of age, rather a dark mulatto, but a bright and smart looking child.

MALCOLM, the youngest, is a boy, four years old, a lighter mulatto than the last, and about equally as bright. He probably also wore a cloth cap. If examined, he will be found to have a swelling at the navel.

Washington and Mary have lived at or near St. Louis, with the subscriber, for about 15 years.

It is supposed that they are making their way to Chicago, and that a white man accompanies them, that they will travel chiefly at night, and most probably in a covered wagon.

A reward of $150 will be paid for their apprehension, so that I can get them, if taken within one hundred miles of St. Louis, and $200 if taken beyond that, and secured so that I can get them, and other reasonable additional charges, if delivered to the subscriber, or to THOMAS ALLEN, Esq., at St. Louis, Mo. The above negroes, for the last few years, have been in possession of Thomas Allen, Esq., of St. Louis.

WM. RUSSELL.

ST. LOUIS, Oct. 1, 1847.

Reward notice for fugitive slaves, St. Louis, October 1, 1847.
Prints and Photographs Division, Library of Congress, Washington, D.C.

and six blacks were killed, and several on both sides were injured. Three of the slaves, including the African, left widows and children, and all the slaves in the area suffered the consequences of their resistance. "[White] people flocked from every quarter, armed to the teeth, swearing vengeance on the defenseless slaves." The most experienced understood that all would suffer for the defiant acts of a few.[4]

The slaves' violent retaliation against slavery, feared by slaveholders and their allies, was a realistic and ever-present danger. Spontaneous violence, an emotional outburst resulting from some long-simmering grievance or suddenly unbearable outrage, was most likely. Overseers were most vulnerable to such attacks because they worked more closely with slaves than other whites, because their job was to force compliance with the work routine and plantation discipline, and because they were the ones most likely to administer punishment. It was during the administration of punishment that overseers were particularly susceptible to angry slave reprisals, as when an overseer punished a young slave in Marksville, Louisiana, for failure to complete assigned work. The slave explained that he had been unable to complete his work because the overseer had sent him on an errand that had taken much longer than either of them had anticipated. The overseer was unmoved by this argument and forced the slave to kneel for a severe whipping. After the first few blows, the slave, smarting from both the whip and the particular injustice, leaped to his feet, grabbed an ax, and hacked the overseer to pieces.[5]

While an angry reaction to some specific injustice or brutal treatment may have triggered violence, rarely was the slave reacting to a single act. More often a long line of such abuses culminated in violent retaliation. Some slaves created detailed plans and organized their movements carefully, as when a group of slaves came together on one South Carolina plantation to plan a strategy for doing away with their abusive overseer. Understanding southern class antagonisms, they planned to take advantage of their master's prejudice against working-class overseers. The slaves surprised the well-armed overseer when he was alone, beat him to death, and carried his body to a nearby swamp and burned it. When the overseer did not arrive for work, his planter employer assumed that he was irresponsible and had simply walked off the job.[6]

The most radical kinds of resistance were those that struck not simply at injustice from an individual slaveholder or overseer but more consciously against the institution itself. There were fewer of these full-blown slave revolts, but they were extremely important for what they symbolized for both master and slave. The Stono rebellion in mid-eighteenth-century South Carolina, the Haitian Revolution at the end of the eighteenth century, and Gabriel's rebellion in early-nineteenth-century Virginia all created fear in white communities. In an effort to guard against revolt, governments sometimes placed severe restrictions on the movements and activities of slaves. Fear drove planters to constant vigilance. Some masters sat up all night, armed and on guard against expected violence, and both masters and slaves understood why. "How can men, who know they are abusing others all day," one slave asked rhetorically, "lie down and sleep quietly at night . . . when they know that men feel revengeful, and might burn their property, or even kill them?"[7]

Such was the fear in the early 1820s when the word was passed in Charleston, South Carolina, that carpenter Denmark Vesey, a former slave who had won his freedom in a lottery, was planning a revolt. In one of the most extensive slave plots in American history, potentially involving up to nine thousand slaves, Vesey and his aides worked for over a year, drawing up plans, fashioning weapons, and participating in West African war rituals under the supervision of slave conjurer Gullah Jack. Their plan to attack Charleston, capture guns and ammunition from the city armory, and march into the countryside liberating slaves as they went was discovered. South Carolina's governor, whose slave had been part of the plot, called out troops to crush the rebellion before it could get under way. The conspirators were captured, thirty-seven were banished from the region, and thirty-five, including Vesey, were executed. The Vesey conspiracy caused near panic in South Carolina as rumors circulated that it had been inspired by northern opponents of slavery and free blacks outside the state. There were theories that educated blacks were the main conspirators. Throughout the region new restrictions were imposed on slaves and free blacks, and old regulations that had languished were rigidly enforced. During such times black southerners were especially vulnerable, and most kept out of public view until white fears had subsided.[8] The most successful slave revolt during the antebellum period took place in Southhampton County, Virginia, in the summer of 1831. Under the leadership of slave preacher Nat Turner, a slave army of seventy or more attacked and killed fifty-seven whites, driving others into the swamps and creating hysteria in the entire region. It took a superior force of some three thousand, including militia from surrounding areas and neighboring states, to end the slave revolt. In a frenzy of retribution, whites killed hundreds of slaves, many of whom had played no role in the rebellion. By early winter, Turner was arrested, tried, and convicted of insurrection and murder, and on November 11, he was hanged in Jerusalem, Virginia. Turner's rebellion was the embodiment of white southern nightmares, swift and deadly, involving more and more slaves as the revolt progressed. Such open violence, however, was the exception in the antebellum South. Slaveholders were protected by a broad array of military forces from other communities, surrounding states, and ultimately the national government. This realization tempered revolutionary actions among most slaves, but some were willing to resort to violence despite the nearly inevitable deadly consequences.[9]

In order to control its slave population in the face of continuous resistance and periodic unrest, the South became a police state. Both slaveholding and nonslaveholding whites were charged with manning the slave patrols that watched transportation routes and gathering places to ensure that slaves were not off plantations without permission and did not meet in unauthorized groups. This martial atmosphere helped encourage a southern attitude of militarism, as John Hope Franklin argued in his classic study *The Militant South*. In order to enslave millions of African people and to maintain them in bondage, southern society was forced to tolerate and came to honor a military social climate that accepted violence as a necessity, brutalizing and dehumanizing all those involved.[10]

Slavery's brutality helped define a general climate of sanctioned violence in southern society and also spawned violence among whites. The historian Bertram Wyatt-Brown, studying pre–Civil War southern culture, argued

Nat Turner, leader
of a slave revolt in
Southhampton, Virginia,
1831.

Prints and Photographs Division,
Library of Congress,
Washington, D.C.

that the concept of honor was the centerpiece of southern relationships, especially among white males.[11] Presumably honorless blacks were the defining
"others" against whom even poor white men could measure their own status. Violence against blacks was a display of white power and a defense of white
honor. Insults to other whites could also lead to the violent defense of a man's
honor. To be without honor was to be lower than a white person, to be more
nearly black, and graphic accounts of heroic violence among southern white
men became part of the regional folklore. "Honor in the Old South applied
to all White classes, though with manifestations appropriate to each ranking."
Among the southern elites, dueling was the classic means of defending
honor, and savage fistfights were common among lower-class men, and both
were tolerated by authorities. Murder and assault rates in the slaveholding
South were ten times or more higher than in New England. The South was
equal in its rates of violence to the West, which had less organized legal authority and a much higher proportion of the young single men who were most
likely to be violent. "Violence in the South," as Wyatt-Brown has argued, "had
its unique source in slavery and the structures of black subordination."[12]

In the face of the formidable power exercised by slaveholders, most
slaves wisely limited their protests to covert actions. It was widely believed
that the most effective and practical protest was action that could not be traced
to its perpetrator. Most slaves asserted themselves in ways less likely to result
in severe punishment. Many resisted the slaveowners' authority by actions

slaveowners viewed as deceitful and dishonest, including such tactics as breaking tools, setting barns afire, or lying to and tricking the master. Stealing was another way slaves could exert control while also obtaining necessities or small luxuries. Slaves frequently justified it with the argument that taking something belonging to the master was simply redistributing the master's property, since they themselves were also the master's property. For slaves, stealing from the master was generally acceptable or even admirable; however, stealing from fellow slaves was not.

To the slaves slavery was more than the absence of freedom, it was the denial of their humanity. Theirs was a constant contention for human dignity and for some measure of autonomy within the plantation society. Masters held the great advantage, of course. Backed by local and national laws, they could punish with impunity or even kill slaves who threatened their authority. Resisting slavery was a complex matter involving many kinds of action and inaction. It was not always a confrontational refusal to submit to the authority of owners or overseers. Resistance was also a matter of surviving, of trying to protect loved ones, and remaining loyal to friends and fellow slaves.

Some earlier historians believed that the master's influence was absolute. It is true that slaves were required to adapt to the culture of the slaveholders, but more recent scholars have uncovered other influences. They have noted a wide variety of "significant others"—people other than the master, who played important roles in a slave's life—and have described the two separate interlocked communities that developed on the plantation. One community revolved around the "big house," where the master and his family had the greatest control and where the slaves were most likely to apparently acquiesce to white authority. This was where most white people gained their impressions of slavery and of southern black people, and this was the plantation community that formed the popular image of the genteel, courtly South in the American imagination. There was another very different plantation community in the slave quarters, however, where white people held far less direct power and the expressions of the slaves were less guarded. It was in this community that slaves could maintain some degree of dignity and control. In view of masters' attempts to be the only significant influence on the slaves, the maintenance of a slave community was a form of resistance to slavery.

By the nineteenth century most slaves lived on large plantations. Although three-quarters of southerners held no slaves, and most slaveholders owned fewer than five, three-quarters of the slaves lived in groups of ten or more, and half lived in slave communities of twenty or more. The growth of the institution, the development of the western South, and more equal numbers of men and women resulted in living arrangements for slaves that ranged from small households or extended "families" to complex slave communities. Solomon Northup's experience of being kidnapped into the Lower South in the 1840s illustrates many of these possibilities. His autobiography gives a remarkable firsthand account of the unpredictable life and degradation of the slave and provides an unusually detailed picture of the lives of slaves in the Lower South during this period.[13]

When first sold in New Orleans, Northup was taken several hundred miles north up the Mississippi River and the Red River to a lumbering camp maintained by his owner, William Ford. There Northup lived near the master's family, with ten other slaves. Working in or around the house were Rose, a slave from Washington who had been there five years; Sally, the mother of two toddlers; John, a sixteen-year-old who worked as the cook; and Eliza, who had been purchased by Ford along with Northup. Eliza had been the slave mistress of a wealthy man near Washington, living for years as his wife and bearing his child. She had the bad fortune, however, to be part of her owner's property, which fell to his lawful wife in their divorce settlement, and was sold. Rose and Eliza became immediate friends on the basis of their both having come from Washington, but the Fords were dissatisfied with Eliza's work, and she was soon sent to the fields. According to Northup's account she was disconsolate and never recovered from being separated from her two young children when they were all sold separately into slavery. In addition to two men who worked at the mill—Sam, also from Washington; and Anthony, a blacksmith from Kentucky who had been with Ford for ten years—there were three slave lumbermen—Northup; Walton, Rose's husband, who had been born a slave on Ford's plantation; and Harry, who was also purchased with Northup. These eleven slaves—some related by birth and some by common background, some many years with the same master, and others newcomers—were all united by their status and lived and worked together in a kind of extended family.[14]

Yet unpredictable change was the awful norm of a slave's life. Northup lived with these people a relatively short time, though he did remain in the same area for his entire time in slavery and so maintained contact with them. After a few years working there, and on Ford's large plantation farther south, he was hired out and eventually sold. He continued to be hired out periodically during slack times on his home plantation or busy times for others, and so worked and lived in different situations. He was employed as a carpenter, hired out to assist a white carpenter or to work on his own, as a fiddler for local plantation parties, and as part of the gang labor cutting cane on large sugar plantations. For most of his remaining ten years in the South, Northup worked on a small cotton plantation as the slave of Edwin Epps, an uneducated and harsh man who had worked as a slave driver and overseer before renting and then purchasing his own plantation. On the plantation where he spent the last eight years, Northup joined an established group of eight other slaves who had been together for many years.

The slaves' fortunes were directly linked to their master's financial stability, and the consequences of a master's insolvency were often dire for his slaves. All but the youngest of Epps's slaves had belonged to a county sheriff in South Carolina named James Buford. When Buford fell on hard times, these seven slaves were put in chains and marched the long distance across the Mississippi River to the plantation of Archy B. Williams, who used them to pay his overseer, Edwin Epps. Five of Epps's nine slaves belonged to the same family. Phebe, her husband Wiley, Phebe's two grown sons by a former husband, and Edward, born to Phebe and Wiley after their purchase by Epps. In addition to this family the small community in the slave quarters included Susan, the elderly Abram, and a young woman named Patsey. Abram was a storyteller and philosopher who had been born in Tennessee and lived there until the 1830s, when a slave trader sold him to Buford in South Carolina. He regaled his fellow slaves with tales of Tennessee's Gen. Andrew Jackson and the exploits of his black soldiers in the War of 1812. Such resourceful slaves could sometimes carve personal space from the largely inflexible world of the plantation.[15]

Special talents or abilities, like Abram's storytelling or Solomon's fiddling, gained some slaves respect and authority among their fellow slaves. Slave conjurers and preachers who ministered to the spiritual needs of the community were influential, although the preacher's role was especially complex. Some slave masters insisted that their slaves convert to Christianity, and large numbers of slaves had professed the Christian faith by the mid–nineteenth century. Yet even converts did not simply adopt European religious beliefs. Many Africans and African Americans never adopted Christian beliefs, and those who did generally adapted them to their own African cultural and spiritual traditions, using them for their own practical purposes. The planters encouraged the acceptance of a religion emphasizing obedience, sin, and gentleness, but slaves were drawn to the Old Testament stories from Exodus, featuring themes of escape from bondage and freedom from oppression. Slave preachers who supported the slaves' longing for freedom were sure to find favor within the slave community. Many relatively benevolent planters saw religion as a vehicle for reinforcing their power, arguing that God commanded slaves to obey their masters and to be loyal, leaving any relief from bondage for the next life. Slaves privately rejected arguments that slavery was the will of God visited on Africans as punishment for an ancient sin. "I was not very long in finding out," recalled Frederick Douglass, that "it was not color, but crime, not God, but man, that afforded the true explanation of the existence of slavery."[16]

African Americans not only adapted Christian beliefs to their previous belief systems and their present condition, they also incorporated African styles of worship into their Christian services. Far less staid and solemn than Europeans in their worship, Africans celebrated their religion with rhythmic song and dance. The ring shout, a ritual circle dance done by the Dahomey, the Kongo, and other societies of West Africa, symbolized a oneness with nature and with ancestors and the solidarity of community. It linked the sacred and the secular worlds and was an important display of religious emotion.[17] As Europeans and Africans met in America, some American religious customs took on African characteristics. This was especially true in the South for blacks and whites, but it was most obvious among African American slaves. As one Virginia slave recalled:

> The way in which we worshiped is almost indescribable. The singing was accompanied by a certain ecstasy of motion, clapping of hands, tossing of heads, which could continue without cessation about half an hour; one would lead off in a kind of recitative style, others joining in the chorus. The old house partook of the ecstasy; it rang with their jubilant shouts, and shook in all its joints.[18]

Whites had different reactions to African American forms of Christian worship. Some found it attractive for what they saw as its unpretentious simplicity. Some were repulsed by what they called its primitive heathenish display. Masters sometimes found it threatening and unnecessary, and a few refused to allow their slaves openly to practice any form of religion. One slaveholder discouraged his slaves' religious interests, saying, "You niggers have no souls, you are just like those cattle, when you die there is an end of you, there is [nothing] more for you to think about than living."[19]

Efforts to curb slave religious worship were generally unsuccessful. A particular brand of African American Christianity remained a central part of slave activity and identity throughout the pre–Civil War period, and the slave preacher remained an important actor in the slave community. The preacher's job was neither comfortable nor safe. Planters who tolerated slave preachers were especially watchful for any hint of their subversion of plantation authority. Thus, most slave preachers were forced to either provide the master's message of obedience, or to speak only indirectly about the worldly concerns of their congregations. Some preachers became expert in a kind of theological doublespeak, or what historian Charles Joyner refers to as the African tradition of "indirection," which allowed strong criticism of authority without direct confrontation. The preacher might appear to be in compliance with the master's wishes but instead provided theological reassurance and expressed the grievances of their fellow slaves.[20] Slaves generally dismissed preachers who appeared to believe the master's message. Frederick Douglass commented, "I could entertain no such nonsense as this [affirmation of the master's beliefs]; and I almost lost my patience when I found any colored man weak enough to believe such stuff." John White, like most slaves, assumed that when a preacher spoke in support of slavery's rules, "the old preacher was more worried about the bullwhip than the Bible." Those who provided support or access to power had standing in the slave community, but those perceived as working for the master were generally dismissed.[21]

While the role of slave preachers gave them distinction in the community, others commanded respect for their strength or skill or their influence with the master or other whites. Some planters took great pride in individual slave athletes who represented the plantation in competitive races and boxing matches. Skilled blacksmiths and carpenters were especially important to plantation maintenance and often had particular leverage with masters. For example, slave musicians who entertained at plantation functions could often use their prestige to influence the master and benefit the community. The same might be said for favored servants or the skilled cooks important to the success of the master's dinner parties. In the fields slave drivers, often slaves themselves, were also important. They worked under the direction of white overseers, and the whips they carried symbolized their power and their responsibility for enforcing plantation rules. They turned slaves out into the fields in the morning, ensured continuous work during the day, and enforced the curfew at night. A driver might have some privileges but was also required to do a share of the work. His was a difficult position because he often lived among those he was expected to discipline. Thus, he often worked out informal agreements with the other slaves, making him and his position useful to the community. Solomon Northup recalled that he developed such skill with the whip that he was able to simulate a whipping by snapping the whip close to but not quite touching the skin, "throwing the lash within a hair's breadth of the back, the ear, the nose, without, however, touching either of them." From a distance he could make a light touch seem like brutal punishment. The victims must play their roles convincingly lest the driver be found out, and all would be punished. "I would commence plying the lash vigorously, when according to arrangement, they would squirm and screech as if in agony." Unfortunately, slaves could not depend on this level of skill or a driver's willingness to risk punishment to spare his fellows, but compromises were often worked out between drivers and community members.[22]

The cluster of interlocking relationships and roles constituting the slave community enabled many to survive the hardships of slavery. Some people were connected by blood, but most were joined by a shared condition and a common place in the power structure. Though all did not agree on the best ways of coping with their situation, the slave community provided important support, helping sustain them in the face of continual assaults on their dignity and humanity. The institution of slavery was predicated on the assumptions that slaves were subhuman and powerless, valuable only for the work they produced. Though, like any human group, the slave community had conflicts, tensions, betrayals, and animosities, it was in the slave quarters that African Americans were likely to find recognition for their accomplishments, respect for their strength of character and virtue, compassion for their suffering, and love. The community was important because it contradicted slavery's message and provided a partial shield from the institution's most devastating effects.

The family was central to the formation of the community, and its maintenance became far more possible as more black women were added to the African American population by the late eighteenth and early nineteenth centuries. The historian Ann Malone found that in Louisiana, two-thirds of the slaves in the 1830s and nearly three-quarters in the 1840s lived in what she called simple family households. Such households were composed of a couple with or without children or a single parent, usually a mother, with children. Family and household composition were greatly influenced by the actions of the slaveholders, who responded to economic difficulties and opportunities by buying or selling slaves. Therefore household composition statistics are an incomplete indication of the history of family formation and dissolution. Still slaves' difficulties and adaptations to adversity are reflected in Malone's findings that fewer than one in five slaves lived alone and fewer than one in ten lived in households of more than two generations. This household data gives little information about the family relationships that may have linked separate households and different plantations, but it confirms earlier studies that found that the nuclear family structure of parents and children was the most common family form among slaves throughout the South before the Civil War.[23]

Slave marriages had no legal standing, and all such unions took place at the pleasure of slaveowners. Planters often encouraged marriages between slaves on their own plantations, since those who married off the plantation would inevitably want the privilege of visiting spouses elsewhere, removing them from the master's direct control. Some masters acquiesced in their slaves' choices of mates from other plantations and attempted to arrange a hire or purchase to unite the couples. When a Colonel Barsdale of Virginia, for example, received a letter asking that he consider hiring or selling a slave woman, the request came from a planter whose slave, Israel, the blacksmith, seemed "much attached to her." Large plantations offered the greatest opportunities for slaves to find mates in their local community, but even there, many sought partners elsewhere. The selection of a partner living off one's planta-tion limited the time a couple could spend together and increased the like-lihood of permanent family separation. Since any offspring became the property of the mother's owner, it also made the father less able to influence his children's upbringing. Yet, many slaves chose marriage partners from other plantations, thereby exercising some control over their lives, and many slave marriages were carried on at a distance.[24] *men of the house can't provide*

Family life for a slave was always problematic, since slaves had no legal rights to protect a family or keep it intact. In marriages between free people, husbands controlled their wives' property and were assumed to protect their rights, standing as the legal representatives of the family. Slave marriages put husbands and wives on an equal footing: Neither had any property rights or legal standing. Slave masters had absolute authority to separate the family and discipline or reward any family member, theoretically making parental authority and marriage rights meaningless. Many families were devastated by the internal slave trade which transported slaves from the eastern Upper South to the plantations of the western Lower South. Even under these circumstances many families managed to maintain contact for decades, many had the sup-port of nuclear families, and some maintained extended kinship networks.[25]

When forced sales made separations unavoidable, some slaves main-tained symbolic contact with lost family members through the names they chose for their children. Many followed African traditions, naming children for their grandparents or other relatives. Although many sons were named after their fathers, slave women whose children were fathered by whites were likely to name sons after black male relatives. Elizabeth Keckley was sepa-rated from her mother at age fourteen and taken from Virginia to North Car-olina, where she eventually had a son by a white man to whom she was hired out. The child was named George, not for his white father, but for his black grandfather, whom Elizabeth had barely known.[26]

The gender assumptions of the white society combined with the laws reg-ulating the slave system and the conditions of servitude to minimize enslaved men's roles as husbands and fathers. Slave women, on the other hand, were often allowed time during the workday to care for their children. Sometimes children were brought to the fields with their mothers, who nursed them and tended to their needs during work breaks. On a few of the larger plantations slaves ran nurseries for the estate's children, often including the white children. On most of the smaller farms, slave mothers provided care for their own children and were sometimes given time off from work to do so. Often husbands worked longer hours to make up for the time allowed their wives for child care.

Although slave parents could frequently make arrangements for caring for their children, when the demands of work were especially great or when

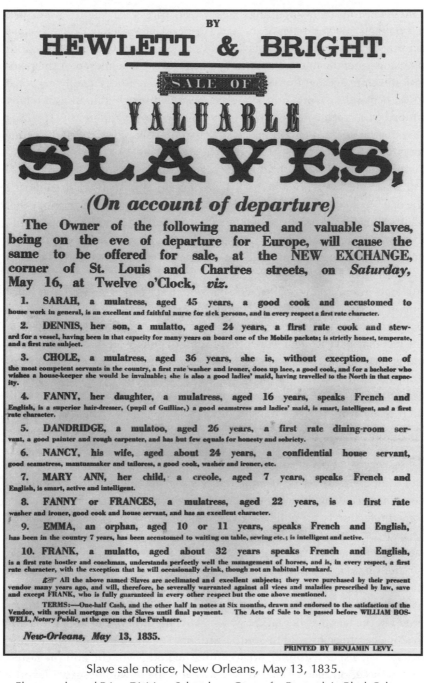

BY
HEWLETT & BRIGHT.

SALE OF

VALUABLE
SLAVES,

(On account of departure)

The Owner of the following named and valuable Slaves, being on the eve of departure for Europe, will cause the same to be offered for sale, at the NEW EXCHANGE, corner of St. Louis and Chartres streets, on *Saturday,* May 16, at Twelve o'Clock, *viz.*

1. SARAH, a mulatress, aged 45 years, a good cook and accustomed to house work in general, is an excellent and faithful nurse for sick persons, and in every respect a first rate character.

2. DENNIS, her son, a mulatto, aged 24 years, a first rate cook and steward for a vessel, having been in that capacity for many years on board one of the Mobile packets; is strictly honest, temperate, and a first rate subject.

3. CHOLE, a mulatress, aged 36 years, she is, without execption, one of the most competent servants in the country, a first rate washer and ironer, does up lace, a good cook, and for a bachelor who wishes a house-keeper she would be invaluable; she is also a good ladies' maid, having travelled to the North in that capacity.

4. FANNY, her daughter, a mulatress, aged 16 years, speaks French and English, is a superior hair-dresser, (pupil of Guilliac,) a good seamstress and ladies' maid, is smart, intelligent, and a first rate character.

5. DANDRIDGE, a mulatoo, aged 26 years, a first rate dining-room servant, a good painter and rough carpenter, and has but few equals for honesty and sobriety.

6. NANCY, his wife, aged about 24 years, a confidential house servant, good seamstress, mantuamaker and tailoress, a good cook, washer and ironer, etc.

7. MARY ANN, her child, a creole, aged 7 years, speaks French and English, is smart, active and intelligent.

8. FANNY or FRANCES, a mulatress, aged 22 years, is a first rate washer and ironer, good cook and house servant, and has an excellent character.

9. EMMA, an orphan, aged 10 or 11 years, speaks French and English, has been in the country 7 years, has been accustomed to waiting on table, sewing etc.; is intelligent and active.

10. FRANK, a mulatto, aged about 32 years speaks French and English, is a first rate hostler and coachman, understands perfectly well the management of horses, and is, in every respect, a first rate character, with the exception that he will occasionally drink, though not an habitual drunkard.

☞ All the above named Slaves are acclimated and excellent subjects; they were purchased by their present vendor many years ago, and will, therefore, be severally warranted against all vices and maladies prescribed by law, save and except FRANK, who is fully guaranteed in every other respect but the one above mentioned.

TERMS:—One-half Cash, and the other half in notes at Six months, drawn and endorsed to the satisfaction of the Vendor, with special mortgage on the Slaves until final payment. The Acts of Sale to be passed before WILLIAM BOSWELL, *Notary Public,* at the expense of the Purchaser.

New-Orleans, May 13, 1835.

PRINTED BY BENJAMIN LEVY.

Slave sale notice, New Orleans, May 13, 1835.

a master insisted on maintaining a steady work pace, slave children were often left on their own for much of the day. Former slave Frederick Douglass characterized the early years of a slave child's life as relatively carefree, spent in play and generally in close association with the white children of the plantation. Before age eight or nine, slave children were not generally expected to do demanding work, and Douglass described his childhood as a happy time.[27] Others remembered their early years in slavery differently, recalling that the work of the plantation was so demanding that parents had little time for child care until evening or Sunday, the slaves' traditional rest day. As J.W.C. Pennington recalled, his childhood was marked by a "want of parental care" as his parents "were not able to give any attention to their children during the day." By necessity, parenting was a community responsibility, with other adults filling in for parents where possible and taking complete responsibility for children separated from their parents. Among slaves, the process of informal adoption helped to provide for children whose parents were absent or incapacitated.[28]

Slavery was harsh for all slaves, but not all slaves experienced that hardship in the same way. "Slavery is terrible for men," explained former slave Harriet Jacobs, "but it is far more terrible for women." Her belief was based on the fact that slave women were often forced to endure all the hardships and indignities imposed on men but were also regularly subject to sexual exploitation. The history of slavery is filled with the stories of masters sexually abusing their female slaves, and plantations were populated with the offspring of such relationships. From trading block to whipping post, slave women's modesty was not respected; they were stripped and exposed to public view. Sexual relationships with slave women marked young white boys' passage into puberty and satisfied the masters' lust. Occasionally slave women could exercise some control over these exploitations. Harriet Jacobs made a conscious decision to take a white lover to shield her from other white men and to give some protection to her child. The vast majority, however, had no choice but to submit to the sexual demands of white men.[29]

Slave women were also vulnerable to the anger of white women who could not punish their husbands, the slave masters, but could and did punish their slaves for these relationships. As a child, Patsey told Solomon Northup, she had been a great favorite around the Epps household in Louisiana. She was proud of the fact that her father was an African, carried, she said, to slavery in Cuba before being sold to South Carolina. She was a skilled teamster and rail-splitter, a speedy runner, an accomplished horsewoman, and the fastest cotton picker on the plantation. She was also the unwilling sexual favorite of frequently drunken Edwin Epps and paid dearly for this in severe whippings at the behest of Epps's extremely jealous wife.[30] Many whites believed that black women were highly sexual and promiscuous, and white men used these stereotypes to absolve themselves of responsibility in these sexual associations. Thus slave women were vulnerable to abuse by planters and punishment by planters' wives, and suffered from the stereotypes that protected white men from guilt.

Both women and men did heavy labor in the fields with little accommodation to gender differences. The specific nature of the work depended on the crop being grown and the time of year, but generally both male and female slaves spent long days in strenuous work. Indeed Solomon Northup reported that some cotton and sugar plantations were worked entirely with female labor. When extra hands were needed at Ford's lumber operation, four black women, Charlotte, Fanny, Cresia, and Nelly, were sent to help the men. They were "excellent choppers," according to Northup, "equal to any man" at piling logs. On the largest plantations slave life was generally more regimented than on small farms or in urban areas. Northup recalled that each workday on the large cotton plantations in Louisiana began with the blowing of a horn about an hour before dawn. After a hurried breakfast (typically warm cornmeal cake) slaves filled gourds with water, packed lunches of cornmeal cake and, occasionally, cold bacon, and went off to the fields to work.[31]

During March and April the ground was prepared for planting. Where Northup labored, a mule pulling a large plow made a straight furrow; a young woman followed sowing cotton seeds from a huge sack hung around her neck. Then came another mule pulling a harrow, which covered the seed. In one pass two mules, two mule drivers—most often men but sometimes women—and one planting woman could plant a row of cotton several hundred yards long. This was the beginning of the process that by fall produced the tens of thousands of pounds of cotton that were the foundation of the South's economy. After planting came the hoeing season, which lasted from April until July, during which time slaves worked their way down each row, cultivating and keeping weeds from choking the growing cotton plants. In August slaves began picking the cotton, the hardest part of the process, as each picker worked with a huge sack on a strap slung around the neck and shoulders. An experienced hand was expected to pick about two hundred pounds of cotton each day.[32]

Landscape architect, abolitionist, and sometime journalist Frederick Law Olmsted reported seeing plantations on which thirty plows and thirty to forty people with hoes, mostly women, moved together across the wide fields of Mississippi well into the night. Often he saw a black slave driver walking along, brandishing a whip and cracking it over the heads of the other slaves. After their work in the fields, slaves had additional tasks, such as gathering wood for supper fires, feeding the animals, and carrying heavy sacks of cotton to be stored or ginned. Slaves had little time to do things for themselves or their families, for at least some planters insisted that their workers be in bed by ten in the evening and forced them to the fields before daylight. One planter told Olmsted, "Well, I don't never start my niggers 'fore daylight except 'tis in pickin' time, then maybe I got 'em out a quarter of an hour before," in this way, confirming his self-image as a kind slave master. Other masters were not so considerate and sent their slaves to the fields as early as necessary to get the day's work done. No matter what time slaves began their day, the work was constant. "I keep 'em right smart to work through the day," Olmsted's informant declared.[33]

Masters and overseers set quotas for the amount of work to be done, generally taking into account the experience, skill, and strength of the individual; and slaves who did not make their quotas were often whipped. According to Northup the most accomplished slaves picked cotton with extraordinary quickness. Patsey, for example, used both hands and could easily pick five hundred pounds of cotton in a single day. When darkness forced slaves from the fields, the day's picking was weighed, a process that provoked extreme anxiety for the slaves. Those who had not picked their quota were whipped, and those who had picked substantially more than expected had their quotas raised. Often slaves cooperated and reduced their pace to protect weaker or slower workers. The fastest and cleverest could always be expected to make their quotas, but others were never able to pick the standard poundage and after repeated beatings were finally removed from the fields, sold, or given other jobs to do. The style of work generally employed on cotton plantations was called gang labor because slaves worked in large gangs, moving through the fields from morning to night, under the threat of the overseer's whip.[34]

In the rice fields of South Carolina and the low country of Georgia, slaves often worked under a task labor system, focused less on the amount of time they labored than on the tasks they completed. Ben Horry, a slave on the Brookgreen plantation in South Carolina, explained that as soon as the fall rice harvest was completed, the slaves started to ready the fields for the next season. Using mules and oxen, they plowed under the remains of the harvested rice plants before the winter arrived. They plowed the fields again in the spring, cut deep trenches into the soil, planted the new rice, and flooded the fields. Then, as the fields were alternately drained and flooded, slaves worked in water or thick mud for the rest of the season, finding respite during the summer only when they moved to higher ground to plant and tend the crops that supplied food for the plantation. In midsummer, when the fields were drained, slaves worked long days in intense heat, with thick mud making their every movement an effort. During the harvest season they gathered the grain with rice hooks and threshed the rice by hand, pounding and fanning it in baskets designed like those used in African rice culture to make it ready for market.[35]

The flies and mosquitoes, the disease and fungal infections, and the general discomfort of working long hours in wet soil in heat and humidity combined to make rice cultivation onerous work. John Brown, a slave who worked in the rice fields of Georgia, thought that rice cultivation was the most unhealthful of all slave agricultural work. He contended that working knee-deep in the foul-smelling water that reflected the heat brought on fevers and contributed to sunstroke. With the constant dampness causing cracks in their skin that allowed insects to lodge just under the flesh, slaves suffered infection, rheumatism, asthma, consumption, and other painful and chronic maladies. Brown also recalled the danger from the water moccasins, which were always plentiful in low-country rice fields. Generally, he said, rice work was "very much more trying than either cotton or tobacco cultivation."[36] Yet the task system employed on most rice plantations provided slaves with some degree of autonomy. A skilled rice worker might complete the assigned work hours before sundown and then have time to perform personal tasks, to grow, gather, or hunt food for his or her own family, to develop a skill that might provide some personal or family advantage, to handle other family matters, or to rest. Completing one's task early could be a backbreaking proposition, but slaves generally preferred the task system of rice over the gang labor of cotton.[37]

Slaves employed in cotton production, although forced to labor in gangs, also found ways to exercise some control over the nature and pace of their work. Many slaves sang their way through the ordeal of gang labor. White observers agreed that slaves seemed to sing all the time they worked. Although a few slaves reported, "Dey didn't allow us to sing on our plantation, cause if we did we just sing ourselves happy and get to shouting and dat would settle de work," slave songs were never successfully banned.[38] These songs ranged from field hollers, like "The Carolina Yell," described as "a loud musical shout, rising and falling, and breaking into falsetto," to more structured combinations of words and complex rhythms.[39] Songs sung during work helped encourage a sense of community among those sharing the hardship of agonizing labor. They helped pass the time during boring work and distracted attention from painful work, but they had an even greater practical value. Slaves working to music set the rhythm for that work. Since on cotton plantations, fast workers often amplified a master's frustration with slower workers and increased the likelihood of their punishment, it was useful for all slaves to maintain a moderate but steady work pace. Work songs helped to coordinate a common pace, allowing the slowest workers to keep up without alerting the master or overseer. This singing also often convinced whites that their slaves were contented and relieved some of their anxieties about the possibility of slave rebellions.[40]

Another way slaves could control their work was by running away for a few days. There were many reasons why slaves left their plantations without permission, including visiting friends and family, courting potential mates, or being angry at masters, but they also ran away to the woods or swamps to rest from their labor when they were exhausted or sick. When Patsey was sick and could not keep up her usual fast pace picking cotton, Northup reported, she ran away. On Epps's plantation slaves faced frequent whipping if they picked too slowly and were whipped again when their pickings weighed too little. Patsey stayed away nearly all summer to recover from an illness, living in the woods a short distance from the plantation and depending on the other slaves to share what little food they had. Her respite was bought at the price of a severe beating, five hundred lashes being the standard punishment at that time in Louisiana for running away. Across the South whipping was universally employed as the punishment for a slave's infraction of the rules, the severity determined by the type of infraction and the mood and temperament of the master or overseer. Northup reported that fifty lashes might be administered for a minor annoyance such as a leaf found in the cotton bag, and one hundred lashes for the offense of "standing idle in the field." Other punishments ranged from longer work hours or loss of the privilege of visiting one's family to more horrifying measures like the amputation of limbs or gruesome, terrifying mutilations that resulted in death. The last was obviously meant to serve as a lesson to other slaves. For controlling slaves, each plantation functioned as an independent fiefdom.[41]

Information was critical to the slaves' ability to exert a measure of control over their situations. Henry Clay Bruce, recalling his slave experience, explained that every plantation had its own spy network. House slaves were particularly well situated to acquire valuable information about the master, his family, his political concerns, and his financial matters. On their breaks from duties in the master's house, domestic slaves often brought news of local, regional, and national events to the slave quarters. News that someone was to be sold or punished, or information about friends or kin on neighboring plantations, might provide the warning that allowed a timely escape or the formulation of a plan of action.[42]

Booker T. Washington reported that what he called the "grapevine telegraph" was a regular and reliable conveyer of information for both slaves and free blacks.[43] Networks of informants included new slaves purchased or hired out from other areas, slave artisans and house slaves who came into regular contact with whites, and any African Americans who traveled to nearby areas or to towns and cities. Slave drivers or personal servants often accompanied planters on business trips or vacations, sometimes even to the free states. Body servants attended the southern planters who regularly visited northern border cities like Cincinnati, and often visited local blacks while their masters did business. The Dumas Hotel in Cincinnati was a favorite gathering place where southern slaves and Ohio free blacks mingled, despite the attempts of many slaveholders to discourage such associations.[44] Slaves returning from such trips faced lengthy interrogation by fellow slaves, seeking word of family members who had gone north, or simply wanting news from the outside world. Information helped break the isolation of the plantation, gave slaves a broader sense of the world, and equipped them with important strategic knowledge. If a cotton broker was about to make an appearance to bid on the plantation's produce, slaves knew that the master might be under special pressure to get the crop baled and shipped to market. As the contract date approached, a planter's dependence on the laborers' efficiency increased, and though his anxiety might lead to additional whippings, it also provided an opportunity that slaves could sometimes exploit to their advantage. At such critical times a work slowdown by slaves could be especially effective.

The internal slave trade threatened the stability of slave families, but it also provided a valuable source of information on distant family members. New slaves brought into an area often carried news of loved ones left behind. Although many plantation slaves lived in relatively isolated areas of the country, the business and social life of the plantation provided many opportunities for the exchange of information. The plantation business brought in new supplies of workers and necessitated contacts with buyers and shippers for agricultural products, and the plantation's social life often brought the personal servants of slaveowners together. Typically slaves from neighboring plantations might gather for holidays like Christmas and, ironically, Independence Day. Through informal networks of information, many slaves managed to maintain family ties. Willie Lee Mathis of Cincinnati, for example, kept in touch with her mother, a slave in Virginia, for thirty years. Others smuggled letters to children, parents, and other relatives in bondage in many areas of the South. Contacts between slaves and between slaves and free blacks, North and South, provided information that enabled some people to escape from slavery. These links created the hazardous informal route to freedom that became known as the underground railroad. Contacts with the world beyond the plantation, as well as cultural memories, family, and other forms of resistance, sustained the hope of freedom for African Americans through desperate times.[45]

Chapter 6

1829 David Walker publishes his *Walker's Appeal to the Colored Citizens of the World,* urging slaves to overthrow slavery

Slavery abolished in Mexico

1830 First national convention of African Americans held in Philadelphia

1831 Nat Turner slave revolt

William Lloyd Garrison begins publishing the *Liberator*

African American Maria W. Stewart delivers the first public lecture by a woman in the United States

1833 British Emancipation Act abolishes slavery in the British Empire

Integrated American Anti-Slavery Society established

1834 British West Indies slaveholders accept compensated emancipation

1837 White abolitionist newspaper editor Elijah P. Lovejoy killed by proslavery mob in Alton, Illinois

1838 Frederick Douglass escapes from slavery in Maryland

1839 Slave rebellion aboard the ship *Amistad.* Supreme Court decision in 1841 frees the surviving slaves, who are represented by former president John Quincy Adams, and thirty-five return to Africa

Antislavery Liberty Party formed in New York State

1841 Slaves aboard *Creole* revolt; bound from Virginia to Louisiana, they sail to freedom in Nassau

1842 Supreme Court, in *Prigg* v. *Pennsylvania,* rules that states may not be compelled to enforce the Fugitive Slave Law of 1793

1845 Frederick Douglass publishes *Narrative of the Life of Frederick Douglass*

1848 Discovery of gold at Sutter's Mill in California begins first gold rush

Frederick Douglass and Martin Delany publish the *North Star*

First Women's Rights Convention held at Seneca Falls, New York; Frederick Douglass seconds the motion for women's suffrage

Free-Soil Party formed, Martin Van Buren is the party's candidate for president, with the slogan "Free Soil, Free Labor, and Free Men"

1849 Harriet Tubman escapes from slavery in Maryland

Free People of Color and the Fight against Slavery

Freedom for African Americans during the era of slavery was an ambiguous status between slavery and full citizenship. It was also precarious, especially in the South, where it generally depended on the sufferance of white authority.[1] There, in reaction to slave revolts and other perceived threats, advocating freedom for African Americans and organizing against slavery became progressively more difficult, even dangerous, during the nineteenth century. In the North, where black freedom was more secure, African American communities established organizations, the foundation for political action designed to broaden their own freedom and to secure the liberty of those enslaved in the South. Protest organizing in northern black communities was aided by African Americans' increasing independence from white control and oversight. More than 70 percent of blacks in Philadelphia and more than 80 percent in Boston lived in independent households by 1820. New York City had a smaller percentage that year, about 60 percent, due to New York State's gradual emancipation provision.[2] The state finally ended slavery completely on July 4 in 1827. African Americans celebrated with parades and festivals, and as the last slaves began to move out of the homes of former white masters, the number of independent black households grew. Many black families that had been torn apart by bondage were reunited, although poverty and the demand for live-in servants still meant that some blacks lived in white households. Yet, in New York as elsewhere, the early decades of the nineteenth century brought increasing numbers of independent black households and a growing black community committed not only to mutual support but also to the struggle for civil rights and black freedom.

In Boston in 1826 African Americans joined to form the Massachusetts General Colored Association, one of the first specifically antislavery black organizations. One of the group's founding members was David Walker, a free black man who came to Boston from North Carolina in the mid-1820s. Walker had never been a slave, but his life and travels in the South had made him intimately familiar with slavery's inhumanity. He described a slave owner forcing a son to whip his own mother to death, and another forcing a husband to beat his pregnant wife until she aborted their child.[3] In Boston, Walker became a community activist, working for abolition and racial justice. In 1827

Samuel Cornish and John Russwurm of New York gave black Americans a public voice when they founded *Freedom's Journal,* the nation's first African American newspaper, and Walker became its Boston agent.

The next year, in a militant speech before the Massachusetts General Colored Association, Walker called for the formation of black organizations to "protect, aid and assist each other to the utmost of our power," and advocated the use of "every scheme we think will have a tendency to facilitate our salvation."[4] In 1829 Walker expanded this message with his publication of *David Walker's Appeal to the Coloured Citizens of the World,* even sending it into the slave South. He condemned the hypocrisy of all those, especially Christians, who professed to love liberty yet supported slavery. He challenged the Jeffersonian thinking that called for freedom while profiting from human bondage and arguing that blacks were intellectually inferior, and he contended that slaves, inflamed by the same thirst for liberty that had moved American Revolutionary patriots, would be justified in revolting against their owners.[5] He saw education as a force for racial defense and uplift, believing it would produce revolutionaries. Southern slaveholders had vivid memories of earlier rebellions and Walker's *Appeal* exacerbated their fear.[6]

A few years later, in 1831, another strong antislavery voice came from Boston when William Lloyd Garrison began to publish his newspaper, the *Liberator.* Garrison, a white man, had good antislavery credentials. He had edited a political reform newspaper in Vermont, worked with Quaker activist Benjamin Lundy in Baltimore editing the *Genius of Universal Emancipation,* and had been jailed on a conviction of libel for accusing a New England shipowner of engaging in the illegal slave trade. Garrison spoke so passionately against slavery that many who had not met him assumed him to be black. Indeed, Garrison counted more blacks among his friends than did most white reformers of his day. He valued the opinions of his black associates and regularly sought their advice. When he was working out his positions on immediate emancipation and African colonization, he often did so with African American friends who criticized and helped him shape his ideas. James Forten and other blacks from Philadelphia provided a sounding board for some of Garrison's early fiery speeches. Speaking before black audiences in New York, New Haven, and Hartford helped him perfect his delivery, which a newspaper in 1830 had described as a bit stiff but admirable in "literary composition and 'philanthropic' concern." His speechmaking improved, and later that year, one enthusiastic observer said that when he spoke, people felt as though they had "heard the groans and viewed the lacerated bodies of the poor sufferers." With the power of an evangelical preacher, Garrison repeatedly announced, "I will not equivocate . . . I will not retreat a single inch—And I WILL BE HEARD." In his newspaper Garrison demanded both the abolition of slavery and the "improvement of the condition of the free people of color." It is no wonder that African Americans came to think of this most unusual white man as a "dearest friend."[7]

Garrison was so influential that those who subscribed to his ideas about immediate emancipation, anticolonization, and not participating in traditional political organizations came to be known as Garrisonians. Since he was a pacifist, Garrison had misgivings about the prospect of African American violence in opposition to slavery. Walker's call for a slave revolt put Garrison in a difficult position, but after some hesitation, he published portions of the *Appeal* in his newspaper. Rumor had it that Walker's southern agents had distributed his pamphlet in the South. In December of 1829 Walker sent thirty copies to Richmond, where they were sold for twelve cents or given away to those who could not afford the price. Many believed that black sailors carried copies south sewn into the linings of the clothing Walker sold in his secondhand clothing store. The *Appeal*'s publication in the *Liberator* gave it a wider circulation and a much higher visibility. In 1831 Nat Turner's deadly slave revolt in Virginia confirmed planters' fears that antislavery propaganda from the North was creating dangerous unrest among the slaves. State laws requiring the confinement of free black sailors when their ships were in port continued to be enforced in the South, despite the fact that the U.S. Supreme Court had declared South Carolina's Negro Seaman's Law unconstitutional in 1823.[8] In a further effort to protect their property, southern authorities put a price on Walker's head and offered substantial rewards for Garrison, his publisher, or any of the *Liberator*'s agents. The mayor of Savannah, Georgia, wrote to the mayor of Boston asking that Walker be arrested and that his writing be suppressed, but Walker's pamphlet had caused less controversy in the North than in the South, and Boston's mayor, unfamiliar with Walker and his writing, denied the request.[9]

The strength of southern animosity toward David Walker led many in the black community to suspect foul play when, later in 1831, he was found dead near the doorway of his clothing shop on Boston's Beacon Hill.[10] In 1835 William Lloyd Garrison, too, felt proslavery's wrath when he was attacked by antiabolitionist forces, seized, and dragged through Boston's streets at the end of a rope. Local blacks saved him in a daring wagon rescue, and city authorities placed him in protective custody. The violent opposition of southern slaveholders and their sympathizers did not deter the abolitionists, however. In 1832 Garrison and other abolitionists organized a meeting at the African Meeting House that established the New England Anti-Slavery Society. Several Boston blacks were among those signing the society's organizing documents. The Massachusetts General Colored Association became an auxiliary to this new society, and prominent black Bostonians John T. Hilton, Samuel Snowden, and Charles Lenox Remond assumed leadership positions. When, at Garrison's instigation, a national antislavery organization was formed in Philadelphia in 1833, seven black men were among the sixty delegates at the founding convention.[11] During the 1830s and 1840s abolitionists created a vast network of antislavery organizations that linked cities and towns in the North and Midwest, joined black communities in coordinated efforts, and tied black organizations to integrated groups. This organization was facilitated by the relatively high and rising black literacy that made pamphlets, newspapers, and handbills effective conduits of information in urban black communities. At midcentury the U.S. Census reported that nearly half of black adults there could read and write; by 1860 the majority were literate. Effective propaganda gained international support for the antislavery cause. Successful organizations also helped enslaved southern blacks escape to freedom.

In 1839 this network of antislavery organizations joined together to work for the freedom of escaped slaves in a celebrated international case. Fifty-three Africans had been captured in Africa and shipped to Cuba aboard a Spanish ship called the *Amistad,* despite the fact that in 1817 Spain had signed a treaty with England outlawing the Atlantic slave trade. Off Cuba the Africans killed the captain and some members of the crew, took over the ship, and attempted to return home. Eventually they were tricked by the crew into sailing into U.S. waters. They were captured, arrested, charged with murder, and imprisoned in Connecticut. The abolitionists went into action with a flurry of activity and publicity. They printed regular accounts in antislavery newspapers; visited the captives; and raised money for their defense, collecting donations at meetings, staging a play in New York, and commissioning and reproducing a portrait of the group's charismatic leader, Joseph Cinque. After sustained effort their case made its way to the U.S. Supreme Court, where former president John Quincy Adams and several prominent abolitionists defended the Africans. The court declared that the defendants had been kidnapped and set them free. In November 1841, finally, the thirty-five people who had survived this ordeal returned to Africa.[12]

Although antislavery societies brought black activists and white activists together, African Americans did not abandon all-black organizations. In 1829 an increase in Cincinnati's African American population had triggered white fears, resulting in a deadly assault on the city's black community. Despite a successful defense, many blacks were driven from the city, some to Canada. Cincinnati officials, bowing to local racist pressure, promised stricter enforcement of Ohio's exclusionary racial laws. Ohio had passed these laws earlier in the century in an attempt to limit black migration to the state. They required black migrants to register with the county, certifying that they were free, and to post a five-hundred-dollar bond to ensure that they would not become dependent on local charity. Anyone who knowingly hired or harbored fugitive slaves could be fined. Other western states also had restrictive laws: Illinois threatened bondage for any black migrant attempting to settle permanently in the state. Black migrants were barred from settling in Michigan, Indiana, Wisconsin, and Iowa. Oregon also prohibited blacks from owning land, and banned further black immigration when it became a state in 1859. In western states generally blacks were prohibited from voting, serving on juries, giving testimony in court cases involving whites, or attending public schools. Though these laws were irregularly enforced, they made African American freedom especially precarious in those states.[13]

In response to the Cincinnati riots and to attacks on black civil rights throughout the North, African Americans from nine states, including New York, Pennsylvania, Maryland, Delaware, and Virginia, met in Philadelphia in the first national convention of black leaders. The delegates meeting at the Mother Bethel Church chose the Philadelphian, Rev. Richard Allen, then seventy years old, to preside over the convention. The main topic on the agenda of this first meeting was the establishment of a Canadian settlement for refugees from American slavery, hostility, and discrimination. Delegates constituted themselves as the American Society of Free Persons of Colour, met annually for six years, then revived their national meetings again in the 1840s. Delegates came from local auxiliary societies organized to combat slavery and its ancillary effects on free black people.[14]

The conventions provided a national forum for African Americans and helped coordinate the actions of the local, state, and regional conventions and organizations of which they were an outgrowth. They also provided opportunities for black leaders to discuss and pass public resolutions on issues concerning their communities and to devise strategies for addressing them. The major concerns of these groups were opposition to slavery, the achievement and protection of civil rights, and the advancement of the race, especially through education and moral reform. The national conventions continued the determined opposition of most black organizations to the African settlement program of the American Colonization Society. Yet their support for Canadian settlements remained strong, especially after Canada abolished slavery in 1833 and refused to return fugitive slaves to the United States.[15]

Some African Americans also considered Haiti an appropriate place for possible settlement. As the first independent black nation in the Western Hemisphere, brought into existence by the defeat of French colonialism, Haiti was a symbol of black freedom and power. In the early 1820s Haitian president Jean-Pierre Boyer invited black Americans to settle in his country, offering free land, four months' provisions, and financial assistance. Haiti needed skilled farmers, and Boyer hoped that American blacks could form a stable rural population. Interest in Boyer's proposal was strong in black communities in the United States. Prince Saunders, a former teacher in Boston's black school, became a strong advocate of the project and worked with Haitian official

Jonathan Granville to recruit African Americans for an American-Haitian settlement. Granville toured New York, Philadelphia, Boston, and Baltimore, speaking to large and enthusiastic black audiences. With Saunders, Granville established the Haitian Emigration Society at a mass meeting in Philadelphia in 1824, and within a few weeks, 60 African Americans set sail from Philadelphia, 120 from New York, and 21 from Baltimore. During the next two years six thousand American blacks made the voyage to Haiti, and by the end of the decade, black communities in the United States had sent between eight and thirteen thousand emigrants.[16]

The venture was not entirely successful, however, and many African Americans returned within a few years. The Haitian government complained that these settlers were not willing to work the land but preferred to rent or sell their holdings and move into the cities. There the language and cultural differences between Catholic French-speaking Haitians and Protestant English-speaking African Americans created an uncomfortable urban coexistence. The most successful and longest-lasting settlement was located in an isolated section of the present-day Dominican Republic. There American blacks created an English-speaking enclave that retained its American identity well into the twentieth century. The reaction of the thousands of migrants who returned to the United States, however, for whom the French culture seemed too foreign, suggests the degree to which these blacks were American in their identity and cultural expectations. By this time almost all American blacks had been born in the United States, and most were several generations away from an African or Caribbean regional or cultural identification. This experience further strengthened the resolve of most American blacks to remain in the United States.

The plan of the American Colonization Society to settle blacks in Liberia was especially unpopular because most of the society's members were prominent slaveholders who, it was believed, simply wanted to remove free blacks from the country. Delegates who met in the national black conventions during the 1830s were particularly opposed to African colonization. In their broad program, they presented a united front—opposing colonization and slavery and supporting moral reform and racial uplift. Yet, the records of these conventions make it clear that free blacks had diverse opinions. All agreed on general aims but not always on the strategies for their accomplishment. Some favored separate all-black organizations and institutions as the major vehicles—advocating establishing all-black schools and encouraging blacks to patronize black businesses—believing that only black-controlled groups could properly speak for and serve the African American community. Others believed that true equality could only come through integrated facilities, organizations, and institutions. Some were committed to bringing about changes through the nonpolitical action of "moral suasion," holding fast to the Garrisonian approach of nonviolence and not participating in inevitably corrupt partisan politics. Others, especially by the 1840s, believed that African Americans would only gain their rights as Americans and have the power to force the society to abolish slavery by participating in politics and forging political alliances.

From the beginning, convention delegates were concerned with establishing the means for independent black achievement in order to escape the restrictions of racial discrimination. Austin Steward, a former slave and delegate from New York State, believed that farming could provide the independence that African Americans needed. To this end he supported the establishment of rural communities in Canada and moved his family to the Wilberforce Colony in Upper Canada for a time, to aid this enterprise. By the end of the 1840s there were such black settlements in Hamilton, Toronto, Chatham, Montreal, and other areas of eastern Canada, as well as a growing black community on Canada's West Coast. African Americans who found security in their new Canadian homes urged others to follow; some prospered in these new settlements. Mary Ann Shadd, daughter of a prominent Philadelphia black abolitionist family, opened a school for blacks in Windsor, just across the border from Detroit, in 1851. During the next decade she edited a newspaper, the *Provincial Freeman,* becoming the first black female newspaper editor in North America. She also published a guide to Canada for fugitives who had escaped from slavery in the United States, and became one of Canada's most effective and prominent abolitionist speakers. In 1856 she married Thomas J. Cary, a black businessman from Toronto. She was determined to remain in Canada herself and passionately urged others to emigrate. "Your national ship is rotten and sinking," she told American blacks. "Why not leave it?"[17]

Canada did seem a haven to many fugitive slaves whose freedom was insecure in the United States. This was true for Henry Bibb, another influential advocate of Canadian emigration. Bibb was a slave in Kentucky who made good his escape a number of times but was recaptured as he attempted to rescue his family. He was finally sold south to New Orleans and then into Texas and Indian Territory, where he became the slave of an Indian owner. In 1841 he escaped again, this time to Detroit, but by then he had given up any hope of rescuing his wife. She had been resold and had become a concubine of her new owner. In 1848 he married black abolitionist Mary Miles, and the couple was forced to flee to Canada when a new federal Fugitive Slave Law was passed in 1850. The Bibbs settled in Sandwich, Canada West (present-day Ontario), where she opened a school and he edited the *Voice of the Fugitive,* an antislavery weekly newspaper that advocated the emigration of American blacks to Canada. Through the efforts of the Bibbs, Mary Ann Shadd Cary, Austin Steward, and other black Americans who had come to see Canada as a land of freedom and opportunity, many Canadian black settlements were established

Reward posters for fugitive slaves often contained
detailed descriptions of runaways.
Mark E. Mitchell Collection of African American History.

in the three decades before the American Civil War ended slavery in the United States.[18]

Although many African Americans came to believe that emigration was their only route to security and independence, most were determined to achieve full freedom in the United States. Richard Allen, for example, argued that independence might also be achieved through practical training in the mechanical trades. When a group of white abolitionists, including Garrison, Lundy, and New York businessman Arthur Tappan, attended the second national convention to propose the establishment of a manual labor school, delegates received them enthusiastically. These schools, where students supported their education by learning and practicing trades, were popular institutions with reformers at the time. In fact the emphasis on the importance of black education for racial uplift was part of a general reform movement that linked black and white reformers in a commitment to antislavery, temperance, and other moral causes.

The convention endorsed the proposal for a racially integrated college and appointed editor Samuel Cornish to head fund-raising for the project. Integrationists also prevailed on decisions about the administration of the college, though it was agreed that African Americans should be in the majority on the board of trustees. When the residents of New Haven, Connecticut, the home of Yale University, learned that the new college was to be located in their city, they quickly organized in opposition. After a town meeting denounced the idea as promoting abolitionism and disorder, white mobs attacked blacks in New Haven and vandalized Tappan's home.[19] This hostile reaction discouraged the initiative for a college in New Haven, but black leaders remained interested in promoting education generally and in manual labor schools in particular. Especially as African Americans faced increased competition for low-level jobs from Irish immigrants in the 1840s and 1850s, there was heightened support for the establishment of educational institutions providing a combination of traditional and practical education.[20]

Although a black-controlled school of higher education was not established during this period, the cooperation between white abolitionists and black abolitionists did lead to the integration of a few institutions established and controlled by antislavery reformers. After 1830, such integrated schools as the Oneida Institute and New York Central College in New York State, and Oberlin Collegiate Institute in Ohio, educated a small but growing number of African American students. Oneida Institute, with a student body of just over one hundred, for example, under the presidency of white abolitionist Beriah Green and supported by the largesse of Arthur Tappan and his brother Lewis, educated fourteen black students between 1832 and 1844. Oberlin had educated one hundred African American students by the 1860s.[21]

Abolitionists' commitment to black education brought many people into the antislavery movement at a young age. In Cincinnati white abolitionist students from Lane Seminary taught black students, mixing lessons in reading and writing with moral and antislavery messages. In Boston black choirs and youth groups, such as the Juvenile Garrison Independent Society, participated in abolitionist programs and conventions.[22] It was common for whole families to be involved in the public programs held by black communities to protest slavery and racial discrimination. Walker Lewis of Boston was a founding member of the Massachusetts General Colored Association and a close associate of David Walker. Lewis's father, Thomas Lewis, had helped found Boston's African Society, an organization that in the early nineteenth century provided aid to African Americans in need and protested against slavery.

Thomas Lewis also helped establish the African Masonic Lodge in Boston, where David Walker was a member during the 1820s. By the 1840s, when Simpson H. Lewis joined the Boston Committee of Vigilance to protect fugitive slaves, three generations of the Lewis family had been active in antislavery and civil rights efforts. Both men and women in the Snowden family were also active in antislavery activity. Samuel Snowden was elected as a counselor to the New England Anti-Slavery Society in 1833, his two sons were part of a group that armed itself against slave catchers, and his daughters were members of the Boston Vigilance Committee.[23]

Women were critical to the antislavery movement in many ways. They held the bazaars and fairs that raised money, providing a major source of financial contributions. Women organized many auxiliaries to male groups, but they also participated in the meetings of the major integrated antislavery associations and were especially active in the moral reform movement. The Female Moral Reform Society, an interracial organization formed in New York in 1834, had sixty-one chapters in New England alone by 1841, and its bimonthly magazine was supported by three thousand subscribers.[24]

The campaign against slavery in the United States created organizations and networks that connected cities and regions, transcended generational divides, crossed racial divisions, and brought men and women together in coordinated and shared efforts. The crossing of so many boundaries often resulted in strong differences of opinion regarding strategy, and it was on the issue of all-black organizations that the black national convention movement floundered in 1835. A strong Philadelphia faction, led by William Whipper, believed that separate organizations undermined arguments for racial integration in American society. Other delegates, especially those from New York, argued that exclusively black groups, in addition to integrated groups, were necessary to fully represent the interests and views of African Americans. The 1835 convention, dominated by the Philadelphia delegation, formed the American Moral Reform Society, and subsequent meetings became embroiled in debates over this issue. The most extreme position was taken by Whipper, Robert Purvis, and other Garrisonians from Philadelphia who objected to any reference to race and opposed the designation of "free people of color" as unwarranted exclusivity. After years of contention the American Moral Reform Society discontinued its meetings in 1841. Although many black activists may have understood the philosophical principle of the moral reformers, most believed their position to be unrealistic and impractical. Samuel Cornish excoriated them for engaging in trivial debates that distracted them from more important endeavors. "They are quarrelling about trifles," he said, "while their enemies are robbing them of diamonds and of gold."[25] Although willing to work with white reformers, most African Americans believed it was important to maintain black organizations in order to be free from the constraints of integrated groups and the subtle prejudice and discrimination they suffered in them. Integrated organizations were more likely to accept gradualist positions and counsel patience, and, given the strength of northern prejudice toward interracial association, there was a greater danger of mob attacks on integrated meetings and economic reprisals on participants.

There were also benefits to working in the integrated antislavery movement, however. Through these groups African Americans asserted their right to equal participation in the society in a concrete way. They also gave black activists access to far greater financial resources and a much wider audience, and white reformers were educated by their contact with blacks. Within the first year of organizing, the integrated American Anti-Slavery Society had forty-seven local societies in ten northern and western states.[26] Although Garrison himself came from a modest background, some prominent white abolitionists—Gerrit Smith and the Tappans of New York, and Wendell Phillips of Massachusetts, for example—were wealthy men who could lend their names, political connections, social networks, and economic resources to the cause. The Tappans underwrote the educational efforts at Oneida Institute, and Smith was the primary supporter of New York Central College. With the assistance of black abolitionists James McCune Smith and Charles B. Ray, Gerrit Smith purchased and distributed more than three thousand land titles for farms near Lake Placid in upstate New York to African Americans from eastern cities. This created thousands of qualified black voters able to meet New York State's property requirement.[27] These were urban workers, cooks, waiters, coachmen, and barbers, ill prepared for farming. The land was poor, either low and swampy or rocky mountain slopes, and the winters were harsh, but the settlers established farms, raised sheep, and initiated a wool trade with Canadian towns. Many of them voted in state and national elections.[28]

Perhaps the greatest contribution of integrated abolition was that it enabled African Americans to speak to sympathetic white audiences. The American Anti-Slavery Society and its supporters published flurries of pamphlets, sermons, and newspapers, but their most effective agents were antislavery speakers. They crisscrossed the North, made forays into the West, and spoke to large gatherings in major cities and more intimate meetings in small villages. Both blacks and whites, men and women, became antislavery speakers, enduring the hardships of long periods away from home. They lived on subsistence wages and the kindness of supporters, collected money for the cause, encouraged local chapters, and often suffered vilification from hecklers and attacks and brickbats from hostile mobs. The most popular speakers by the early 1840s were African Americans who had been slaves, many of whom were still fugitives. For many whites attending these lectures, it was the first time they had heard a black speaker.

The first full-time paid black traveling abolitionist speaker was free-born Charles Lenox Remond, who was employed by the Massachusetts society in 1838. Yet, the best-known black American abolitionist was an escaped slave hired by the American Anti-Slavery Society in 1841. Born Frederick Bailey, a slave, on Maryland's Eastern Shore in 1818, Frederick Douglass grew up on the plantation of Edward Lloyd, former governor of Maryland and U.S. senator. With a hunger for knowledge encouraged by his grandmother, Douglass seized every opportunity to learn to read and write. From his young white playmates being tutored by a teacher from New England, from his owner's sister-in-law, who tutored him directly, and through his own efforts, Douglass acquired the beginnings of the education that he continued to expand throughout his life. When, as a young man, he was hired out in Baltimore, his curiosity about the world turned to a determination to secure his own freedom. At twenty, in the late summer of 1838, with the help of a free black woman named Anna and carrying identification papers borrowed from a black sailor, Douglass escaped.[29]

Traveling through Philadelphia and continuing northward, Douglass made his way to the New York home of underground railroad activist David Ruggles, where later Anna joined him and they were married. The couple moved farther north, settling in New Bedford, Massachusetts, where Douglass worked as a dock laborer. He became a lay preacher in the African Methodist Episcopal Zion church and attended local antislavery meetings, at which he occasionally told the story of his own bondage.[30] In August 1841 he attended an antislavery convention on Nantucket Island. White abolitionist William C. Coffin had heard him speak to a small gathering in New Bedford and asked him to give his personal testimony to the Nantucket meeting. Douglass was nervous standing before the crowd, but soon his powerful story captured and greatly moved the audience. William Lloyd Garrison and the other prominent abolitionists were so impressed that they offered him a position as an antislavery agent for the Massachusetts Anti-Slavery Society. Late that fall Douglass, Anna, and their two children moved to Lynn, Massachusetts, a Quaker community near Boston that was believed to be safe for a fugitive. Over the next two years Douglass gave antislavery speeches in more than sixty towns in New England and became an accomplished speaker whose power to affect and inspire his audience had few equals.[31]

As abolitionists continued formal organizing, less structured, more spontaneous activity carried on in secret liberated thousands of slaves from bondage. The modern technology of the steam locomotive provided the language for this underground railroad. Its safe houses were called stations, its operators were called conductors, and the fugitives were called passengers. Its function became legendary, and whites as well as blacks participated. Although some of its work was directed and financed by formally organized abolitionist societies, underground railroad activity extended far beyond the formal organizations. Its varied actions included everything from raids on southern plantations to desperate bids for freedom by individual slaves. Fugitive settlements, maroon communities, and blacks allied with the Seminole Indians of Florida struck from the cover of swamps and protective wilderness at the plantations of Georgia and South Carolina. Fugitives moved south as well as north. In the regions of the Deep South or the Southwest, fugitives fled toward Mexico, which had abolished slavery by the mid-1820s, or westward into the frontier territories.

In the southern interior, fugitives might seek temporary safety in deep woods, swamps, or mountains. In the Upper South, the North was the logical favored destination. The mythology of the underground railroad has emphasized the efforts of northern white abolitionists, mainly Quakers. While their support was important, the underground railroad radiated out from the South in all directions, and escape was generally a slave initiative. The initial hours and the first few miles, before a runaway reached the relative safety of free territory or a protective community, were the most critical. Generally unfamiliar with areas outside the immediate proximity of the plantation, fugitives were at a great disadvantage, easy prey for pursuers with tracking dogs or local patrols that routinely stopped blacks unescorted by whites. In this early phase fugitives were dependent on other slaves, friends, and family to shelter, feed, and guide them on their way. Later, in southern towns or in the North, contact with the free black community became increasingly significant, and along with it an increased possibility for contact with organized underground railroad activity.

James Williams escaped slavery in Virginia, headed north, and finally reached Carlisle, Pennsylvania, where he found a number of free blacks. When he inquired about employment, they surmised that he was a runaway from the South. "They knew that I was from Virginia, by my pronunciation of certain words [and] that I was probably a runaway slave," he recounted. He confided in these people, placing his fate in their hands in part because they were black. Later Williams explained that he was informed "that I need not be alarmed as they were friends, and would do all in their power to protect me." They sheltered him and "treated [him] with the utmost kindness." He was taken by wagon to Harrisburg to meet others, and from there he was taken to Philadelphia. To this point Williams had been cared for by strangers concerned for his safety. Only in Philadelphia did he contact the formally organized underground railroad.[32]

The Philadelphia Vigilant Association, formed in 1837, specialized in assisting fugitives and maintained contacts throughout the North. Through its resources Williams traveled to New York. But apparently Williams's master was so determined that he be recaptured that he had employed slave catchers, who

William Still

William Still was the son of former slaves. His father freed himself by self-purchase, but his mother escaped from slavery in 1807. In doing so, she was forced to leave her two sons behind. Fourteen years later, William was born free in New Jersey. As an adult, Still, one of the nation's most important abolitionists, lived in Philadelphia. He operated an elaborate network of safe houses and conductors, as part of the most extensive underground railroad system in the country.

In a letter written on August 8, 1850, from his office in Philadelphia, William Still described an astounding encounter with a man who called himself Peter Freedman from Alabama. Freedman sought information about his family, who had come north some years before, and as his story progressed, Still recognized much of the detail. "My feelings were unutterable," he explained. "I could see in the face of my newfound brother, the likeness of my mother."* Peter Freedman was William's brother left in slavery when his mother escaped. The brothers had never met.

"I told him I could tell him all about his kinfolk," William recalled, and the next day Peter was reunited with the family. Their father was dead by this time, but Peter met five brothers and three sisters that he had never known. "I shall not attempt to describe the feelings of my mother and the family on learning the fact that Peter was one of us," William wrote.[†] Slavery, a central social and economic feature of the South and a legal and political fact of American life, regularly created these and other hardships for families.

This family's struggle was not over, however. When Peter left Alabama, he had left behind a wife and children whom he was determined to free. Members of the underground railroad secured their escape to Indiana, but they were recaptured and returned to slavery. When Peter attempted to purchase their freedom, their master demanded the almost impossible sum of five thousand dollars. With the assistance of many of William's abolitionist friends, Peter began a lecture tour, telling his story and that of his enslaved family in order to raise money

William Still, abolitionist and underground railroad operative in Philadelphia. Photographs and Prints Division, Schomburg Center for Research in Black Culture, The New York Public Library, Astor, Lenox, and Tilden Foundations.

(continued)

for their freedom. It took four additional years of fund raising for Peter to gather the money, but in October 1854 he accomplished his goal.

Once free, Peter Still and his family settled on a ten-acre farm in Burlington, New Jersey, where they lived until Peter died of pneumonia in 1868. WIlliam Still continued his underground railroad activities and worked for civil rights in Philadelphia throughout the Civil War. During and after the war, he raised funds to assist former slaves who had gained their freedom in the South. He also served on Philadelphia's Board of Trade and helped establish a Young Men's Christian Association (YMCA) for the city's blacks. He lived into the twentieth century, dying in 1901. Many descendants of the Still family continue to live in southern New Jersey, where they hold regular family reunions.

---

*"William Still to James Miller McKim," Philadelphia, August 8, 1850, in Peter C. Ripley, Roy E. Finkenbine, Michael F. Hembree, and Donald Yacovone, eds., *The Black Abolitionist Papers*, vol. 4 (Chapel Hill: University of North Carolina Press, 1991), 53–58.
†Ibid.

searched for the fugitive as far north as Boston. When they were seen in New York, the New York Committee of Vigilance arranged for Williams to be sent to England. By this time the fugitive was under the protection of the formal underground, with international connections.[33]

Such black abolitionists as Jacob C. White and William Still in Philadelphia, David Ruggles in New York, and Leonard Grimes and Lewis Hayden in Boston, major figures in underground activities, represent the range of personal experiences that people brought to this dangerous and demanding work. The White family was important to much of Philadelphia's black abolitionist action. Jacob was a wealthy businessman and longtime activist, and his wife, Elizabeth, was a member of the Female Vigilance Committee. Jacob operated a free-produce store (selling products grown by free workers) and led a boycott of cotton, sugar, rice, tobacco, and other products grown by slaves. Their son, Jacob C. White, Jr., later continued this work. David Ruggles was born free in Connecticut and came to New York City as a teenager. After working in several businesses, he became an agent for the antislavery newspaper, the *Emancipator,* and for the American Anti-Slavery Society. Later he opened a bookstore specializing in antislavery publications. When a proslavery mob burned his store in 1835, Ruggles became an officer of the New York Committee of Vigilance, the chief arm of the city's antislavery underground. Over the next five years he and his associates facilitated the escape of more than six hundred fugitives, poor health finally forcing him to limit his underground work.[34]

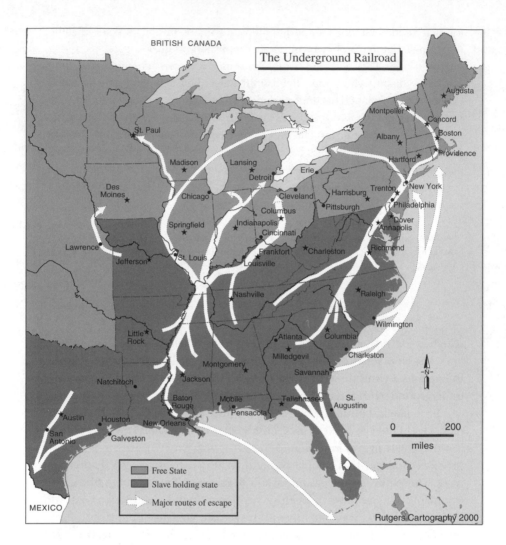

Leonard Andrew Grimes was born in northern Virginia in the small town of Leesburg in the early winter of 1815. He was free, and although his racially mixed heritage was readily apparent to many, he was light enough sometimes to be mistaken for a white person. As a young boy, he traveled to nearby Washington, D.C., where he worked first at a butcher shop and then for a druggist, before a slaveholder hired him to be a hack driver. In this employ, Grimes traveled through the South, where his observations led him to hate slavery and encouraged him to become active in the underground railroad. He saved his money and prospered in his business while using his wits, his money, and his horse-drawn hacks to assist fugitives to escape from bondage. After aiding one family that escaped to Canada from Virginia, Grimes was arrested in Richmond, found guilty of "stealing slaves," and sentenced to two years in prison. His prison term was hard on him both physically and emotionally, but after serving his time, he emerged, with his spirit intact and a powerful devotion to religion. He became a preacher and traveled north, settling first in New Bedford, where he ministered to a small congregation for two years. Then, in 1846, the Twelfth Baptist Church in Boston called Grimes to be its minister. From this pulpit he continued his abolitionist work, becoming a major leader of underground activity in the city. His church attracted so many runaways that it become known as the fugitive slave church.[35]

For most free blacks involvement in the underground railroad was a natural outcome of their personal relationships. Since nine of every ten African Americans were slaves, almost every free black person either had been a slave or had family members or friends in slavery. As one historian explained, "Practically every clump of Negro settlers in the free states was an underground depot by definition."[36] Fugitive slaves were some of those most directly involved in underground railroad activities, thereby risking their own recapture. Lewis Hayden was a fugitive from Kentucky who settled in Boston, opened a small clothing shop, and became active in antislavery and the underground. He often sheltered fugitives in his home and confronted slave catchers who attempted to capture people under his protection.[37] The story of Harriet Tubman, underground railroad conductor, is legendary. She was born into slavery on the Eastern Shore of Maryland, the property of one of the largest plantation owners in the region. At six years of age she was doing domestic work, and by her teens she worked full-time in the fields doing heavy labor. Her owner struck Harriet in the head while she was attempting to protect another slave from punishment. The blow left her severely injured, and thereafter she suffered short episodes of unconsciousness.

When her master died and it became clear that his slaves would be sold away from the area and possibly into the Deep South, she determined to escape. Failing to convince other slaves, even her own husband, to follow her, she set out alone and finally reached Philadelphia. There she found work as a domestic but soon determined to devote her life and the little money she was able to accumulate to freeing her family and other slaves. She was encouraged in this project by William Still, the leader of the underground railroad in Philadelphia. In late 1850 Tubman traveled to Baltimore on the first of many clandestine ventures into the South. This first trip was occasioned by word that her sister and her sister's two children were about to be sold and separated from their husband and father, a free black man on the Eastern Shore of Maryland. As the sale was about to commence, the husband broke into the room where the slaves were being held for auction, gathered up his

Harriet Tubman (*left*) and seven unidentified persons.
Photographs and Prints Division, Schomburg Center for Research in Black Culture,
The New York Public Library, Astor, Lenox, and Tilden Foundations.

family, and brought them to Baltimore, where Tubman waited to escort them to freedom.

With forged papers and elaborate plans that included rescues on Saturday evening so as to delay the publication of advertisements for escaped slaves until the Monday-morning newspapers, Tubman worked with free blacks and white abolitionists. During the 1850s Tubman made at least twenty trips south rescuing members of her family and other slaves, perhaps as many as three hundred in all.[38] Although white abolitionists contributed much to the movement, as white activist James G. Birney observed, "such matters [as direct contact with and assistance of fugitives] are almost uniformly managed by the colored people, I know nothing of them generally till they are past." Birney understated the role of white reformers, but it was true, nevertheless, as Cincinnati Quaker Levi Coffin remembered, that "fugitives often passed through [town] generally stopping among the colored people."[39]

Even so, at its most organized levels the underground railroad was very much an interracial enterprise. It was most formally organized and most interracial in the North, where the law and local sentiment were less hostile toward antislavery activity, but some antislavery whites were willing to go South, risking their freedom, even their lives, to assist fugitives. Calvin Fairbank and Delia Webster, students at Oberlin College, were arrested and jailed for assisting fugitives (one of whom was Lewis Hayden) to escape from Kentucky. Many of these fugitives worked to win their release, but Fairbank became so notorious for his actions that Kentucky finally sentenced him to fifteen years in prison, where he was tortured unmercifully.[40]

Jonathan Walker, a New England sea captain, was apprehended by authorities off the Florida coast in the summer of 1844 with fugitives whom he was attempting to transport to freedom in the Bahamas. His ship was captured, and he was arrested and taken to Pensacola. He was jailed, fined, whipped, and branded with a double S for "slave stealer." After seven months several of his friends, including a number of free blacks, secured his release from prison. Frederick Douglass praised Walker's actions, saying that abolitionists would make the double *S* a symbol for "slave-savior."[41]

Fugitives often sought the assistance of seamen who they thought were particularly willing to provide aid. With cosmopolitan knowledge and access to the means of long-distance travel, sailors could provide a fugitive with valuable services. After Frederick Douglass escaped slavery in Baltimore with false seaman's papers, another sailor in New York City facilitated his contact with the vigilance committee. The culture of seagoing men often encouraged defiance of shoreside social, legal, and even racial conventions. Perhaps it is too much to say that "there seemed to have been an entire absence of prejudice against the blacks as shipmates among the crew," as one nineteenth-century observer claimed, but historian William Jeffrey Bolster has documented the interracial comradeship on shipboard and the willingness of sailors, black and white, to assist fugitives. In the South sailors were always regarded with suspicion. One southern newspaper asserted that sailors actually kidnapped slaves who might otherwise be unwilling to leave the South.[42]

Seamen and riverboatmen were also crucial to the underground communication network that kept free blacks in the North in touch with friends and relatives in the slave South. In their regular trips up and down the Mississippi River or the Atlantic coast, these men often carried personal messages and antislavery literature and provided information to southern free blacks and slaves, breaking the isolation of southern society. Information about routes of travel, underground contacts in northern communities, and antislavery activities buoyed those held in bondage and helped to make escape a realistic aim.[43]

This communication network facilitated personal interaction on either side of the cotton curtain. When Henry Williams escaped from slavery in Louisiana during the 1830s, he left his wife behind. He settled in Cincinnati, where he was able to secure work and establish a new life in freedom. After several years Williams met and married a woman from a neighboring town. Members of his church who considered him already married were outraged. The congregation charged Williams with bigamy, and he was accused of having deserted his wife in slavery. The church demanded a signed release from her before it would sanction the new marriage. This posed a difficult and

Broadside announcing reward for the return of black children
kidnapped and feared sold into slavery.
Graphics Division, Rhode Island Historical Society.

dangerous situation for an escaped slave, who might face reenslavement if he
returned to the South. The underground communication network provided
the answer to Williams's dilemma. He sent a message to his first wife by way
of a boatman who regularly traveled to southern port cities on the Mississippi
River. The boatman obtained her *X* and her enthusiastic expression of support for dissolving the marriage. The church was satisfied and recognized
Williams's new marriage.[44]

In addition to organized groups and extensive communication networks,
the underground railroad was sometimes specific, sometimes isolated, acts of
conscience that transcended political philosophy. The chief justice of the Ohio
Supreme Court, Joseph R. Swan, in his legal opinion supporting the constitutionality of the 1850 Fugitive Slave Law, explained, "As a citizen I would
not deliberately violate the Constitution or the law." Yet, if confronted by a
slave pleading for protection, the chief justice admitted, "I might momentarily
forget my allegiance to the law and the Constitution and give him covert [*sic*]
from those who were on his track."[45]

For African Americans the fight against slavery was both personal and
philosophical. It was about the liberty promised by the Revolution and the
Declaration of Independence, and the freedom denied to family and friends
bound in slavery. It was also about defending black people from an institu-

tion that by its very existence threatened the human rights of all African Americans. Resistance to slavery not only included overt physical confrontation with masters and overseers but also meant defeating slavery's attempt to control its victims and to hold them in debilitating isolation. The underground communication network was as much a part of antislavery activity as the underground railroad or formal abolitionist protest. In both formal and informal ways, blacks, often joined by progressive whites, engaged in a long-term agitation against slavery.

A call for a meeting in Buffalo, New York, in 1843 to reconvene the black national convention sparked a great deal of debate among black leaders. Their philosophical differences had become more public, their disagreements over strategy more strident, and meeting in New York State signaled a change that was partly generational, partly a reflection of changing political and social circumstances. All but one of the previous meetings had been held in Philadelphia, which, like Boston, was a stronghold of Garrisonian opinion. Many blacks had grown impatient with the tools of moral suasion, nonparticipation in politics, and nonviolence that had been so influential in the previous decade. Pacifism had always been a controversial philosophy among blacks. Many of their most loyal allies, including Quakers and William Lloyd Garrison, were pacifists, but few African Americans were committed to this belief. In 1837 a meeting of New York blacks had challenged the theory of nonviolence as impractical for "persons who are denied the protection of equitable law, and when their liberty is invaded and their lives endangered by avaricious kidnappers."[46] Samuel Cornish, editor of New York's *Colored American,* confessed that when faced with kidnappers or "a midnight incendiary with a lighted torch in his hand" he had trouble believing in the virtue of "using moral weapons."[47]

From the start it was clear that nonviolence would be a major point of contention at the 1843 meeting. Fearing acrimonious debate and conclusions they could not support, the Philadelphians opted not to attend. Samuel Davis of Buffalo, chair of the convention, opened the meeting by urging blacks not to wait for others to act on their behalf. Citing uprisings in Greece and Poland as illustrations of the need to strike for liberty, he asserted that "if we are not willing to rise up and assert our rightful claims, and plead our own cause, we have no reason to look for success."[48] On the second day Henry Highland Garnet took the podium and delivered a rousing speech, one of the most militant calls for slave uprisings since David Walker's *Appeal.* He argued that patience should be no virtue for black people and proposed a resolution urging African Americans to wait no longer for freedom and justice. The time for action had come, he declared, and for free blacks this meant the use of violence if necessary to defend their rights, their families, and the freedom of those who had been illegitimately held in bondage. For slaves this might mean open rebellion to secure freedom. "You cannot suffer greater cruelties than you have already. Rather die freemen," he urged, "than live to be slaves."[49]

Other New Yorkers echoed Garnet's sentiments and supported his call to action, but the Boston delegates and other Garrisonians dissented. Frederick Douglass and Charles Lenox Remond pointed out that openly encouraging slave rebellions provided an excuse for proslavery retaliation against both slaves and free blacks. They argued that it was reckless to jeopardize the entire abolitionist movement with such calls. Other delegates made counter-arguments, sentiment was closely divided, and the resolution failed by just one vote.[50]

A second issue—the wisdom of black involvement in partisan politics—also sharply divided black opinion. Garrison urged abolitionists not to participate in politics, arguing that party politics required compromises that would dilute antislavery principles and voting expressed tacit approval for the constitutional system that sanctioned slavery. Nevertheless many black abolitionists voted, and African Americans were powerful advocates for political reform even in states that prohibited black voting. In New York State the fact that there were property requirements for black voters but not for white voters made some African Americans more determined to participate in politics, if only to challenge this law.

In 1839 abolitionists from western New York had organized the Liberty Party, and antislavery hopes for political power were raised when the new party ran antislavery men for state and national offices. The Liberty Party nominated a former Kentucky slaveholder turned Ohio abolitionist, James G. Birney, for the presidency and attracted considerable black support. The *Colored American* endorsed the party's national slate, calling Birney "a better man in every possible respect to be President of the United States" than the current Democratic president Martin Van Buren or Whig candidate William Henry Harrison.[51] Black delegates attended the party's convention in 1840, but black support was equivocal. At the 1840 New York State convention of African Americans, a resolution endorsing the party was hotly debated before it was finally withdrawn.[52] Though strongly opposed to slavery, the Liberty Party attempted to broaden its appeal beyond antislavery circles by linking the evil of slavery with the injustice of poverty. "Pity not only the enslaved poor and the colored poor, but all poor," urged a broadside advertising its meeting in Peterboro, New York, in 1846.[53] Though some remained wary of any political party's ability to remain ardently antislavery, black support for the Liberty Party was substantial throughout the 1840s. Several blacks traveled the campaign circuit, combining stories of their slave experience with a partisan political message. In 1844 the minister and former slave Jermain Wesley Loguen agreed to merge fund-raising efforts for his church in Bath, New York, with tours on behalf of the Liberty Party. One contemporary recalled the effectiveness of Loguen's presentation in the small town of Cortland, maintaining that "no prayer ever made . . . melted the people like that." Liberty Party officials did remain committed to broadening the black franchise, not incidentally, increasing the number of their potential supporters. After his unsuccessful 1840 presidential candidacy, Birney wrote to Lewis Tappan suggesting a petition campaign to secure equal suffrage for blacks in New York State.[54] This was the context for abolitionist Gerrit Smith's distribution of farmland in upstate New York to black families, allowing more blacks to meet the property requirement for voting.[55]

The establishment of the Liberty Party seemed to many to indicate the growing power of the antislavery movement, but there were also ominous indications that slavery was expanding its territory and its power. In 1836 prominent slaveholders in northern Mexico rebelled against their government's restrictions on slavery and established the independent republic of Texas. In 1845 the United States annexed Texas as a slaveholding territory with the prospect of statehood. In his address to the Buffalo convention in 1843, Henry Garnet had anticipated just such an expansion of slaveholder influence, warning of the "propagators of American slavery spending their blood and treasure, that they may plant the black flag in the heart of Mexico and riot in the halls of Montezuma."[56] When President James K. Polk asked Congress to declare war against Mexico in 1846, Boston blacks denounced "any war which may be occasioned by the annexation of Texas, or . . . any other war . . . designed to strengthen or perpetuate slavery."[57] Douglass scolded Massachusetts, "the brightest of every other state," for becoming "the tool of Texas" when it offered men to fight and die in the unjust war, a war he saw as a hypocritical ruse to rob Mexico.[58] African Americans were alarmed that the slave power seemed strong enough to push the federal government into a proslavery war.

Meanwhile blacks in the late 1840s in northern cities worried about the wave of immigration that increased job competition among those at the bottom of the economic ladder. Economic competition threatened to create racial violence and provided potential converts for the antiabolitionist Democratic Party. As national political parties took up contentious issues directly related to the antislavery cause, and members of black communities felt under increasing political and economic attack, black abolitionists debated the most expeditious course of action. There were many disagreements over specific strategies, but all agreed that their responsibility to those still suffering under slavery and to those growing up in the limited northern freedom demanded their steadfast commitment to racial justice.

1850   Congress passes major compromise legislation containing harsher federal Fugitive Slave Law, admitting California as a free state and outlawing the slave trade in the District of Columbia

1851   Mary Ann Shadd Cary publishes the newspaper *Provincial Freeman* in Ontario, Canada

1852   Harriet Beecher Stowe publishes *Uncle Tom's Cabin*

1854   Congress passes the Kansas-Nebraska Act; armed conflict erupts over the slave or free status of the future state of Kansas

African American singer Elizabeth Greenfield gives a command performance before Queen Victoria

Fugitive Anthony Burns is returned to slavery from Boston

Republican Party formed

1855   William C. Nell publishes *The Colored Patriots of the American Revolution*

1857   In the case of *Dred Scott* v. *Sanford,* the Supreme Court upholds the right of slavery to expand into the territories, refuses to free Scott, and denies black people the right to U.S. citizenship

1858   Senatorial election debates between Abraham Lincoln and Stephen A. Douglas in Illinois; Douglas wins election

1859   John Brown leads thirteen whites and five blacks in an abortive raid on Harpers Ferry, Virginia

1860   Abraham Lincoln elected president

U.S. population 31,443,790; black population 4,441,830 (14 percent)

1861–1865   Civil War; more than 180,000 African Americans serve in combat roles and 200,000 as support troops; twenty-four receive Congressional Medal of Honor

1862   Compensated emancipation pays slave owners for freeing their slaves in the District of Columbia

1863   Abraham Lincoln issues the Emancipation Proclamation

From Militancy to Civil War

$\mathcal{B}$ y the 1847 national black convention, debates were more pessimistic, more militant, and even more bellicose. Educate your sons in the "art of war," urged one resolution. Calls for patience and faith in rational debate were replaced by arguments favoring the use of violence to discourage slaveholding and the kidnapping of free blacks. The next year in Cleveland, the convention passed resolutions advocating women's rights and the right of violent self-defense. The delegates supported speakers who urged that additional committees of vigilance be formed "to measure arms with assailants without and invaders within."[1] Ohio blacks reinforced that message in 1849 when their meeting urged "the slave [to] leave [the plantation] immediately with his hoe on his shoulder" and made plans to publish five hundred copies of a volume pairing Walker's *Appeal* with Garnet's 1843 address.[2] Even Frederick Douglass, previously opposed to violence in the antislavery cause, could see justice in slaves' killing slaveholders. In the winter of 1849 Douglass asked, "Who dare say that the criminals deserve less than death at the hands of their long-abused chattels?"[3]

Events during the 1850s confirmed blacks' growing conviction that the federal government was unlikely to support the cause of freedom. The U.S. victory over Mexico brought large tracts of land under federal authority, again raising the inflammatory question of whether the new lands would be open to slavery. This issue had broad political consequences, since the common wisdom among northern white working men was that their labor was cheapened and their opportunities severely limited in regions that tolerated slavery. Although most white workers would not disturb slavery in the South, they were strongly opposed to allowing slavery in the western territories, fearing it would deprive white working people of access to the new lands that were the core of the American future. White southerners agreed that the nation's future lay in the western territories but asserted their right to bring slavery, an institution basic to their way of life, into that future. To forestall a clash between regions, Kentucky representative Henry Clay engineered a political compromise in Congress. California would be admitted as a free state, but the other southwestern territories taken from Mexico would be organized without a decision on slavery. For the antislavery forces the compromise promised the abolition of the slave trade in the nation's capital. For proslavery interests, the compromise offered the strictest fugitive slave law ever enacted, far stronger than the 1793 provision. This measure was so harsh that even President Millard Fillmore, who signed it into law in the fall of 1850, questioned its constitutionality.[4]

The Fugitive Slave Law of 1850 infuriated African Americans, who considered it definitive evidence that proslavery forces had taken over the federal government. This new law made it easier for slaveholders to retrieve runaways who sought asylum in the North. They were not even required to bring accused fugitives before a court but could take possession of their human property simply by presenting an affidavit drawn up by a southern court, with a physical description of the runaway, to any federal commissioner. Further, any bystander who refused to help recover a fugitive could be fined one thousand dollars and sentenced to up to six months in jail. This law not only struck down northern states' personal liberty laws, which prohibited the use of local and state officials or facilities in the capture of fugitives, but it even threatened the freedom of blacks who were legally free. Since alleged fugitives could not speak in their own defense, free blacks could more easily be kidnapped into slavery. Thus, even where abolitionists were strongest, no African American was beyond the reach of the slave power.[5]

Free blacks immediately swore to defy the new federal law. Meeting in Chicago only a few days after its passage, African Americans strongly denounced it. The city council in Chicago called it unconstitutional, deemed its supporters traitors, and refused to order city police to enforce it.[6] At Boston's Faneuil Hall abolitionists vowed that no fugitive would be taken from that city, and Frederick Douglass asserted that the streets "would be running red with blood" before the law could be enforced in Boston.[7] Pittsburgh blacks, stating their intention to make the recovery of fugitives in that city a costly proposition, bought one store's entire inventory of handguns and knives.[8] In Cazenovia, a town in the middle of New York State, abolitionists and fugitive slaves met defiantly in a "Fugitive Slave Convention" and called for slave rebellion. Anticipating a confrontation, leaders in Ohio and Massachusetts called for the formation of black military companies to be ready to take up arms against slavery.[9]

Despite such strong reactions, the federal government, prodded by southern political pressure, was determined to enforce the law. James Hamlet, who was arrested in New York City and taken to Baltimore, had the dubious distinction of being the first to be returned to slavery under its provisions. The New York abolitionists, who had been unable to prevent his capture, collected the eight hundred dollars demanded by Hamlet's master, bought his freedom, and returned him to the city. Others were not so fortunate and were returned to slavery from northern cities during the early 1850s. Many, even those who had lived in the North for several years, fled to Canada. Commu-

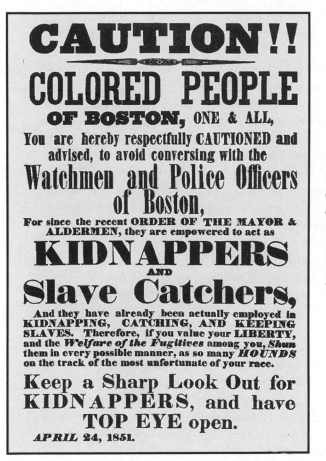

Broadside warning of the presence of slave catchers in Boston.

Photographs and Prints Division, Library of Congress, Washington, D.C.

nities closest to the South felt this emigration most acutely. According to contemporary accounts, small towns in southern Pennsylvania were "almost deserted of black fellows, since they have heard of the new law. It is supposed that more than a hundred have left for Canada and other parts." The black population of Columbia, Pennsylvania, decreased by more than half in a matter of months.[10] One observer in Pittsburgh reported that "nearly all the waiters in the hotels have fled to Canada." According to his tally, "Sunday 30 fled; on Monday 40; on Tuesday 50; on Wednesday 30 and up to this time the number that has left will not fall short of 300."[11] Fugitive or free, blacks not well known in their local communities were especially vulnerable to capture or kidnapping.[12] Things were not much better farther north—in Buffalo one black church lost 130 members of its congregation, Rochester's black Baptist church lost 114 members, and Boston's Twelfth Baptist Church and Albany, New York's, Hamilton Street Church each lost one-third of its members to Canadian migration.[13] Shortly after the fugitive slave provision was signed into law, the

Anti-Slavery Society of Canada estimated that between four and five thousand African Americans had crossed the Canadian border, and many of them were free blacks.[14]

Most blacks, however, did not go to Canada. Free blacks were critical in the fight against the Fugitive Slave Law, and the historical record is filled with their defiance of authority, as they endangered themselves and their property in attempts to prevent the recapture of fugitives. Before the passage of the new law, William Craft and his wife, Ellen, had escaped slavery in Georgia. They had made their way to Philadelphia and then to Boston, using an ingenious disguise, with the light-complexioned Ellen posing as an ill young white man and the darker William as her slave attendant. After their escape they traveled widely as antislavery speakers, mesmerizing audiences with their story. While in Boston, the couple stayed with Lewis Hayden, the escaped slave and active abolitionist. Though one of the best-known centers of antislavery activity in the country, Boston was not beyond slavery's reach. In early November 1850 the *Liberator* warned of "the appearance of two prowling villains . . . from Macon, Georgia, for the purpose of seizing William and Ellen Craft, under the infernal Fugitive Slave Bill, and carrying them back to the hell of Slavery."[15]

Abolitionist pressure led to the temporary arrest of the slave hunters, but eventually they descended on Hayden's home intending to recover the fugitives. Hayden confronted the slave hunters on the front porch of his house where he had placed barrels of explosives. He made clear his intention to blow up the house and anyone who might enter rather than allow the fugitives to be taken back to slavery. Meanwhile a number of Boston's blacks met to consider their course of action, and it was the overwhelming sense of the meeting that the fugitives would not be taken without a fight. Yet, realizing it was only a matter of time before the federal government would prevail even in Boston, abolitionists raised funds to send the Crafts to England, where they were taken in by British abolitionists and remained safe from capture.[16]

In Springfield, Massachusetts, John Brown, a deeply religious—some said fanatical—white activist, organized the U.S. League of the Gileadites. This group of black men and women armed themselves and intended to act as a guerrilla force to defend fugitives and attack slavery. Defiant abolitionist action spread across the North, but federal officials grew more determined as resistance increased. When an integrated group of abolitionists successfully rescued a fugitive named Shadrach Minkins from a Boston courtroom, President Filmore ordered the prosecution of the rescuers. Eight Bostonians, four blacks and four whites, were arrested, but none was convicted. In Syracuse, New York, in a case that became known as the Jerry Rescue, William ("Jerry") McHenry, a fugitive from Missouri, was arrested, but abolitionists rescued him from authorities and delivered him to Canada.[17]

Resistance in many northern cities made enforcing the Fugitive Slave Law costly. In New York City two hundred policemen were required to guard a single chained fugitive and return him to slavery. An attempt to recapture a fugitive in Christiana, Pennsylvania, resulted in the "Battle of Christiana," which left one slaveholder dead and another injured.[18] The failed rescue of Anthony Burns, a fugitive from Virginia, in Boston in 1854 was one of the most dramatic and costly actions. Attempting to free Burns, several hundred abolitionists armed with stones, ax handles, guns, and knives attacked a federal courthouse and murdered a U.S. deputy marshal, and it took two military companies to quell the riot. Thousands of antislavery supporters came from the surrounding area to witness Burns's trial and return to slavery, proceedings that required more than two thousand police and military troops and cost the federal government one hundred thousand dollars.[19]

One attempt to recapture fugitives in Ohio was especially tragic. Margaret Garner was one of a group of seventeen fugitives from Kentucky, including her husband, her four children, and her husband's parents, who found sanctuary in Cincinnati in January 1856. Underground Railroad operatives were able to send nine of the fugitives on to Canada, but Garner and her family remained in Cincinnati while a relative attempted to arrange their passage. Before this could be accomplished, however, Kentucky slave hunters arrived, secured the assistance of the U.S. marshal, and surrounded the house where the fugitives had taken shelter. Although Garner's husband attempted to protect his family by firing on the slave hunters, capture seemed inevitable. Desperately determined not to allow herself and her children to be taken back into slavery, Garner killed her three-year-old, cutting her throat with a kitchen knife. Before her relatives could stop her, she had also severely injured two of her other children. Questioned later, Garner said that she had intended to kill all of her children and herself. "God did not appear to save us," she recounted calmly. "I did the best I could." Although state authorities indicted Garner for murder, federal law prevailed, and the court upheld the slaveholder's right to the return of his human property.[20]

The legal arguments of abolitionists, including Ohio governor Salmon P. Chase, could not prevent the fugitives' return to slavery. They were taken first to Kentucky, and then while en route farther south, their ship was involved in an accident. Garner and one of her remaining children fell overboard into the river; she was saved, but the child drowned. This final tragedy in the Garner case further inflamed northern opinion against the Fugitive Slave Law. The Ohio legislature, calling the law unconstitutional, ordered state officials to remove fugitives from the custody of federal authorities upon the state's issuance of a writ of habeas corpus.[21]

Attempts to enforce the Fugitive Slave Law heightened African American resistance, strengthened abolitionist resolve, and seemed to increase northern

Margaret Garner

In 1987 black writer Toni Morrison took the literary world by storm with a wrenching and haunting novel. *Beloved* was the story of Sethe, a fugitive slave woman who killed her baby rather than allow the child to grow up under slavery. The novel and the movie made from it were loosely based on an actual incident in 1856. Margaret Garner, her husband, their four children, and her in-laws escaped from slavery in Kentucky. It was winter, and they walked across the frozen Ohio River to the free state of Ohio. There they joined nine other fugitives from Kentucky and made their way to Cincinnati. Within sight of slaves across the river, Cincinnati was a virtual magnet for runaways. They were drawn there and to other towns on the north side of the river by the hope of safety within a free black community and aid from abolitionists. Nevertheless slave catchers trapped Garner and her children, but before they could seize her, she cut her baby girl's throat. Had she had time, Garner later said, she would have killed all of her children and herself. The prospective return of her children to slavery was too much for her to bear. The best efforts of Cincinnati abolitionists could not prevent her being returned to the South. Still, Garner was determined that she and her children would not be reenslaved. On a ship bound for their sale in the Deep South, she threw one child overboard and leaped in herself. Sailors pulled Garner from the water still alive, but the child drowned. Eventually she was sold in a New Orleans slave market.

One can hardly imagine a slavery so horrible that a mother would kill her children to save them from it. Defenders of slavery often claimed that slaves were contented. They contended that masters were benevolent, and they romanticized the master-slave relationship. The power of Margaret Garner's tragic story was not lost on the abolitionists. They told it again and again as heartbreaking proof of the inhumanity of slavery and the incredible lengths to which some would go to free themselves and those they loved from its grip.

Margaret Garner, escaped slave, killed her child rather than submit her children to slavery. Photographs and Prints Division, Library of Congress, Washington, D.C.

opposition to the inhumanity of keeping human beings in bondage. Highly publicized fugitive slave cases gave human form to what previously had been abstractions in the minds of many white northerners. Seeing some of these people returned to slavery evoked the sympathy of many formerly apathetic people, and the tragedies attending the enforcement of federal law galvanized the abolition movement. Harriet Beecher Stowe was a writer from a northern white abolitionist family whose sister urged her to use her literary talent to combat the Fugitive Slave Law. Stowe's 1852 novel *Uncle Tom's Cabin* caught the imagination and stirred the emotions of northern readers. Her melodramatic depiction of the plight of the fugitive and the horrors of slavery became the single most influential piece of antislavery literature in the century. Its authenticity was bolstered by consultation with people who had actually experienced slavery. Prominent among them was Frederick Douglass, whom Stowe admired and with whom she developed a close friendship. Douglass was effusive in his praise of Stowe's intelligence, philosophy, and character, and he called her novel *"the master book* of the nineteenth century."[22]

The moral discomfort the book caused in the North was not strong enough to unite northern whites in the antislavery cause. It and the Fugitive Slave Law did, however, convince many northerners that the expansion of slave power posed a threat to the civil rights of *all* Americans. *Uncle Tom's Cabin* sold out its first printing of five thousand copies in the first two days and sold three hundred thousand copies in the United States and two hundred thousand in England during the first year.[23] *The Times* of London reported on its wild popularity among the British. Lord Palmerston, who became British prime minister during the 1860s, claimed to have read the entire book three times, the only novel he had read in thirty years. This book's impact was so powerful that it influenced British authorities to keep the Canadian border open to people fleeing from slavery. Partly because of Stowe's novel and partly in response to the fugitive slave cases, many northerners who had supported slaveholders' property rights were forced to confront the morality of their position.

The novel was widely read even in the South. In Charleston, South Carolina, the stores could not keep it on their shelves, but reaction was decidedly negative. "I would have the review as hot as hellfire, blasting and searing the reputation of the vile wretch in petticoats who could write such a volume," the editor of the *Southern Literary Messenger* wrote to instruct his reviewer. In the two years after the publication of *Uncle Tom's Cabin,* southern authors wrote at least fifteen novels whose premise was that slavery was more benevolent than Stowe's depiction. Many argued that slavery compared favorably to the conditions of free labor in the North. Clearly Stowe's novel accentuated the growing rift between North and South, and it led President

Lincoln a decade later to address Stowe as "the little lady who wrote the book that made this great war."[24]

By the 1850s most of the South had become a closed society—a police state that barred dissent—where concurrence with slavery was the price of social acceptance and individual safety. Slavery was claimed to be a superior, more progressive, more humane system than free labor.[25] The abolitionist arguments that the South was controlled by proslavery forces bent on shaping national policies to their needs was made more credible by southern reactions to the rise of the antislavery movement in the North. White northern anxiety strengthened with each southern attempt to block the delivery of the U.S. mail for fear that it carried antislavery literature. Each act of violence meant to prohibit the public expression of antislavery ideas, and each reward for killing antislavery leaders offered or sanctioned by southern legislators, heightened northerners' concerns about their own rights. By the middle of the nineteenth century, northern support for the antislavery cause had broadened to include those "likely to be more concerned for the welfare of white men than they were for the rights of free black men and slaves."[26]

Sectional disputes erupted in violence as Congress began to organize the Kansas and Nebraska territories. Although the Missouri Compromise of 1820 had prohibited slavery in the territories held by the federal government north of the state of Missouri, the question was opened again in the 1850s. The discovery of gold in California in 1848 had spurred the desire for constructing a transcontinental railroad to the West Coast. When the U.S. Senate began to organize the territories in preparation for this construction, an agreement was struck between southern Democrats and the chair of the Committee on Territories, Illinois senator Stephen A. Douglas. In return for the southerners' support for a railroad route through Chicago in his home state, Douglas's bill left the issue of slavery's existence in the territories to the settlers, effectively rescinding the Missouri Compromise. The bill outraged African Americans. Many gathered in Philadelphia to denounce it, and all over the North abolitionists condemned Senator Douglas as a "sectional traitor." Angry antislavery supporters burned Douglas in effigy, and when he tried to explain the bill to a Chicago audience, he was hooted down. The Kansas-Nebraska Act was signed into law in the spring of 1854, and *Frederick Douglass' Paper* lamented the triumph of "the audacious villainy of the slave power" over "the most explicit and public pledges of both the great parties."[27]

The popular-sovereignty provision of the Kansas-Nebraska Act set the stage for a confrontation between antislavery and proslavery forces who rushed to settle Kansas. Planters sponsored proslavery emigrants from Missouri, who flooded into Kansas and were confronted by Free-Soilers from New England and New York. Frederick Douglass proposed raising funds to encourage black emigration to Kansas, but scarce resources discouraged such efforts. A large black migration would have been an especially risky project, since black settlers in the territory were often in mortal danger from proslavery forces. Free-Soil whites who took up residence in Kansas ultimately did battle with "border ruffians" from Missouri in bitter unrestrained conflicts that earned the territory the name "Bleeding Kansas." In 1856 warring forces killed some two hundred people. Despite his shocking execution of five proslavery men at Pottawatomie Creek, white abolitionist John Brown became a heroic figure in some antislavery circles for his battles against supporters of slavery.[28]

At the same time, in February 1854, a diverse group of abolitionists, Liberty Party people, Free-Soilers, and disaffected Whigs formed a new political party. They were joined by some northern Democrats appalled at the growing influence of southern planters within the Democratic Party. Within two years, this new Republican Party ran John C. Frémont as its first presidential candidate. Mainstream Republicans sought to keep the western territories free from slavery, and the party's slogan, "Free Labor, Free Soil, Free Men," was attractive to both African Americans and to land-hungry white workers. Yet the Republican plan was for slavery's containment within the borders of the South, not for its abolition. Especially troubling was the link between this Free-Soil stand and the philosophy of white supremacy, as Frederick Douglass noted in his 1856 essay, "The Unholy Alliance of Negro Hate and Anti-slavery."[29]

The pervasiveness of racism encouraged Republicans to filter their message through appeals to white racial chauvinism. Many of those attracted to the new party were also those who packed audiences in blackface minstrel shows. In these immensely popular performances by white men such as T. D. Rice, Dan Emmett, and Dan Bryant, working-class northern whites could measure their self-worth against caricatured degraded images of black people. Before the Civil War these performances by white actors who darkened their faces to assume stereotypical black styles became the embodiment of white ambivalence toward the interracial American culture. Many whites were attracted to black music, dance, and humor but feared and disdained black people. Appealing to this constituency while maintaining an antislavery stance was no simple proposition.[30] Thus the platform of the Republican convention in 1856 committed the party to freedom in Kansas but was silent on other issues of interest to African Americans, such as the Fugitive Slave Law, slavery in the District of Columbia, the interstate slave trade, and the abolition of slavery.

Most African Americans were more inclined to support the Liberty Party. It stood for abolition and civil rights for blacks, included several prominent African Americans in its leadership, and by 1855 was considering changing its name to the Radical Abolition Party. But the Liberty Party had no chance of electing candidates to office. The Republican Party was not an antislavery party, but it might at least be successful in limiting slavery's spread and curbing its power. Given the practical political choice between Republicans and Democrats, the "avowed supporters of the enslavement of [the] race," there really was no choice.[31] In Boston, African Americans, including Garrisonians, resolved to give Frémont their qualified support. As one speaker made clear, "We do not pledge ourselves to go further with the Republicans than the Republicans will go with us."[32] Before the November elections black meetings in Brooklyn, New York; throughout New York State; and in Ohio and Pennsylvania endorsed the Republican Party and its candidate, but their ambivalence was apparent. As one delegate from New York put it, "[W]e do not for a single moment endorse all the political tenets of that party."[33]

Even qualified political support from African Americans was a mixed blessing for the Republicans, and they came under harsh criticism from their opponents. Blacks, on the other hand, were encouraged when the Democrats attacked the party as "Black Republicans" and accused it of favoring radical abolitionists and race mixing. Republican candidates made a respectable showing in the election of 1856. Frémont lost to the Democratic presidential candidate, James Buchanan, by fewer than one-half million votes out of a total of four million cast.[34] Frederick Douglass took hope from these results. "We have turned Whigs and Democrats into Republicans," he wrote to abolitionist Gerrit Smith; "we can turn Republicans into Abolitionists."[35] Others, less optimistic about political change, concluded that "the peaceful annihilation of slavery [was] hopeless" and that the slaveholder's "execution only waits the finish of the training of his executioners."[36]

A Supreme Court case in the fall of 1857 made it even more difficult for African Americans to be optimistic about ending slavery and about their future. After a series of decisions and reversals in lower courts, a case involving a Virginia-born slave named Dred Scott reached the high court. Scott brought suit against his master, demanding freedom on the basis of their having lived in the free territories of Wisconsin and Illinois for a number of years. Scott had originally brought his case in Missouri, where other slaves had been successful in similar actions, but after winning his case initially, he lost on appeal, and the case moved to the Supreme Court. In his opinion in this case, southern-born Chief Justice Roger B. Taney went far beyond the simple decision. Taney declared that Congress had no authority to exclude slavery from the territories, essentially striking down the central plank in the Republican platform and finishing off the Missouri Compromise. Further, he stunned African Americans by attacking them directly, declaring that they were not and could not be American citizens and thus had no rights guaranteed under the U.S. Constitution—or, as Taney put it, "no rights which the white man was bound to respect."[37]

The Department of State, under Secretary Lewis Cass of Michigan, responded quickly and denied passports to blacks, a change in policy despite the department's insistence to the contrary. Defiantly the *Boston Daily Bee* pointed to several instances in which blacks previously had received passports. Protesting the Supreme Court's decision, the Massachusetts legislature instructed its secretary of state to issue passports to black citizens of the state. African Americans continued to exercise a right of citizenship by voting in five New England states and in New York (with property requirement restrictions). Many whites also denounced the court decision, and many state and federal officials expressed outrage at the obvious inequity.[38]

This federal assault on their rights led some blacks to reconsider emigration. In the summer of 1858 a group of blacks, led by Henry Highland Garnet, established the African Civilization Society to encourage settlement of American blacks in Liberia, which had become an independent West African nation in 1847. The society was not racially restricted and counted several white reformers as part of its membership, but unlike the earlier American Colonization Society, this was largely a black-controlled venture that condemned slavery and American hypocrisy and focused on expanding opportunities for black freedom and independence. It also reflected the desire of society members, many of whom were black ministers, to spread the faith among West Africans. But African colonization was not popular with many American blacks, some of whom reasoned that emigration to Canada or the West Indies was more practical for continuing the fight against slavery. James T. Holly, born free in Washington, D.C., returned from a visit to Haiti in the mid-1850s with glowing reports of the opportunities there for African Americans willing to take up residence. Perhaps aware of the earlier attempt at Haitian settlement, few American blacks agreed to emigrate there, but Canadian emigration continued.[39]

As the decade progressed, emigration seemed less likely, and the sequence of events encouraged African Americans to prepare themselves for military action. Boston blacks had petitioned the Massachusetts legislature in 1855 to charter a black military company, and when their request was denied, they had formed the Massasoit Guard without state sanction. In November 1857, after the Dred Scott decision was announced, the guard, armed and in full uniform, paraded through the streets of Boston.[40] At a meeting of Massachusetts African Americans in 1858, black lawyer Robert Morris called on his fellows to stand together against the federal attack: "If any man comes here to New Bedford and they try to take [any fugitive] away, you telegraph us in Boston, and we'll come down 300 strong, and stay with you; and we won't go until he's safe."[41] Cincinnati African Americans formed the Attucks Guards, named for Crispus Attucks, the black sailor who was the first to die in the American Revolution. African Americans in New York also called one of their units the Attucks Guards. Ohio blacks demanded that racial restrictions be removed from the state militia, and the Ohio convention of 1857 resolved that independent military companies should be established wherever blacks were denied places

Dred Scott, Harriet Scott, and their daughters,
newspaper article on the family, 1857.

in the state militia.[42] In cities and towns in the North, blacks anticipated war and readied themselves. "Captain" J. J. Simmons of the New York City unit prophesied that soon northern black military units would be called to march through the South with "a bible in one hand and a gun in the other."[43]

Through the spring and summer of 1858, a group of black abolitionists and white abolitionists met in the United States and Canada to discuss the feasibility of attacking slavery directly. John Brown, the leader of Kansas abolitionist guerrilla forces, devised a daring plan to strike against slavery in Virginia. With the financial backing of wealthy abolitionists from New England and New York, Brown gathered a band of eighteen men—thirteen whites and five blacks. As what had been plans for a small guerrilla action grew to plans for a full-scale assault, African Americans' doubts about the wisdom of the scheme also grew. Although Frederick Douglass had taken part in the early discussions, by the time of the raid he was convinced it was a noble folly. Later Douglass wrote that although he had prior knowledge of the raid, he had never intended to join it. "Let every man work for the abolition of slavery in his own way," he declared. "I would help all and hinder none."[44]

On October 16, 1859, Brown and his men raided the federal arsenal at Harpers Ferry, Virginia, in an effort to obtain weapons and ammunition to arm slaves on nearby plantations. With this expanded force, Brown intended to move against the slaveholders, freeing their slaves, and enlisting some of the slaves in a vast abolitionist army. Despite their doubts many blacks encouraged the mission and supported it. Of the twenty-one men who followed Brown to Harpers Ferry, five were African American: Shields Green, a fugitive slave from South Carolina; Osborne Anderson, a printer from Chatham, Canada; Lewis Sheridan Leary, from Oberlin, Ohio; Sheridan's nephew, John Copeland, a student at Oberlin College; and Dangerfield Newby, a freed slave from Virginia. Forty-four-year-old Newby, the oldest of the five, had personal reasons for participating in the raid. A fugitive himself, Newby hoped to free his wife, Harriet, and their six children, who were enslaved in Virginia near Harpers Ferry. Before the raid Harriet had written to him begging that he come for them. "If I thought I should never see you this earth would have no charms for me," she wrote. "[Come] this fall without fail."[45]

Newby never reached his family. John Brown and his raiders were trapped by federal troops under the command of Col. Robert E. Lee, and most of Brown's men, including Newby and Leary, were killed. Brown and four others, Copeland and Green among them, were captured, tried, convicted of treason, and sentenced to be hanged. Anderson escaped, while authorities sought other conspirators. A telegraph operator in Philadelphia warned Frederick Douglass three hours before delivering to the sheriff an order for Douglass's arrest. Douglass escaped to Canada and, near the end of November, sailed for England. Several of those identified as Brown's financial backers also fled to Canada.[46]

The raid on Harpers Ferry shocked the South and confirmed southern beliefs that only a strong proslavery federal government could protect slavery from abolitionist aggression. Among African Americans, John Brown was a hero. In a letter to his wife, Mary, a group of black women from New York called him "our honored and dearly-loved brother."[47] On the day of Brown's execution, blacks in Cincinnati, Pittsburgh, Philadelphia, and New York mourned his death. Three thousand gathered in Boston's Joy Street Church to hear the Reverend John Sella Martin, a former slave, condemn slavery and praise noble efforts to end that evil institution.[48] A solemn crowd in Detroit listened to a message on "Brown's Christian Fortitude" and his devotion to antislavery and heard the Brown Liberty Singers offer a musical selection entitled "Ode to Old Capt. John Brown."[49]

Reaction to John Brown's raid and his martyrdom reflected the growing conviction among abolitionists that only violence would bring an end to slavery. One black abolitionist from Boston, John Rock, expressed his certainty that "sooner or later, the clashing of arms will be heard in this country" and contended that "the black man's service will be needed . . . to strike a genuine blow for freedom [with a] power which white men 'will be bound to respect.'"[50] In early December 1859 broadsides called Canadian blacks to local meetings to consider ways to honor "Brown and his confederates . . . martyrs to the cause of Liberty," and Thomas Hamilton, editor of the *Weekly Anglo-African,* compared Brown's raid with Nat Turner's slave rebellion, the deadliest of nineteenth-century North America.[51]

By the end of the 1850s sectional considerations pervaded virtually every political decision in the United States, and sectional considerations involved slavery either directly or indirectly. Confrontations grew ever more bellicose, and violence reached even into the halls of Congress when a proslavery congressman from South Carolina attacked and beat Massachusetts senator Charles Sumner on the floor of the Senate chamber. Gun- and knife fights broke out in the House of Representatives, and one congressmen was killed by political rivals. In the presidential election year of 1860, sectional animosities split the Democratic Party between proslavery southerners who selected John C. Breckenridge of Kentucky as their standard bearer and northern Democrats who remained loyal to Stephen A. Douglas. Other southerners who refused to accept Breckenridge formed the Constitutional Union Party under the leadership of John Bell of Tennessee. Republicans nominated the politically moderate Abraham Lincoln as their presidential candidate.

African Americans continued to view Republicans as essentially the lesser of potential political evils. They found the Democratic proslavery position completely unacceptable, but they were also realistic about the shortcomings of the Republican Party. Blacks had observed the Republican rush to denounce John Brown and disassociate themselves from his raid. They had angrily noted Massachusetts Republican governor Nathaniel P. Banks's veto of legislation allowing blacks to enlist in the state militia. They knew that despite the black support that had helped elect Republican governor Edwin D. Morgan in New York, he had failed "to utter an anti-slavery sentence" during his annual message. Republicans had introduced a bill to repeal the Fugitive Slave Law, but it had failed when twelve Republicans voted against it and forty-three abstained. Further, in an effort to combat the "black Republican" label, some Republicans had declared themselves "a white man's party."[52]

Some black leaders argued that the Republicans' pretense of friendship was more dangerous to African American rights than the Democrats' animosity. John Rock asserted that Republicans "[aimed] to place white men and white labor against black men and black labor" and thus were "no better than" the Democrats.[53] Others considered Abraham Lincoln and his moderate wing of the Republican Party to be only Free-Soilers, not genuinely antislavery. Although Douglass and other black leaders expressed their misgivings, African Americans in New York, Brooklyn, Boston, and several other northern cities formed Republican clubs, and the vast majority of black voters cast their ballots for the victorious Lincoln.[54]

Lincoln's election precipitated a crisis. Before he could take office, South Carolina demanded that President Buchanan remove federal troops from the forts in Charleston Harbor and led the seven states of the Lower South (South Carolina, Mississippi, Florida, Alabama, Georgia, Louisiana, and Texas) in declaring their withdrawal from the United States. On February 4, 1861, representatives from all the seceding states—except Texas, whose delegates arrived later—met as a constitutional convention in Montgomery, Alabama, to define the political structure of the Confederate States of America. Lincoln reacted cautiously during his first days in office, trying to hold on to the slave states of the Upper South. In his inaugural address he firmly opposed the right of states to withdraw from the federal union but pledged that he would not interfere with slavery, the institution that was the foundation of Southern economic and social life. Attempted conciliation did not dissuade the states of the Confederacy, and war came on April 12, 1861, when Confederate batteries in Charleston Harbor opened fire on the federal Fort Sumter. Within days Lincoln issued a call for seventy-five thousand volunteers to put down the rebellion in South Carolina. Fearing a federal invasion that would threaten slavery, four states of the Upper South (Virginia, Arkansas, Tennessee, and North Carolina) withdrew from the United States, leaving Maryland, Delaware, Kentucky, and Missouri as the only slave states loyal to the U.S. government. Lincoln's increased need for federal troops was exacerbated by the fact that almost one-third of the nation's army officer corps, including important West Point–trained men, left to fight with the rebellion against the United

States. During the first year of the war the U.S. Army expanded from just over sixteen thousand men to more than seven hundred thousand. Blacks volunteered immediately, but the federal government refused them, and none of the new recruits was African American.[55]

African Americans in Washington, D.C., Pittsburgh, Boston, New York, and elsewhere, answered Lincoln's call. Through their military units and as individuals, they sent letters and petitions to the War Department expressing their eagerness to serve, but all their offers were rejected. Most whites and governmental officials, including Lincoln, questioned blacks' bravery. Many believed that ex-slaves in particular would be too submissive and cowardly to be good soldiers. One white corporal from a New York regiment bluntly summed up the general feeling among white recruits: "We don't want to fight side and side with the nigger. We think that we are too superior race for that."[56] Outraged black leaders pointed to the fact that black troops had served with distinction in the American Revolution and in the War of 1812. "Colored men were good enough . . . to help win American independence," Douglass noted angrily, "but they are not good enough to help preserve that independence against treason and rebellion." Why would the American government attempt to fight "rebels with only one hand?"[57]

Before the war many radical abolitionists had supported the idea of disunion, that is, withdrawing the free states from their union with slaveholders. Frederick Douglass had begun to reconsider when Lincoln's election had brought, as Douglass wrote, "at least an antislavery reputation to the Presidency." He was less hopeful, though, when Lincoln attempted to compromise with the South by proposing constitutional protections for slavery. "If the Union can only be maintained by new concessions to the slaveholders," Douglass had declared, "let the Union perish." Southern secession, however, changed abolition's prospects—southern slavery was no longer protected by the military might of the United States. Slave rebellion had a much better chance of success, and runaway slaves might be safe in free states.[58] Despite Abraham Lincoln's equivocation, African Americans agreed that the war ignited by the firing on Fort Sumter was "a war for and against slavery," and the United States could not win it without destroying slavery. Yet federal military commanders continued for two years to refuse the thousands of blacks who volunteered to be soldiers.[59]

The South recognized the value of black participation in the Confederate war effort. Slave labor produced most of the food for the troops, and the Confederacy impressed free blacks and slaves into service as laborers, teamsters, cooks, and servants to support southern troops. Despite their value to the southern war effort, however, U.S. commanders continued to return runaway slaves to their southern masters until Congress passed the Confiscation Act in August 1861. This act set Confederate slaves free once they came under

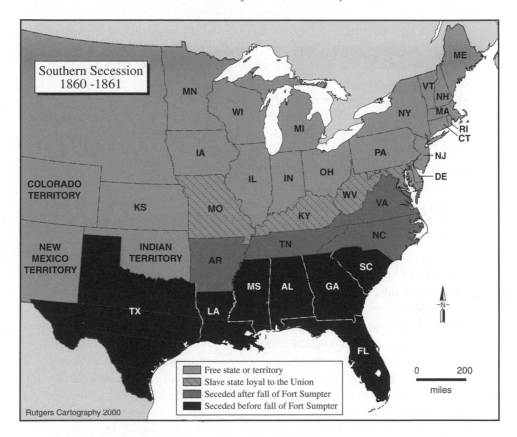

Southern Secession 1860-1861

ME
VT
NH
MN
MA
WI
NY
MI
RI
CT
IA
PA
NJ
DE
OH
COLORADO
TERRITORY
IL
IN
WV
VA
KS
MO
KY
TN
NC
NEW
MEXICO
TERRITORY
INDIAN
TERRITORY
AR
SC
MS
AL
GA
TX
LA
FL

- Free state or territory
- Slave state loyal to the Union
- Seceded after fall of Fort Sumpter
- Seceded before fall of Fort Sumpter

0   200
miles

Rutgers Cartography 2000

the control of federal forces, but it did not free slaves who might escape from slaveholders in states such as Delaware and Maryland, which had remained loyal to the United States. African Americans were insulted by the government's refusing their service, and many, like Henry Cropper of the Philadelphia black military company, urged African Americans to maintain their dignity and self-respect by withdrawing their offer.[60]

Meanwhile the early years of the war brought enormous losses to the United States. At Shiloh, Tennessee, in April 1862, 63,000 United States troops fought the largest battle in American history and suffered more than thirteen thousand casualties. The United States lost sixteen thousand dead, wounded, or missing two months later, during the Seven Days Battle in Virginia, and more than fourteen thousand at the Second Battle of Manassas. By early summer 1862 it was clear that this would not be a short and relatively painless war. In the face of such losses, and with support for the Confederacy said to be building in Britain and Western Europe, Congress and the president decided to take desperate measures. In July Congress passed legislation allowing the president to enlist black troops should he deem it "necessary and proper for the suppression of this rebellion." By November the first black regiment had been raised, composed of ex-slaves in South Carolina who had been freed within U.S. lines. Thomas Wentworth Higginson, a white abolitionist who had participated in a daring attempt by blacks to rescue a fugitive slave in Boston before the war, was appointed to command these troops. By year's end the First South Carolina was engaged in combat along the Georgia-Florida border. Witnessing their courage and ability, Higginson wrote, "Nobody knows anything about these men who has not seen them in battle. . . . No officer in this regiment now doubts that the key to the successful prosecution of this war lies in the unlimited employment of black troops."[61]

In the summer of 1862, Lincoln had announced his intention to strike directly at slavery in the South, an attempt to redirect and rejuvenate the war effort, to enlist northern antislavery sentiment, and to make it more difficult for the British and Europeans to support the Confederacy. The president was true to form; Lincoln's timing and words were cautious: a U.S. victory would precede the public announcement, and he would pursue his political and military purpose with the least disruption for slaveholders in loyal states. In September Gen. George McClellan, commander of the U.S. Army of the Potomac, defeated Confederate forces under Robert E. Lee at Antietam Creek in Sharpsburg, Maryland. Lincoln moved swiftly, and five days after the victory, on September 22, he made the preliminary announcement of his Emancipation Proclamation. As of January 1, 1863, all slaves in areas controlled by people in rebellion against the United States would be declared "forever free." The declaration of freedom did not apply to slaves held by those loyal to the United States or to slaves held by rebels who had been subdued before January 1, 1863. Certainly a limited emancipation, but it reinforced Congress's abolition of slavery in the District of Columbia the previous April and seemed to be part of an abolitionist trend.

African Americans had waited anxiously for the promised New Year's proclamation. They were not confident of Lincoln's commitment. He had denounced slavery but had protected it to secure southern loyalty to the United States before the war. He had finally enlisted blacks into the military but had promised emancipation only to Confederate slaves. In August 1862 he had been the first American president to invite a delegation of African Americans to meet with him at the White House, but he had told them that black people were a burden on the nation and it would be better if they left the country and settled in Africa or the West Indies. Across the North, African Americans in small towns and large cities held mass meetings to await the proclamation. When it came they broke into wild celebration, greeting it with singing, dancing, prayers, lofty rhetoric, and plain speaking about family and friends still in slavery. Although it was a halfway measure, the Emancipation Proclamation transformed the war's purpose and made Lincoln the "Great Emancipator."[62]

The war's new moral purpose and the dedication and success of black soldiers influenced racial sentiment in the North. By late winter 1863, a second black unit from South Carolina, commanded by Col. James Montgomery, had been formed, and in March some of Montgomery's and Higginson's African American troops captured and occupied the Confederate stronghold of Jacksonville, Florida. Gen. David Hunter informed his superiors that his troops were "hardy, generous, temperate, strictly obedient, possessing remarkable aptitude for military training, and deeply imbued with that religious sentiment which made the soldiers of Oliver Cromwell invincible." He also wrote that he had detected the racist attitudes of many of the white soldiers who had come into contact with black troops "rapidly softening or fading out."[63] Newspapers challenged racial bigots with the "facts" of "good conduct and gallant deeds of the men they persecute and slander."[64] One white Illinois soldier who had voted Democratic before the war wrote to his wife, "So long as [my] flag is confronted by the hostile guns of slavery . . . I am as confirmed an abolitionist as ever was pelted with stale eggs." In the Eighty-sixth Indiana Regiment one officer reported that although many of his men had denounced what they called an "abolition war," by March 1863 they were expressing support for emancipation and for black combat troops. An Indiana sergeant who admitted that he did not like free blacks declared himself in favor of the Emancipation Proclamation if it would end the war. A poll of one Iowa regiment showed that only one-quarter of the white soldiers opposed the proclamation, while half favored it and the rest registered no opinion.[65]

There was still resistance to blacks' participation in the war, however. In Pennsylvania the governor refused to recruit them, and John Mercer Langston's offer to raise black troops in Ohio met an icy response from Governor David Tod. "Do you know[,] Mr. Langston," Tod asked, "that this is a white man's government; that white men are able to defend and protect it?" He continued, "When we want you colored men we will notify you."[66] Yet, now that Lincoln had committed the nation to the cause of freedom, and Congress had authorized raising black troops, there seemed reason for optimism. In January 1863 Governor John A. Andrew of Massachusetts was authorized to form the Fifty-fourth Massachusetts Volunteers, the first black military regiment recruited from the North. Governor Andrew, an abolitionist, placed Col. Robert Gould Shaw, a young man from a prominent white abolitionist family, at its head. He also appointed several black leaders, including Frederick Douglass, Charles Lenox Remond, Thomas Morris Chester, and Martin Delany, as recruiting agents, but the effort was slow at first. Many blacks were reluctant to join a force that had recently rejected their offers to serve. Chester presided over a meeting in Harrisburg, Pennsylvania, where blacks demanded a guarantee of fair treatment. If they were to serve, it must be with dignity and equality. Although most state and local officials accepted black military assistance only under the most dire circumstances, by April thirty or forty men a day were enlisting in the Massachusetts Fifty-fourth.[67]

African Americans who enlisted were refused positions as officers, and blacks in uniform risked being attacked and harassed by northern whites. A white gang and policemen attacked Cpl. John Ross in the streets of Washington, D.C., in the summer of 1863, and one police officer explained that he would shoot a "nigger recruit" as easily as he would a mad dog.[68] The greatest insult black soldiers faced, however, came from the Confederacy. In May the Confederate congress resolved that any black U.S. troops captured would be killed or enslaved, not treated as prisoners of war. White officers leading black troops were to be treated as criminals and might be executed. Chester gave up his recruiting efforts in disgust and left the United States for Britain in the fall of 1863, but African Americans continued to enlist despite the injustices they faced.

As an added insult, black troops were expected to serve for inferior pay. Initially the War Department pledged equal pay, and the first recruits enlisted with that understanding. But until 1864, when Congress actually authorized equal pay, black troops were paid at a rate less than half that paid to white soldiers. A white private was paid thirteen dollars per month plus a uniform allowance, and a regimental sergeant received twenty-one dollars per month plus allowances, while blacks at all noncommissioned ranks earned only ten dollars per month, from which three dollars were subtracted for uniforms. Black soldiers, their families, and many of their white officers complained bitterly, pointing out that soldiers could not provide for their families on this sub-standard pay. Black civilians employed by the military could earn as much as twenty-five dollars per month.[69] Some black soldiers' wives and children were forced into poorhouses while their men were defending the country. Some blacks refused to serve without full pay, some requested discharges so they could support their families, and others served without pay rather than accept inferior pay. For more than a year almost all of the Fifty-fourth Massachusetts refused to accept unequal pay. Protest was widespread, with black regiments from Michigan, Kansas, Rhode Island, and South Carolina joining in. The black women of Boston held fairs to raise money and gather supplies for soldiers' families. Black soldiers resented both the pay differential and the symbolic refusal to recognize their role as soldiers: it was about more than money. "To say we are not soldiers [even if they paid] us $20 would be injustice," wrote one black corporal from the Fifty-fourth Massachusetts, "for it would rob a whole race of their title to a manhood."[70] Pay inequities rooted in practicality and prejudice were not easy to change. One New Yorker expressed the prevailing sentiment, "[I]t is unjust in every way to the white soldier to put him

Broadside: "Men of Color to Arms."

on a level with the black."[71] Black protest met a swift military response. In the fall of 1863, when one company of the Third South Carolina Volunteers, led by Sgt. William Walker, refused to perform their duties until they were properly paid, the army charged the entire company with mutiny and executed Sergeant Walker.[72]

Although not admitted as soldiers, black women also served the war effort. *Provincial Freeman* editor Mary Ann Shadd Cary moved from Canada to Indiana during the war to help in black recruitment. Harriet Tubman, the best-known conductor on the underground railroad, expanded her activities to include spying for the government and bringing recruits to the army. In March 1863 she brought 750 black men out of slavery and into the federal forces. Thousands of other black women did everything from camp chores to taking up arms when circumstances warranted. Susie King, born a slave in Georgia, worked as a teacher of freed people and as a nurse during the war. She spent part of her time with her husband's unit, the First South Carolina Volunteers, doing the laundry and learning to handle a gun.[73]

Men, women, and children flocked to the Union lines to escape slavery as the U.S. Army moved through the South. Commanders quickly learned that black enlistees were far more willing to serve if the army guaranteed the protection of their families, and small shanty settlements of civilians sprang up on the fringes of military camps. The wives of black soldiers often did cooking and laundry for the officers, and although this allowed black women to be close to their husbands, it posed problems as well. White men in authority generally regarded black women as inferior and fair game for sexual exploitation. At one camp the harassment was so bad that a black soldier complained, "We have a set of officers here who apparently think that their commissions are license to debauch and mingle with deluded freedwomen, under cover of darkness."[74]

About 29,000 black sailors (about one-quarter of the navy) and more than 186,000 African American soldiers, in 166 black regiments, fought for the United States during the Civil War. One in every five black adult males in the entire country served in the U.S. forces, constituting one-tenth of the nation's military force. About half of those who served were former slaves. In battle black troops were often given the most dangerous jobs. Coupled with the Confederate treatment of captives, this resulted in a casualty rate roughly twice that of white troops. Despite their sacrifices and their service in previous wars, black troops were continually challenged to prove their courage and capability in battle. African Americans fought their first major Civil War battle at Port Hudson, Louisiana, in May 1863. The First and Third Louisiana regiments, a Native Guard composed of free, educated, affluent blacks from New Orleans, advanced under the command of black officers who gave orders in

Susie King

Susie King was born in 1848, the daughter of a domestic slave and the great-grandaughter of a slave midwife. She traced her lineage in America to her great-great-grandmother Dolly, five of whose children had fought in the Revolutionary War. Susie's grandmother took advantage of the family's favor with their master. He allowed her to take young Susie and her brother from the plantation to her home in Savannah. She supported them by doing odd jobs and laundry, and carrying on a trade between the farms and the city. Susie was fourteen when the Civil War began and her uncle took her to South Carolina's Sea Islands. There she saw northern soldiers, the first whites who did not treat her like a slave. Since she had attended school in Savannah, she was able to serve the army by teaching children and newly freed adults. Eventually she married Edward King, a former slave who was a sargeant in the U.S. First South Carolina Volunteers. She continued to work without pay as a laundress and as a nurse, ministering to white as well as black troops. She also handled weapons and learned to shoot, clean, and disassemble them.

For a time the regiment was stationed a mile from Fort Wagner, where in 1863 the black Fifty-fourth Massachusetts Regiment had lost more than 250 men. King visited the former Confederate fort, then under federal control, and watched U.S. guns shelling Charleston. As she remembered the gruesome sight, there were "many skulls lying about. Some thought they were the skulls of our boys; others thought they were the enemies'."* When the regiment entered Savannah in early 1865, King remained there, running a school until her husband's death the following year. She alternately operated her school and worked for a white Savannah family until she secured her husband's military pension. King eventually moved to Boston, married Russell Taylor, and organized a relief organization for Civil War veterans. In 1902 Susie King published her memoir, illustrating the varied and important roles that black women played in the Civil War and in the black community.

Susie King Taylor, Civil War nurse. Photographs and Prints Division, Schomburg Center for Research in Black Culture, The New York Public Library, Astor, Lenox, and Tilden Foundations.

*Dorothy Sterling, *Speak Out in Thunder Tones* (Garden City, N.Y.: Doubleday & Company, Inc., 1973), 355.

Charge of the Fifty-fourth Massachusetts Colored Regiment
on Fort Wagner, South Carolina, July 1863.
Mark E. Mitchell Collection of African American History.

both English and French. Seven successive charges on Confederate fortifications left one of five black soldiers dead or wounded. The siege by white and black regiments lasted for forty-eight days, and the United States lost nearly ten thousand men. Witnesses were effusive in their praise of the black troops. "No regiment behaved better than they did," reported one white officer. "Nobly indeed, they have acquitted themselves," read the *New York Times,* and poet George H. Boker commemorated their heroism with a verse distributed in English and German.[75]

About the same time, two regiments of African Americans beat back a Confederate attack at Milliken's Bend on the Mississippi River near Vicksburg. At one point, 840 black soldiers and 160 white soldiers defended the U.S. position against almost two thousand Confederates. The Confederate advance pushed U.S. forces to the edge of the river, and Confederates summarily executed captured black troops. Finally, with the arrival of a gunboat, the U.S. forces made a desperate stand, with soldiers using their rifles as clubs in hand-to-hand combat. Even the defeated Confederates praised this predominately black force, and one U.S. officer declared that, "[b]y their coolness and determination in battle," blacks had moved themselves into "high standing

Sergeant
W. H. Carney,
Company C,
Fifty-fourth
Massachusetts
Colored Regiment,
winner of the
Congressional
Medal of Honor.

Photographs and Prints
Division, Schomburg
Center for Research
in Black Culture,
The New York Public
Library, Astor, Lenox,
and Tilden Foundations.

as soldiers."[76] Finally that summer, the famous assault by the Fifty-Four Massachusetts at Fort Wagner in Charleston Harbor brought further proof of
black valor. They suffered enormous losses in this futile attack on the Confederate stronghold, but they fought with courage and skill. Leading the
charge, Colonel Shaw fell on the ramparts and was killed. For his part in the
attack, Sgt. William H. Carney received the Congressional Medal of Honor,
and the *New York Tribune* praised the Fifty-fourth's performance in this "test
of black troops." The *Tribune*—its editor apparently ignorant of the black soldiers who had fought in that famous Revolutionary War battle—compared the
bravery of the Fifty-fourth at Fort Wagner to the courage of white troops at
the Battle of Bunker Hill. By the end of the summer of 1863, Abraham Lincoln was convinced of the value of enlisting black troops and urged Gen.
Ulysses S. Grant to increase enlistments, saying, "I believe [they are] a resource
which, if vigorously applied now, will soon close the contest." Finally the federal government had acceded to black demands that African Americans be relied
on to strike a blow for freedom.[77]

Notes

Introduction

1. William L. Andrews, *To Tell A Free Story: The First Century of Afro-American Autobiography, 1760–1865* (Urbana, Ill.: University of Illinois University Press, 1986).
2. R.J.M. Blackett, *Beating Against the Barriers: Biographical Essays in Nineteenth-Century Afro-American History* (Baton Rouge, LA: Louisiana State University Press, 1986); James Oliver Horton and Lois E. Horton, *Black Bostonians: Family Life and Community Struggle in the Antebellum North* (New York: Holmes and Meier Publishers Inc., [1979] revised edition, 1999).
3. John Hope Franklin, *George Washington Williams: A Biography* (Chicago: University of Chicago Press, 1985).
4. Northwestern University awarded the Ph.D. in history to Rufus Clement in 1930, Benjamin Quarles received his doctorate from the University of Wisconsin in 1940, and John Hope Franklin received his Ph.D. in history from Harvard University in 1941.
5. Ira Berlin, *Many Thousands Gone: The First Two Centuries of Slavery in North America* (Cambridge, Mass.: The Belknap Press of Harvard University Press, 1998); Philip D. Morgan, *Slave Counterpoint: Black Culture in the Eighteenth-Century Chesapeake & Lowcountry* (Chapel Hill: The University of North Carolina Press, 1998); James Oliver Horton and Lois E. Horton, *In Hope of Liberty: Culture, Community and Protest Among Northern Free Blacks, 1700-1860* (New York: Oxford University Press, 1997).

Chapter 1 ▪ *Africa and the Atlantic Slave Trade*

1. Olaudah Equiano, *The Interesting Narrative of the Life of Olaudah Equiano, or Gustavus Vassa, the African* (1789), reprinted in *Great Slave Narratives*, edited by Arna Bontemps (Boston: Beacon Press, 1969), 7. Recently discovered documents have led scholars to question whether Equiano's description of Africa was based on personal experience or oral history. See Vincent Carratta, "Olaudah Equiano or Gustavas Vasa? New Light on an Eighteenth-Century Question of Identity," *Slavery and Abolition* 20:3 (1999), 96–105.
2. Philip Curtin, Steven Feierman, Leonard Thompson, and Jan Vansina, *African History*, 9th ed. (New York: Longmans, 1991); A. J. Arkell, *A History of Sudan from the Earliest Times to 1821* (University of London Athlone Press, 1961).
3. Basil Davidson, *The Search for Africa: History, Culture, Politics* (New York: Random House, 1994), 73; Colin A. Palmer, *Passageways: An Interpretive History of Black America, 1619–1863*, vol. 1 (Fort Worth, Tex.: Harcourt Brace College Publishers, 1998), 5.
4. Quoted from Philip S. Foner, *History of Black Americans*, vol. 1 (Westport, Conn.: Greenwood Press, 1975), 40–41. See also Jean Rouch, *Les Songhay* (Paris: Presses Universitaires de France, 1954), and R. E. Bradbury, *The Benin Kingdom and the Edo-speaking Peoples of Southwestern Nigeria* (London: International African Institute, 1957).

5. John Hope Franklin and Alfred P. Moss, Jr., *From Slavery to Freedom: A History of Negro Americans*, 6th ed. (New York: Knopf, 1988).
6. Foner, *History of Black Americans*, vol. 1, 43–47.
7. David Brion Davis, *The Problem of Slavery in Western Culture* (Ithaca, N.Y.: Cornell University Press, 1966), 52; Ronald Sanders, *Lost Tribes and Promised Lands: The Origins of American Racism* (New York: Harper Perennial, 1992); Curtin et al., *African History*, 183–189.
8. Philip D. Curtin, "Migration in the Tropical World," *Immigration Reconsidered*, edited by Virginia Yans-McLaughlin (New York: Oxford University Press, 1990), 21–36.
9. Slaves in Africa retained an acknowledged humanness, for slavery was a condition of their lives and a status of the society into which they had fallen. Slavery was not, as it would later become in the United States, a racially defined, permanent state connoting a supposed genetic inferiority.
10. Equiano in Bontemps, *Great Slave Narratives*, 11.
11. Donald R. Wright, *African Americans in the Colonial Era: From African Origins through the American Revolution* (Arlington Heights, Ill.: Harlan Davidson, Inc., 1990). Dahomey was most transformed by its access to firearms and became committed to the slave trade as the principle foundation of its national economy by the early sixteenth century. The Dutch established trade in Allada, the major trading state in the region, before the end of the century. See I. A. Akinjogbin, *Dahomey and Its Neighbors, 1708–1818* (Cambridge, England: Cambridge University Press, 1967).
12. Colin Palmer, "African Slave Trade: The Cruelest Commerce," *National Geographic* 182:3 (September 1992), 67–68.
13. Akinjogbin, *Dahomey*.
14. Sanders, *Lost Tribes*, 17.
15. Davis, *The Problem of Slavery*, 53.
16. Winthrop D. Jordan, *White over Black: American Attitudes Towards the Negro, 1550–1812* (Chapel Hill, N.C.: University of North Carolina Press, 1968), 7.
17. Equiano in Bontemps, *Great Slave Narratives*, 28–29.
18. Ibid., 30.
19. Jay Coughtry, *The Notorious Triangle: Rhode Island and the African Slave Trade, 1700–1807* (Philadelphia: Temple University Press, 1981).
20. Alexander Falconbridge, *An Account of the Slave Trade on the Coast of Africa* (London, 1788), 16–22.
21. William Loren Katz, *Eyewitness: The Negro in American History* (Belmont, Calif.: Fearon Pitman Publishers, Inc., 1974), 6.
22. "Samuel Waldo to Captain Samuel Rhodes, 1734," in *Documents Illustrative of the History of the Slave Trade in America*, vol. 3, edited by Elizabeth Donnan (Washington, D.C.: Carnegie Institution of Washington, 1932), 45.
23. Vincent Harding, *There Is a River: The Black Struggle for Freedom in America* (New York: Harcourt Brace Jovanovich, Publishers, 1981), 12–13.
24. Ivan van Sertima, *They Came before Columbus* (New York: Random House, 1976).
25. William D. Piersen, *From Africa to America: African American History from the Colonial Era to the Early Republic, 1526–1790* (New York: Twayne Publishers, 1996), 37–44.
26. Germany later broadened its participation in the slave trade but never became a dominant player, in large part because it did not develop substantial American holdings.
27. Wright, *African Americans in the Colonial Era*, 40.
28. Darold Wax, "Preferences for Slaves in Colonial America," *Journal of Negro History* 58:4 (1973), 375–376.
29. Curtin, Feierman, Thompson, and Vansina, *African History*, 219–221.

Chapter 2 ▪ *The Evolution of Slavery in British North America*

1. Winthrop D. Jordan, *White over Black: American Attitudes toward the Negro, 1550–1812* (New York: W. W. Norton, 1977), 75, 79.
2. Jordan, *White over Black,* 75.
3. Jordan, *White over Black,* 81.
4. David Brion Davis, *The Problem of Slavery in Western Culture* (Ithaca, N.Y.: Cornell University Press, 1966), 102.
5. Paul C. Palmer, "Servants into Slaves: The Evolution of the Legal Status of the Negro Laborer in Colonial Virginia," *South Atlantic Quarterly* 65 (Summer 1966).
6. *Pennsylvania Gazette,* October 8, 1747; *Journal and Baltimore Advisor,* October 10, 1779.
7. Carl N. Degler, "Slavery and the Genesis of Race Prejudice," *Comparative Studies in Society and History* 2 (1959), 61.
8. Edward Pearson, "From Stono to Vesey: Slavery, Resistance, and Ideology in South Carolina, 1739–1822" (Ph.D. dissertation, University of Wisconsin, 1991). Pearson provides an account of the establishment of slavery in South Carolina and the transition from timber producing and herding to rice cultivation. He offers a fascinating argument on the impact of this transition on the gender conventions of African slaves. Donald R. Wright, *African Americans in the Colonial Era: From African Origins through the American Revolution* (Arlington Heights, Ill.: Harlan Davidson, Inc., 1990), 67; Ira Berlin, *Many Thousands Gone: The First Two Centuries of Slavery in North America* (Cambridge, Mass.: Harvard University Press, 1998), 149, 370. Slaveholders believed that Africans were immune to malaria. This was not true, but many Africans did display a resistance to the disease that was greater than that of Europeans.
9. Philip D. Morgan, *Slave Counterpoint: Black Culture in the Eighteenth-Century Chesapeake & Lowcountry* (Chapel Hill: University of North Carolina Press, 1998), 394, 264–265.
10. William Loren Katz, *Eyewitness: The Negro in American History* (Belmont, Calif.: Fearon Pitman Publishers, Inc., 1974), 22.
11. Darold Wax, "Georgia and the Negro before the American Revolution," *Georgia Historical Quarterly* 51 (March 1967), 63–75.
12. Berlin, *Many Thousands Gone,* 369–370.
13. William D. Piersen, *From Africa to America: African American History from the Colonial Era to the Early Republic, 1526–1790* (New York: Twayne Publishers, 1996), 57–65; Philip S. Foner, *History of Black Americans,* vol. 1 (Westport, Conn.: Greenwood Press, 1975), 228; Clement Alexander Price, *Freedom Not Far Distant: A Documentary History of Afro-Americans in New Jersey* (Newark: New Jersey Historical Society, 1980), 35. Population numbers are estimates, since there was no official Pennsylvania census during the colonial period.
14. Gary Nash, *Forging Freedom: The Formation of Philadelphia's Black Community, 1720–1840* (Cambridge, Mass.: Harvard University Press, 1988); Israel Acrelius, *A History of New Sweden; or, The Settlements on the Delaware* (Philadelphia: Historical Society of Pennsylvania, 1874); Katz, *Eyewitness,* 23.
15. Jean R. Soderlund, *Quakers and Slavery: A Divided Spirit* (Princeton, N.J.: Princeton University Press, 1985), 15–16.
16. New York and New Jersey blacks frequently spoke both English and Dutch because the area was controlled by the Netherlands until the 1660s. *Pennsylvania Gazette,* September 24, 1741; June 6, 1746; July 31, 1740; July 4, 1745; September 20, 1764; *New York Gazette,* July 31, 1766.
17. A. Leon Higginbotham, Jr., *In the Matter of Color: Race and the American Legal Process: The Colonial Period* (New York: Oxford University Press, 1978); Joyce D. Goodfriend, *Before the Melting Pot: Society and Culture in Colonial New York City,*

1664–1730 (Princeton, N.J.: Princeton University Press, 1992), 111–132. See also Shane White, *Somewhat More Independent: The End of Slavery in New York City, 1770–1810* (Athens: University of Georgia Press, 1991), and Edgar J. McManus, *Black Bondage in the North* (Syracuse, N.Y.: Syracuse University Press, 1973), 57–58.

18. Ira Berlin, "Time, Space, and the Evolution of Afro-American Society," *American Historical Review* 85 (February 1980), 44–78; McManus, *Black Bondage,* 84.

19. McManus, *Black Bondage,* 208–211; White, *Somewhat More Independent,* 3.

20. James Oliver Horton and Lois E. Horton, *In Hope of Liberty: Culture, Community, and Protest among Northern Free Blacks* (New York: Oxford University Press, 1977), 10, 37.

21. Jane G. Austin, *Dr. LeBaron and His Daughters* (Cambridge, Mass.: Riverside Press / Boston: Houghton, Mifflin & Co., 1892), 55.

22. Austin, *Dr. LeBaron,* 91.

23. Arthur Zilversmit, *The First Emancipation: The Abolition of Slavery in the North* (Chicago: University of Chicago Press, 1967), 33; James A. Henretta, "Economic Development and Social Structure in Colonial Boston," *William and Mary Quarterly* 22 (1965), 75–92; Lorenzo J. Greene, *The Negro in Colonial New England 1620–1766* (1942; reprint, N.Y.: Atheneum Press, 1968), 84.

24. Greene, *The Negro in Colonial New England;* Piersen, *Black Yankee;* Nash, *The Urban Crucible.* See also Robert C. Twombly and Robert M. Moore, "Black Puritan: The Negro in Seventeenth Century Massachusetts," *William and Mary Quarterly,* 3rd series, 24 (April 1967), 224–242.

25. Higginbotham, *In The Matter of Color,* 203.

26. The Stono Rebellion is described in chapter 3.

27. Peter Wood, *Black Majority: Negroes in Colonial South Carolina from 1670 through the Stono Rebellion* (New York: W. W. Norton, 1974), 152.

28. Free blacks were taxed more heavily than whites and had to pay a poll tax from age twelve. Whites did not have to pay the poll tax until age sixteen. After 1760 blacks were required to possess fifty acres of land in order to be eligible to vote. There is reason to believe that some free blacks in South Carolina voted. See Higginbotham, *In the Matter of Color,* 204.

29. See examples of conspiratorial free blacks in Robert Olwell, "Becoming Free: Manumission and the Genesis of a Free Black Community in South Carolina, 1740–90," in Jane Landers, ed., *Against the Odds: Free Blacks in the Slave Societies of the Americas* (Portland, Ore.: Frank Cass, 1996), 1–19.

30. *New England Weekly Journal,* May 1, 1732.

31. Katz, *Eyewitness,* 24.

32. Winthrop Jordan, *White over Black,* 139; Greene, *The Negro in Colonial New England;* Debra L. Newman, "Black Women in the Era of the American Revolution in Pennsylvania," *Journal of Negro History* 61:3 (July 1976), 276–289.

33. Horton and Horton, *In Hope of Liberty,* 30–54; Katz, *Eyewitness,* 27.

34. Horton and Horton, *In Hope of Liberty,* 39.

35. Jack D. Forbes, *Black Africans and Native Americans: Color, Race, Cast in the Evolution of Red-Black Peoples* (New York: Basil Blackwell, 1988).

36. Lamont D. Thomas, *Rise to Be a People: A Biography of Paul Cuffe* (Urbana: University of Illinois Press, 1986).

37. Horton and Horton, *In Hope of Liberty.*

38. Alice Morse Earle, *Colonial Days in Old New York* (1896; reprint, New York: Empire Book Company, 1926), 196–200. See also White, *Somewhat More Independent;* and Sterling Stuckey, *Slave Culture: Nationalist Theory and the Foundations of Black America* (New York: Oxford University Press, 1987).

39. Albert J. Raboteau, *Slave Religion: The "Invisible Institution" in the Antebellum South* (New York: Oxford University Press, 1978), 15; Berlin, *Many Thousands Gone.*

40. Samuel E. Morrison, "A Poem on Election Day in Massachusetts about 1760," *Proceedings of the Colonial Society of Massachusetts* 18 (February 1915), 54–61.
41. Eileen Southern, ed., *Readings in Black American Music* (New York: W. W. Norton, 1971), 41.
42. Wood, *Black Majority.*
43. Reports by eighteenth-century European doctors traveling in West Africa and anthropological studies in the twentieth century confirm that inoculation was an ancient practice in West Africa. For an important recent argument on the impact of African medicine on American medicine see William D. Piersen, *Black Legacy: American's Hidden Heritage* (Amherst: University of Massachusetts Press, 1993), 101–102.
44. Ibid.

Chapter 3   ▪   **Slavery and Freedom in the Age of Revolution**

1. Robert Olwell, *Masters, Slaves and Subjects: The Culture of Power in the South Carolina Low Country, 1740–1790* (Ithaca, N.Y.: Cornell University Press, 1998), 22–23.
2. These Africans are generally referred to as Angolans, but John Thornton provides a convincing argument that they were most likely to have been from the Kingdom of Kongo in modern Angola. See John K. Thornton, "African Dimensions of the Stono Rebellion," *American Historical Review* 96:4 (October 1991), 1101–1114.
3. Jane G. Landers, "Acquisition and Loss on a Spanish Frontier: The Free Black Homesteaders of Florida, 1784–1821," in Jane G. Landers, ed., *Against the Odds: Free Blacks in the Slave Societies of the Americas* (Portland, Ore.: Frank Cass, 1996), 85–101.
4. Olwell, *Masters, Slaves and Subjects,* 22.
5. Thornton, "African Dimensions of the Stono Rebellions," 1111.
6. Olwell, *Masters, Slaves and Subjects,* 24.
7. Ibid., 26–29.
8. Ira Berlin, *Many Thousands Gone: The First Two Centuries of Slavery in North America* (Cambridge, Mass.: Harvard University Press, 1998), 171–173.
9. Ibid.; James Oliver Horton and Lois E. Horton, *In Hope of Liberty: Culture Community, and Protest among Northern Free Blacks, 1700–1860* (New York: Oxford University Press, 1997), 42–43.
10. Alan Gallay, "Planters and Slaves in the Great Awakening," in *Masters and Slaves in the House of the Lord: Race and Religion in the American South, 1740–1870,* edited by John B. Boles (Lexington: University Press of Kentucky, 1988), 19–36; Nathan O. Hatch, *The Democratization of American Christianity* (New Haven, Conn.: Yale University Press, 1989).
11. Leonard W. Labaree, "The Conservative Attitude toward the Great Awakening," *William and Mary Quarterly* 1 (1944), 339, 336.
12. *New York Weekly Journal,* August 9, 1742.
13. Daniel Horsemanden, *The New York Conspiracy,* edited by Thomas J. Davis (Boston: Beacon Press, 1971); Thomas J. Davis, *A Rumor of Revolt: The Great Negro Plot in Colonial New York* (New York: Free Press, 1985).
14. Davis, *A Rumor of Revolt.*
15. Gary Nash, "Up from the Bottom in Franklin's Philadelphia," *Past and Present* 77 (1977), 57–83; Eric Foner, *Tom Paine and Revolutionary America* (New York: Oxford University Press, 1976), 48.
16. For a description of the process of the concentration of colonial wealth and political power see James A. Henretta, *The Evolution of American Society, 1700–1815: An Interdisciplinary Analysis* (Lexington, Mass.: D. C. Heath, 1973). Gary Nash has analyzed the tax records for Boston, New York, and Philadelphia from the

late seventeenth to the late eighteenth century and found that in all three cities the rich increased their share of the community's wealth. See Nash, *The Urban Crucible.*

17. Josiah Quincy, Jr., *Reports of Cases Argued and Adjudged in the Superior Court of Judicature of the Province of Massachusetts Bay, between 1761 and 1772*, edited by Samuel M. Quincy (Boston: Little Brown, 1865), 237–238; Nash, *Urban Crucible*, 8.

18. Benjamin Colman to Mr. Samuel Holden, Boston, May 8, 1737, "Colman Papers," unpublished papers, vol. 2, Massachusetts Historical Society.

19. Jesse Lemisch, "Jack Tar in the Streets: Merchant Seamen in the Politics of Revolutionary America," *William and Mary Quarterly* 25 (1968), 371–407; Howard Zinn, *A People's History of the United States* (New York: Harper & Row, 1980), 51; Nash, *Urban Crucible*, 221–223.

20. Roi Ottley and William J. Weatherby, eds., *The Negro in New York: An Informal Social History, 1626–1940* (New York: New York Public Library, 1967), 36–37.

21. William C. Nell, "Crispus Attucks Once a Slave in Massachusetts," *Liberator*, August 5, 1859, 124. See the *Boston Gazette and Weekly Journal*, October 2, November 13, and November 20, 1750, for the runaway ad for Attucks.

22. Ibid.

23. John Adams, quoted in Howard Zinn, *A People's History of the United States* (New York: Harper & Row, 1980), 67. See *Boston Gazette*, March 12, 1770, for an eyewitness account of this event.

24. Benjamin Thatcher, *Traits of the Tea Party, Being a Memoir of George R. T. Hewes* (New York, 1835), 103–104. See also William Cooper Nell, *The Colored Patriots of the American Revolution* (Boston: Robert F. Wallcut, 1855; reprint, Salem, N.H.: Ayer Company, 1986).

25. One of those initially wounded died later. Thatcher, *Traits of the Tea Party*, 123–124.

26. John Adams's diary, July 1773, in Sidney Kaplan, *The Black Presence in the Era of the American Revolution, 1770–1800* (Washington, D.C.: Smithsonian Institution Press, 1973), 9. The original diary is housed at the Massachusetts Historical Society, Boston, Massachusetts.

27. Jack P. Greene, ed., *The Reinterpretation of the American Revolution* (New York: Harper & Row, 1968), 169. There is evidence that Revolutionary leaders such as Samuel Adams tended to disqualify African Americans from consideration as persons deserving freedom from British rule, conveniently separating the actual slavery of blacks from the metaphorical slavery of white colonists. See Patricia Bradley, *Slavery, Propaganda, and the American Revolution* (Jackson: University of Mississippi Press, 1998).

28. Sidney Kaplan, *The Black Presence in the Era of the American Revolution, 1770–1800* (Greenwich, Conn.: New York Graphic Society, 1973), 11–13.

29. James Otis, *The Rights of the British Colonies Asserted and Proved* (Boston: Edes and Gill, 1764), 37; Abigail Adams to John Adams, September 22, 1774, in Lyman H. Butterfield, ed., *Adams Family Correspondence* (Cambridge, Mass.: Harvard University Press, 1963), vol. 1, 162, 12–14.

30. The Boston Tea Party in 1773 was part of the protest over England's tax on tea. Revolutionaries dressed as American Indians boarded a vessel in the port and dumped the ship's cargo of tea overboard. Philip S. Foner, *History of Black Americans: From Africa to the Emergence of the Cotton Kingdom*, vol. 1 (Westport, Conn.: Greenwood Press, 1975), 307.

31. Benjamin Quarles, *The Negro in the American Revolution* (Chapel Hill: University of North Carolina Press, 1961).

32. Zinn, *A People's History of the United States*, 81.

33. *Pennsylvania Gazette,* June 12, 1780; Clement Alexander Price, *Freedom Not Far Distant: A Documentary History of Afro-Americans in New Jersey* (Newark, N.J.: Historical Society, 1980), 68; for information about the banditti, see Rachel N. Klein, *Unification of a Slave State: The Rise of the Planter Class in the South Carolina Backcountry, 1760–1808* (Chapel Hill: University of North Carolina Press, 1990), 95–99.
34. Paul Finkelman, *Slavery in the Courtroom: An Annotated Bibliography of American Cases* (Washington, D.C.: Library of Congress, 1985); Foner, *History of Black Americans,* vol. 1, 296–297; Bradley, *Slavery, Propaganda,* 66–80.
35. Wilson, *The Loyal Blacks,* 21; Franklin and Moss, *From Slavery to Freedom,* 70.
36. Quotes in Foner, *History of Black Americans,* vol. 1, 316. Benjamin Quarles suggested that Washington was also moved by black requests to be included in the American forces, and although this undoubtedly did play a role in his decision, we agree with Philip Foner that military considerations were mainly responsible for the change in policy. See Benjamin Quarles, *The Negro in the American Revolution,* and Foner, *History of Black Americans.*
37. Revolutionary War Pension Records, Prince Hazeltine, Records of the Veteran's Administration, Record Group #15, National Archives and Record Service, Washington, D.C.
38. Quarles, *The Negro in the American Revolution,* ix; Sylvia R. Frey, *Water from the Rock: Black Resistance in a Revolutionary Age* (Princeton, N.J.: Princeton University Press, 1991), 121–122.
39. "The Negro in the Military Service of the United States: A Compilation of Official Records, State Papers, Historical Records, Etc.," National Archives, Washington, D.C.: 206–214, 220, cited in Foner, *History of Black Americans,* vol. 1, 333.
40. British slaveholders in the West Indies or those in North America who remained loyal to the Crown expressed similar fears about Lord Dunmore's arming slaves to fight for the British Empire. Many believed that before the war was over British troops would have to be used to defend against the armed rebellion of their slave allies. See "The Negro in the Military Service of the United States: A Compilation of Official Records, State Papers, Historical Records, Etc.," National Archives, Washington, D.C.
41. Revolutionary War Pension Records, Cato Cuff, Samuel Coombs, Prince Whipple, Oliver Cromwell, and Prince Bent.
42. Wilson, *Loyal Blacks;* Robin W. Winks, *The Blacks in Canada: A History* (Montreal: McGill–Queen's University Press, 1997).
43. Quarles, *The Negro in the American Revolution,* 172; Wilson, *Loyal Blacks,* 42; Ottley and Weatherby, *The Negro in New York,* 40.
44. Wilson, *Loyal Blacks,* 70–77, 135–153.
45. John H. Watson, "In Re Vermont Constitution of 1777 . . . ," *Proceedings of the Vermont Historical Society, 1919–1920,* cited in Foner, *History of Black Americans,* vol. 1, 347.
46. Foner, *History of Black Americans,* vol. 1, 347. In 1857 free blacks were also declared to be full citizens of the state of New Hampshire. For a similar petition from Connecticut, see Herbert Aptheker, ed., *A Documentary History of the Negro People in the United States* (New York: New Citadel Press, 1951), 10–12.
47. Zilversmit, *The First Emancipation;* Horton and Horton, *In Hope of Liberty,* 80.
48. Ira Berlin, *Slaves without Masters: The Free Negro in the Antebellum South* (New York: Pantheon Books, 1974); *Negro Population in the United States, 1790–1915* (New York: Arno Press, 1968).
49. Paul Finkelman, *An Imperfect Union* (Chapel Hill: University of North Carolina Press, 1981), 80.

50. "Removal to the South, 1818," quoted in Price, *Freedom Not Far Distant,* 85–86.
51. For quotes see Jacqueline Bernard, *Journey toward Freedom: The Story of Sojourner Truth* (New York: Feminist Press at the City University of New York, 1990), 71. Also see Bert James Loewenberg and Ruth Bogin, eds., *Black Women in Nineteenth-Century American Life* (University Park: Pennsylvania State University Press, 1976), 234–242; Harriet Beecher Stowe, "Sojourner Truth, The Libyan Sibyl," *Atlantic Monthly* (April 1863), 473–481.
52. Revolutionary War Pension Records, Cato Howe; James Deetz, *In Small Things Forgotten: The Archeology of Early American Life* (Garden City, N.Y.: Anchor Doubleday, 1977), 138–161.

Chapter 4 ▪ **The Early Republic and the Rise of the Cotton Kingdom**

1. James Oliver Horton and Lois E. Horton, *In Hope of Liberty: Culture, Community and Protest Among Northern Free Blacks, 1700–1860* (New York: Oxford University Press, 1997), 69–70; Gary Nash, *Forging Freedom: The Formation of Philadelphia's Black Community, 1720–1840* (Cambridge, Mass.: Harvard University Press, 1988), 52.
2. Gary B. Nash, *Race and Revolution* (Madison, Wis.: Madison House, 1990), 6.
3. Ibid.; David P. Szatmary, *Shays' Rebellion: The Making of an Agrarian Insurrection* (Amherst: University of Massachusetts Press, 1980); Horton and Horton, *In Hope of Liberty,* 177. The African Americans' petition for funds to transport them to Africa was unsuccessful. In 1787 Shays's followers won control of the Massachusetts legislature and later secured a pardon for their leader.
4. Thomas Jefferson attempted to include the southwestern territories as part of the area in which slavery was outlawed, but his recommendation failed to be adopted by Congress by a single vote. Apparently the New Jersey representative who would have voted for its inclusion missed the vote because of illness. Had slavery been prohibited from taking root in the Southwest as well as the Northwest, the course of American history during the nineteenth century and beyond might well have been considerably different. See Staughton Lynd, *Class, Conflict and Slavery, and the United States Constitution* (Indianapolis, Ind.: Bobbs-Merrill, 1967); Emma Lou Thornbrough, *The Negro in Indiana: A Study of a Minority* (Indianapolis, Ind.: Bobbs-Merrill, 1957); and Paul Finkelman, "Slavery and the Northwest Ordinance: A Study in Ambiguity," *Journal of the Early Republic* 6 (Winter 1986), 343–370.
5. Leon Litwack, *North of Slavery: The Negro in the Free States, 1790–1860* (Chicago: University of Chicago Press, 1961), 72. Indiana's black population increased from less than three hundred in 1800 to fourteen hundred by 1820, to more than eleven thousand by 1850. Ohio's blacks, numbering less than four hundred in 1800, stood above twenty-five thousand by mid–nineteenth century. *Negro Population in the United States, 1790–1915* (Washington, D.C.: Government Printing Office, 1918; reprint, New York: Arno Press, 1968), 45.
6. James Walvin, *An African's Life: The Life and Times of Olaudah Equiano, 1745–1797* (New York: Cassell, 1998).
7. Equiano's narrative style influenced the nineteenth-century antislavery autobiographies of former slaves such as Frederick Douglass. See the introduction by Henry Louis Gates, Jr., to *The Classic Slave Narratives* (New York: Penguin Books, 1987), xiii.
8. C.L.R. James, *The Black Jacobins* (1938; reprint, New York: Vintage Books, 1963); Donald R. Hickey, "American's Response to the Slave Revolt in Haiti, 1791–1806," *Journal of the Early Republic* 2 (Winter 1982), 361–379.
9. Gary B. Nash and Jean R. Soderlund, *Freedom by Degrees: Emancipation in Pennsylvania and Its Aftermath* (New York: Oxford University Press, 1991).

Philadelphia was the seat of the national government from 1790 to 1800, when Washington became the capital.

10. Paul A. Gilje, *The Road to Mobocracy* (Chapel Hill: University of North Carolina Press, 1987), 149.

11. Douglas R. Egerton, "Gabriel's Conspiracy and the Election of 1800," *Journal of Southern History* 56 (May 1990), 191–214. See also Douglas R. Egerton, *Gabriel's Rebellion: The Virginia Slave Conspiracies of 1800 and 1802* (Chapel Hill: University of North Carolina Press, 1993). Egerton speculates that Gabriel favored the Republicans in any struggle with the Federalists, failing to appreciate that the Republican commitment to freedom and liberty did not apply to blacks. This interpretation is intriguing in light of the fact that in Philadelphia, New York, and even in the Upper South, Federalists were those who founded the antislavery societies of the late eighteenth century. If Gabriel was aware of the international tensions between the United States and France, it seems likely that he would have also been aware of the antislavery leanings of many Federalists in Philadelphia and Virginia. See also Gerald W. Mullin, *Flight and Rebellion: Slave Resistance in Eighteenth-Century Virginia* (New York: Oxford University Press, 1972), and Stuckey, *Slave Culture*.

12. Donald R. Wright, *African Americans in the Early Republic, 1789–1831* (Arlington Heights, Ill.: Harlan Davidson, 1993); Edward W. Phifer, "Slavery in Microcosm: Burke County, North Carolina," in Allan Weinstein and Frank Otto Gatell, eds., *American Negro Slavery: A Modern Reader* (New York: Oxford University Press, 1968), 74–97.

13. Richard B. Morris and Jeffrey B. Morris, eds., *Encyclopedia of American History* (New York: Harper & Row, 1976), 757, 759; Douglas C. North, *The Economic Growth of the United States, 1790–1860* (New York: W. W. Norton, 1966), 128.

14. North, *The Economic Growth of the United States*, 75–76.

15. Ann Patton Malone, *Sweet Chariot: Slave Family and Household Structure in Nineteenth-Century Louisiana* (Chapel Hill: University of North Carolina Press, 1992), 52; Charles Duncan Rice, *The Rise and Fall of Black Slavery* (New York: Harper & Row, 1975), 286–287.

16. Gavin Wright, *The Political Economy of the Cotton South: Households, Markets and Wealth in the Nineteenth Century* (New York: W. W. Norton, 1978).

17. Lewis Clarke, *Narrative of the Sufferings of Lewis Clarke, during a Captivity of More than Twenty-Five Years among the Algerines of Kentucky* (Boston: D. H. Eli, 1845), 121; James Williams, *Narrative of James Williams, An American Slave, Who Was for Several Years a Driver on a Cotton Plantation in Alabama* (New York: American Anti-Slavery Society, 1838), 32; Benjamin Drew, ed., *A North-Side View of Slavery: The Refugee, or the Narratives of Fugitive Slaves in Canada Related by Themselves* (Boston: John P. Jewett, 1856; reprint, New York: Negro Universities Press, 1968), 178; Israel Campbell, *Bond and Free; or, Yearnings for Freedom, from My Green Briar House; Being the Story of My Life in Bondage and My Life in Freedom* (Philadelphia, 1861), 18.

18. Michael Tadman, *Speculators and Slaves: Masters, Traders, and Slaves in the Old South* (Madison, Wis.: University of Wisconsin, 1989), 21–46; Malone, *Sweet Chariot*, 15, 193.

19. Gary B. Nash, "Forging Freedom: The Emancipation Experience in the Northern Seaport Cities, 1775–1820," in Ira Berlin and Ronald Hoffman, eds., *Slavery and Freedom in the Age of the American Revolution* (Charlottesville: United States Capitol Historical Society/University Press of Virginia, 1983), 3–48; quote, 7; Leonard P. Curry, *The Free Black in Urban America 1800–1850* (Chicago: University of Chicago Press, 1981), 244–248. In addition to these free blacks,

Philadelphia still had about fifty slaves and New York City nearly three thousand slaves in 1800.

20. Thomas, *Rise to Be a People: A Biography of Paul Cuffe* (Urbana: University of Illinois Press, 1986).

21. James B. Browning, "The Beginnings of Insurance Enterprise among Negroes," *Journal of Negro History* 22:4 (October 1937), 417–432; Robert L. Harris, Jr., "Early Black Benevolent Societies, 1780–1830," *Massachusetts Review* 20:3 (Autumn 1979), 603–625.

22. Harris, "Early Black Benevolent Societies, 1780–1830," 603–625; Browning, "The Beginnings of Insurance Enterprise among Negroes," 417–432; "Colored Population of Philadelphia," *National Enquirer and Constitutional Advocate of Universal Liberty* 1:7 (October 22, 1836), 27.

23. Horton and Horton, *Black Bostonians* (New York: Holmes & Meier, 1999), 41–55; see also C. Eric Lincoln and Lawrence H. Mamiya, *The Black Church in the African American Experience* (Durham, N.C.: Duke University Press, 1990); Edward Smith, *Climbing Jacob's Ladder: The Rise of Black Churches in Eastern American Cities, 1740–1877* (Washington, D.C.: Smithsonian Institution Press, 1988).

24. Charles V. Hamilton, *The Black Preacher in America* (New York: William Morrow, 1972); David E. Swift, *Black Prophets of Justice: Activist Clergy before the Civil War* (Baton Rouge: Louisiana State University Press, 1989).

25. Ira Berlin, *Slaves without Masters: The Free Negro in the Antebellum South* (New York: Pantheon, 1974), 284–315.

26. Ibid. Berlin argues that the role of free blacks differed from one region of the South to another and over time. Also see Horton and Horton, *In Hope of Liberty,* for important distinctions between the role of free blacks, especially mulattoes, in the North and in the South.

27. Thomas, *Rise to Be a People.*

28. Foner, *History of Black Americans,* vol. 1, 485.

29. *New York Evening Post,* August 20, 1814, quoted in Shane White, *Somewhat More Independent* (Athens: University of Georgia Press, 1991), 150.

30. Quoted in Foner, *History of Black Americans,* vol. 1, 486.

31. Ibid., 487.

32. William Cooper Nell, *Colored Patriots of the American Revolution* (Boston: Robert F. Wallcut, 1855; reprint, New York: Arno Press, 1968), 190–191. Sailors were commonly called tars.

33. W. Jeffrey Bolster, *Black Jacks: African American Seamen in the Age of Sail* (Cambridge, Mass.: Harvard University Press, 1997), 127.

34. Donald E. Everett, "Emigrés and Militiamen: Free Persons of Color in New Orleans, 1803–1815," *Journal of Negro History* 38:4 (October 1953), 377–402.

35. James Roberts, *The Narrative of James Roberts: Soldier in the Revolutionary War and at the Battle of New Orleans* (Chicago, 1858), 32.

36. Arnett G. Lindsay, "Diplomatic Relations between the United States and Great Britain Bearing on the Return of Negro Slaves, 1783–1828," *Journal of Negro History* 5 (October 1920), 391–419.

37. William S. McFeely, *Frederick Douglass* (New York: W. W. Norton, 1991), 318.

Chapter 5 ▪ **Slavery and the Slave Community**

1. Peter Kolchin, *American Slavery, 1619–1877* (New York: Hill & Wang, 1993), 242.

2. Solomon Northup, *Twelve Years a Slave* (Auburn, N.Y.: Derby and Miller, 1853; reprint, edited by Sue Eakin and Joseph Logsdon, Baton Rouge, La.: Louisiana State University Press, 1968).

3. Walter M. Brasch, *Black English and the Mass Media* (Amherst: University of Massachusetts Press, 1981), 26–31; Charles Joyner, *Down by the Riverside: A South Carolina Slave Community* (Urbana: University of Illinois Press, 1984).

4. Austin Steward, *Twenty-Two Years a Slave and Forty Years a Freeman* (Rochester, N.Y.: W. Alling, 1857), 33–38. For a description of retribution taken against Virginia slaves after the Nat Turner rebellion see Jacobs, *Incidents in the Life of a Slave Girl*.

5. William F. Cheek, *Black Resistance before the Civil War* (Beverly Hills, Calif.: Glencoe Press, 1970), 99.

6. Norrece T. Jones, Jr., *Born a Child of God Yet a Slave: Mechanisms of Control and Strategies of Resistance in Antebellum South Carolina* (Hanover, N.H.: University Press of New England, 1990).

7. Benjamin Drew, ed., *North-Side View of Slavery, the Refugee; or, The Narrative of Fugitive Slaves in Canada. Related by Themselves* (Boston: John P. Jewett, 1856), 223.

8. Bernard E. Powers, *Black Charlestonians: A Social History, 1822–1885* (Fayetteville: University of Arkansas Press, 1994), 31–33.

9. Eric Foner, ed., *Nat Turner* (Englewood Cliffs, N.J.: Prentice-Hall, 1971); Ira Berlin, *Slaves without Masters: The Free Negro in the Antebellum South* (New York: Pantheon Books, 1974), 188–189, 195; Henry Irving Tragle, *The Southampton Slave Rebellion of 1831: A Compilation of Source Material* (Amherst: University of Massachusetts Press, 1971).

10. John Hope Franklin, *The Militant South, 1800–1860* (Cambridge, Mass.: Harvard University Press, 1956); Sterling Stuckey, *Slave Culture: Nationalist Theory and the Foundation of Black America* (New York: Oxford University Press, 1987); Eugene D. Genovese, *Roll, Jordan, Roll: The World the Slaves Made* (New York: Pantheon Books, 1974).

11. Bertram Wyatt-Brown, *Southern Honor: Ethics and Behavior in the Old South* (New York: Oxford University Press, 1982). Wyatt-Brown describes the violence in Southern society but attributes it to cultural factors imported from ancient Ireland. Although he may well be correct, slavery almost certainly necessitated its regular practice and helped to create the atmosphere in which this violence took on a racial dimension.

12. Ibid., 88, 366. Wyatt-Brown has interesting information comparing northern and southern crime rates generally and concludes that northern society's lower crime rate reflected its less violent culture. One might ask if the early abolition of slavery in the North, an institution that was never as widespread or as significant there as in the South, was not a major factor in this cultural difference.

13. Northup, *Twelve Years a Slave*.

14. Ibid., 61–69.

15. Ibid., 122–144.

16. Quoted in James Oliver Horton and Lois E. Horton, "Black Theology and Historical Necessity," in Miles L. Bradbury and James B. Gilbert, eds., *Transforming Faith: The Sacred and Secular in Modern America* (Westport, Conn.: Greenwood Press, 1989), 25–37; quote, 28.

17. Melville J. Herskovits, *Dahomey* (New York: Augustin, 1938); Robert Farris Thompson, *The Four Movements of the Sun* (Washington, D.C.: National Gallery of Art, 1981). For an important interpretation of the ring shout and its significance as a link between West African culture and that of African America see Stuckey, *Slave Culture*.

18. James Lindsay Smith, *Autobiography of James Lindsay Smith* (Norwich, Conn: Press of the Bulletin Co., 1881), 27.

19. Francis Fedric, *Slave Life in Virginia and Kentucky* (London: Wertheim, MacIntosh, and Hunt, 1863), 5.
20. Charles Joyner, *Down by the River Side: A South Carolina Slave Community* (Urbana: University of Illinois Press, 1984), 232.
21. Quoted in Horton and Horton, "Black Theology and Historical Necessity," 29.
22. Northup, *Twelve Years a Slave*, 172.
23. Ann Patton Malone, *Sweet Chariot: Slave Family and Household Structure in Nineteenth-Century Louisiana* (Chapel Hill: University of North Carolina Press, 1992), 16–17. See also Herbert Gutman, *The Black Family in Slavery and Freedom* (New York: Pantheon Press, 1976), and Leslie Howard Owens, *This Species of Property: Slave Life and Culture in the Old South* (New York: Oxford University Press, 1976).
24. Owens, *This Species of Property*, 198.
25. Brenda Stevenson, "A Heroine's Heroine: Slave Women Choose," paper presented at the Intercollegiate Department of Black Studies' Conference, Claremont Colleges, Claremont, California, January 1994.
26. Gutman, *Black Family in Slavery and Freedom*, 191. Elizabeth's father and mother belonged to different masters, and before her father was moved to the West he was able to visit only twice a year.
27. Frederick Douglass, *My Bondage and My Freedom*, edited and with an introduction by William L. Andrews (Urbana: University of Illinois Press, 1987), 27–32.
28. James W. C. Pennington, *The Fugitive Blacksmith*, in Arna Bontemps, ed., *Great Slave Narratives* (Boston: Beacon Press, 1969), 193–267; quote, 207.
29. Harriet A. Jacobs, *Incidents in the Life of a Slave Girl, Written by Herself*, edited by Jean Fagan Yellin (Cambridge, Mass.: Harvard University Press, 1987), 77.
30. Northup, *Twelve Years a Slave*, 151–152.
31. Ibid., 116, 123–125.
32. Ibid.
33. Frederick Law Olmsted, *The Slave States: Before the Civil War* (1856; reprint, revised and enlarged, New York: Capricorn Books, 1959), 203.
34. Northup, *Twelve Years a Slave*, 125.
35. Joyner, *Down by the River Side*, 23–24, 42. See also John Michael Vlach, *The Afro-American Tradition in Decorative Arts* (Athens: University of Georgia Press, 1990).
36. John Brown, *Slave Life in Georgia: A Narrative of the Life, Suffering, and Escape of John Brown, A Fugitive Now in England* (London: W. M. Watts, 1855), 186–187.
37. Joyner, *Down by the River Side*, 43–45. Joyner gives a detailed description of the task system and its advantages to the slaves over the gang system used in cotton cultivation.
38. Charles Joyner, "The World of the Plantation," in Edward D. C. Campbell, Jr., with Kim S. Rice, eds., *Before Freedom Came* (Charlottesville and Richmond: University Press of Virginia and The Museum of the Confederacy, 1991), 51–99; quote, 82.
39. Olmsted, *The Slave States*, 115.
40. Lawrence W. Levine, *Black Culture and Black Consciousness: Afro-American Folk Thought from Slavery to Freedom* (New York: Oxford University Press, 1977), 5–19; see also Miles Mark Fisher, *Negro Slave Songs in the United States* (1953; reprint, New York: Carol Publishing Group, 1990).
41. Northup, *Twelve Years a Slave*, 135–136.
42. Henry Clay Bruce, *The New Man: Twenty-nine Years a Slave, Twenty-nine Years a Free Man: Recollections of H. C. Bruce* (York, Pa.: P. Anstadt and Sons, 1895).
43. Booker Taliaferro Washington, *Up from Slavery: An Autobiography* (1900; reprint, New York: Dell, 1965), 26.

44. James Oliver Horton, *Free People of Color: Inside the African American Community* (Washington, D.C.: Smithsonian Institution Press, 1993), 66.

45. James Oliver Horton, "Links to Bondage," ibid., 53–74.

Chapter 6 ▪ *Free People of Color and the Fight against Slavery*

1. Just before the Civil War, the South Carolina legislature considered a provision that would have deprived all free blacks in the state of their freedom. See James Roark and Michael Johnson, *Black Masters: A Free Family of Color in the Old South* (New York: W. W. Norton, 1984).

2. Gary B. Nash, "Forging Freedom: The Emancipation Experience in the Northern Seaport Cities, 1775–1820," in *Slavery and Freedom in the Age of the American Revolution*, Ira Berlin and Ronald Hoffman, eds. (Charlottesville: University Press of Virginia, for the United States Capitol Historical Society, 1983), 3–48; quote, 32–33.

3. David Walker, *David Walker's Appeal to the Coloured Citizens of the World* (1829), introduction by Sean Wilentz (New York: Hill & Wang, 1995), 21.

4. *Freedom's Journal*, March 16, 1827.

5. Walker, *David Walker's Appeal*.

6. Peter P. Hinks, *To Awaken My Afflicted Brethren: David Walker and the Problem of Antebellum Slave Resistance* (University Park: Pennsylvania State University Press, 1997).

7. Henry Mayer, *All on Fire: William Lloyd Garrison and the Abolition of Slavery* (New York: St. Martin's Press, 1998), 101; *Liberator*, January 1, 1831.

8. James O. Horton and Lois Horton, *In Hope of Liberty: Culture, Community, and Protest among Northern Free Blacks* (New York: Oxford University Press, 1997), 213, chap. 9, n. 1.

9. James Oliver Horton and Lois E. Horton, *Black Bostonians: Family Life and Community Struggle in the Antebellum North* (New York: Holmes & Meier Publishers, 1999).

10. Donald M. Jacobs, "David Walker: Boston Race Leader, 1825–1830," *Essex Institute Historical Collection* 107 (January 1971), 94–107.

11. Philip S. Foner, *History of Black Americans*, vol. 2 (Westport, Conn.: Greenwood Press, 1983), 399, 401.

12. Horton and Horton, *In Hope of Liberty*, 244–245.

13. Ibid., 102–103.

14. Ibid.

15. Howard Holman Bell, ed., *Minutes of the Proceedings of the National Negro Conventions 1830–1864* (New York: Arno Press / New York Times, 1969). For an account of the Cincinnati race riot see Richard Wade, *The Urban Frontier: The Rise of Western Cities, 1790–1830* (Cambridge, Mass.: Harvard University Press, 1959), 222–229.

16. Horton and Horton, *In Hope of Liberty*, 193–196.

17. Ibid., 262.

18. C. Peter Ripley, Roy E. Finkenbine, Michael F. Hembree, and Donald Yacovone, eds., *The Black Abolitionist Papers: Canada, 1830–1865*, vol. 2 (Chapel Hill: University of North Carolina Press, 1991), 109–112.

19. Dorothy Sterling, *Speak Out in Thunder Tones: Letters and Other Writings by Black Northerners, 1787–1865* (New York: Da Capo Press, 1998); James Stewart, *William Lloyd Garrison and the Challenge of Emancipation* (Arlington Heights, Ill.: H. Davison Press, 1992).

20. Former slave and renowned abolitionist speaker Frederick Douglass promoted the manual-labor-school idea for blacks both at conventions and in his newspapers during this later period. See Horton and Horton, *Black Bostonians*, 84.

21. Carlton Mabee, *Black Education in New York State* (Syracuse, N.Y.: Syracuse University Press, 1979), 108–166; C. Peter Ripley, Roy E. Finkenbine, Michael F. Hembree, and Donald Yacovone, eds., *The Black Abolitionist Papers*, vol. 3 (Chapel Hill: University of North Carolina Press, 1991), 337 n.; Nat Brandt, *The Town That Started the Civil War* (Syracuse, N.Y.: Syracuse University Press, 1990), 38.

22. "Report of the Condition of the People of Color in the State of Ohio" (April 1835), reprinted in Aptheker, *Documentary History*, 157–158; Horton and Horton, *Black Bostonians*, 33.

23. Horton, *Free People of Color*, 49–50.

24. Christine Stansell, *City of Women* (New York: Alfred A. Knopf, 1982), 63–73; Barbara Meil Hobson, *Uneasy Virtue* (New York: Basic Books, 1987), 51–54.

25. *Colored American*, March 15, 1838.

26. Stewart, *Garrison*, 82.

27. Ripley, Finkenbine, Hembree, and Yacovone, eds., *The Black Abolitionist Papers*, vol. 3, 482.

28. Horton and Horton, *In Hope of Liberty*, 243.

29. Frederick Douglass, *Narrative of the Life of Frederick Douglass*, edited by David W. Blight (New York: Bedford Books, 1993).

30. William McFeely, *Frederick Douglass* (New York: W. W. Norton, 1991).

31. Ibid., 82–92; see also Blight, *Narrative of the Life of Frederick Douglass*.

32. John G. Whittier, *Narrative of James Williams an American Slave* (New York: Isaac Knapp, 1838), 97–99.

33. Ibid.

34. Dorothy B. Parker, "David B. Ruggles, An Apostle for Human Freedom," *Journal of Negro History* (January 1943), 23–50.

35. Ripley, Finkenbine, Hembree, and Yacovone, *The Black Abolitionist Papers*, vol. 4, 184–185 n.

36. J. C. Furnas, *Goodbye to Uncle Tom* (New York: William Sloane Associates, 1956), 214.

37. Horton and Horton, *Black Bostonians*.

38. Sarah H. Bradford, *Scenes in the Life of Harriet Tubman* (Auburn, N.Y., 1869).

39. "James G. Birney to Lewis Tappan, February 27, 1837," in Dwight L. Dumond, ed., *Letters of James Gillespie Birney* (1938; Gloucester, Mass.: Peter Smith, 1966), vol. 2, 379; Levi Coffin, *Reminiscences of Levi Coffin* (Cincinnati: Western Tract Society, 1876), 106. Coffin was speaking specifically of Newport, Indiana, but it was also more generally true.

40. Calvin Fairbank, *How the Way Was Prepared* (1890; reprint, New York: Negro University Press, 1969), 46–93.

41. Jonathan Walker, *Trial and Imprisonment of Jonathan Walker* (1845; reprint, Gainesville: University Presses of Florida, 1974); John W. Blassingame, *The Frederick Douglass Papers, 1841–1846* (New Haven, Conn.: Yale University Press, 1979), vol. 1, 226.

42. William Jeffrey Bolster, *Black Jacks: African American Seamen in the Age of Sail* (Cambridge, Mass.: Harvard University Press, 1997); *Richmond Enquirer*, November 15, 1850.

43. Horton, *Free People of Color*, 68–71.

44. "Original Records of the Union Baptist Church, Cincinnati, Ohio, 1834," Cincinnati Historical Society.

45. Brandt, *The Town That Started the Civil War*, 212.

46. *Colored American*, December 9, 1837.

47. *Colored American*, September 9, 1837.

48. "Minutes of the National Convention of Colored Citizens, Held in Buffalo, 1843," in Howard Holman Bell, ed., *Minutes of the Proceedings of the National*

Negro Conventions, 1830–1864 (New York: Arno Press and *New York Times,* 1969), 7.

49. Henry Highland Garnet, *Walker's Appeal, with a Brief Sketch of His Life, and Also Garnet's Address to the Slaves of the United States of America* (New York: J. H. Tobitt, 1848), 90–96.

50. "Minutes of the National Convention . . . ," 23.

51. *Colored American,* April 18, 1840.

52. *Colored American,* August 29, 1840.

53. "The Poor Man's Party" broadside dated October 17, 1846, Peterboro, N.Y., Cornell University Archives, Ithaca, N.Y.

54. In October 1845 blacks from western New York State held a meeting in Geneva, New York, to protest racial restrictions on voting. They alerted the state's blacks to be ready to act if a convention was called to amend the state constitution. Among those attending were William Wells Brown and Samuel Ringold Ward. See *Ithaca Chronicle,* October 1, 1845.

55. "Gift of Land and Money to Negroes" (undated list of names) and "To Gerrit Smith Grantees" (broadside dated October 4, 1854), box 145, Gerrit Smith Papers, George Arents Research Library, Syracuse University, Syracuse, NY.

56. Ripley, Finkenbine, Hembree, and Yacovone, *The Black Abolitionist Papers,* vol. 3, 409.

57. Foner, *History of Black Americans,* vol. 2, 543.

58. *National Anti-Slavery Standard,* October 15, 1846, 77.

Chapter 7 ■ *From Militancy to Civil War*

1. Quoted in James Oliver Horton and Lois E. Horton, *Black Bostonians: Family Life and Community Struggle in the Antebellum North,* rev. ed. (New York: Holmes and Meier, 1999), 102.

2. "State Convention of Colored Citizens of Ohio, Columbus," in Philip S. Foner and George W. Walker, eds., *Proceedings of the Black State Conventions, 1840–1865* (Westport, Conn.: Greenwood Press, 1979), 229.

3. *North Star,* February 9, 1849, quoted in Robert C. Dick, *Black Protest: Issues and Tactics* (Westport, Conn.: Greenwood Press, 1974), 138.

4. Fillmore is not known for antislavery sentiments, but his past indicated that he had some sympathy for the fugitives. When Fillmore was a lawyer in Buffalo during the 1830s, according to William Wells Brown, he served without charge as defense counsel for a fugitive slave. William E. Farrison, "William Wells Brown in Buffalo," *Journal of Negro History* 39:4 (October 1954), 298–314.

5. William Loren Katz, *Eyewitness: The Negro in American History,* 3rd ed. (Belmont, Calif.: Fearon Pitman Publishers, 1974), 189; James Oliver Horton and Lois E. Horton, "A Federal Assault: African Americans and the Impact of the Fugitive Slave Law of 1850," *Chicago-Kent Law Review* 68:3 (Fall 1993), 1179–1197; Carol Wilson, *Freedom at Risk: The Kidnapping of Free Blacks in America, 1780–1865* (Lexington: University Press of Kentucky, 1994).

6. Olivia Mahoney, "Black Abolitionist," *Chicago History* 20:1–2 (1991), 22–37.

7. *Liberator,* October 18, 1850.

8. *Liberator,* October 25, 1850.

9. Foner and Walker, *Proceedings,* 318; Horton and Horton, *Black Bostonians,* 130–131.

10. Fred Landon, "The Negro Migration to Canada after the Passing of the Fugitive Slave Act," *Journal of Negro History* 5:1 (January 1920), 22–36.

11. *Liberator,* October 4, 1850.

12. *Pennsylvania Telegraph,* October 2, 1850.

13. Horton and Horton, *Black Bostonians*, 112. See also Mechal Sobel, *Trabelin' On: The Slave Journey to an Afro-Baptist Faith* (Princeton, N.J.: Princeton University Press, 1988), 216; *Liberator*, April 25, 1851; James K. Lewis, "Religious Nature of the Early Negro Migration to Canada and the Amherstburg Baptist Association," *Ontario History* 58 (1966), 117–132.

14. *Liberator*, December 13, 1850; Michael F. Hembree, "The Question of 'Begging': Fugitive Slave Relief in Canada, 1830–1865," *Civil War History* 37:4 (December 1991), 314–327; quote, 315.

15. "Slave-Hunters in Boston," *Liberator*, November 1, 1850.

16. For a more complete account of the Crafts in Boston see Horton and Horton, *Black Bostonians*, 112–113.

17. Gary Collison, *Shadrach Minkins: From Fugitive Slave to Citizen* (Cambridge, Mass.: Harvard University Press, 1997); Foner, *History of Black Americans*, vol. 3, 35–36.

18. Foner, *History of Black Americans*, vol. 3, 35–36; Thomas P. Slaughter, *Bloody Dawn: The Christiana Riot and Racial Violence in the Antebellum North* (New York: Oxford University Press, 1991).

19. Horton and Horton, *Black Bostonians*, 120–123; Albert J. Von Frank, *The Trials of Anthony Burns: Freedom and Slavery in Emerson's Boston* (Cambridge, Mass.: Harvard University Press, 1998).

20. Foner, *History of Black Americans*, vol. 3, 87–91; Julius Yanuck, "The Garner Fugitive Slave Case," *Mississippi Valley Historical Review* 40 (June 1953), 47–66; Steven Weisenburger, *Modern Medea: A Family Story of Slavery and Child-Murder from the Old South* (New York: Hill & Wang, 1998).

21. Yanuck, "The Garner Fugitive Slave Case"; Weisenburger, *Modern Medea*.

22. Philip S. Foner, ed., *The Life and Writings of Frederick Douglass*, vol. 4 (New York: International Publishers, 1950), 227.

23. Donald E. Liedel, "The Antislavery Publishing Revolution in the 1850s," *Library Journal* 2 (1972), 67–80.

24. Ripley, Finkenbine, Hembree, and Yacovone, *The Black Abolitionist Papers*, vol. 4, 144; James M. McPherson, *Battle Cry of Freedom: The Civil War Era* (New York: Oxford University Press, 1988), 90.

25. Eugene D. Genovese, *The Slaveholders' Dilemma* (Columbia: University of South Carolina Press, 1992).

26. Merton L. Dillon, *The Abolitionists: The Growth of a Dissenting Minority* (DeKalb: Northern Illinois University Press, 1974), 86.

27. *Frederick Douglass' Paper*, May 26, 1854.

28. Benjamin Quarles, *Allies for Freedom: Blacks and John Brown* (New York: Oxford University Press, 1974), 32–36.

29. Eric Foner, *Free Labor, Free Soil, Free Men* (New York: Oxford University Press, 1970); Frederick Douglass, "The Unholy Alliance of Negro Hate and Antislavery," *Frederick Douglass' Paper*, April 5, 1856.

30. David R. Roediger, *The Wages of Whiteness: Race and the Making of the American Working Class* (New York: Verso, 1991); Eric Lott, *Love and Theft: Blackface Minstrelsy and the American Working Class* (New York: Oxford University Press, 1993).

31. Benjamin Quarles, *Black Abolitionists* (New York: Oxford University Press, 1969), 189.

32. *Liberator*, September 5, 1856.

33. *Liberator*, October 1, 1858.

34. Millard Fillmore, former president, ran on the nativist American Party (Know-Nothing) ticket and got just under nine hundred thousand votes.

35. Quoted in Foner, *History of Black Americans*, vol. 3, 213.

36. Foner, *Life and Writings of Frederick Douglass,* vol. 2, 406.
37. *Dred Scott* v. *Sanford* (1857), 19 Howard, 393.
38. Leon F. Litwack, *North of Slavery: The Negro in the Free States, 1790–1860* (Chicago: University of Chicago Press, 1961), 57.
39. Wilson Jeremiah Moses, *The Golden Age of Black Nationalism, 1850–1925* (New York: Oxford University Press, 1978).
40. *Frederick Douglass' Paper,* September 7, 1855; *Liberator,* November 27, 1857.
41. *Liberator,* August 13, 1858.
42. "Proceedings of the State Convention of Colored Men of the State of Ohio, Held in the City of Columbus, January 21st, 22d & 23d, 1857," in Foner and Walker, *Proceedings,* vol. 1, 320.
43. Ripley, Finkenbine, Hembree, and Yacovone, *The Black Abolitionist Papers,* vol. 4, 319.
44. *Liberator,* November 11, 1959.
45. Benjamin Quarles, *Allies for Freedom: Blacks and John Brown* (New York: Oxford University Press, 1974), 86–87.
46. McFeely, *Frederick Douglass,* 198–203; Quarles, *Allies for Freedom.*
47. *Weekly Anglo-African,* December 1859.
48. *Liberator,* December 9, 1859.
49. Benjamin Quarles, ed., *Blacks on John Brown* (Urbana: University of Illinois Press, 1972), 20–21.
50. *Liberator,* March 12, 1858.
51. Broadside signed by Harvey C. Jackson, Simcoe, Canada West, December, 7, 1859, in Boyd B. Stutler Collection of the John Brown Papers, Mss. 42, Roll 5, Ohio Historical Society; *Weekly Anglo-African,* December 31, 1859.
52. Quoted in Foner, *History of Black Americans,* vol. 3, 270–271.
53. *Liberator,* January 27, 1860, quoted in James M. McPherson, *The Negro's Civil War: How American Negroes Felt and Acted during the War for the Union* (New York: Vintage Books, 1965), 5.
54. *Anglo-African,* February 4, 1860; *Liberator,* October 19, 1860. See also McPherson, *The Negro's Civil War,* 10.
55. Hondon B. Hargrove, *Black Union Soldiers in the Civil War* (Jefferson, N.C.: McFarland & Co., 1988).
56. Quoted in McPherson, *Negro's Civil War,* 163.
57. *New York Tribune,* February 12, 1862; *Douglass' Monthly,* September 1861.
58. Quoted in McPherson, *Negro's Civil War,* 11. See also James O. Horton, "'Making Free': African Americans and the Civil War," in Frances H. Kennedy, ed., *The Civil War Battlefield Guide* (Boston: Houghton Mifflin Co., 1990), 261–263.
59. McPherson, *Negro's Civil War,* 17–18.
60. *Pine and Palm,* May 25, 1861, also quoted in McPherson, *Negro's Civil War,* 29.
61. Quoted in McPherson, *Negro's Civil War,* 166–167.
62. R.J.M. Blackett, ed., *Thomas Morris Chester: Black Civil War Correspondent* (Baton Rouge: Louisiana State University Press, 1989).
63. Quoted in McPherson, *Negro's Civil War,* 168.
64. *New York Tribune,* March 28, 1863.
65. James M. McPherson, *What They Fought For, 1861–1865* (Baton Rouge: Louisiana State University Press, 1994), 66–67.
66. Blackett, *Thomas Morris Chester,* 33.
67. Ibid., 34–38. Only when Harrisburg, Pennsylvania, faced Confederate invasion were black defenders considered. They were quickly rejected after the threat receded.
68. McPherson, *Negro's Civil War,* 178–179.

69. Although in 1864 Congress authorized equal pay for blacks who had been free before the war, until March 1865 it did not include those who had been slaves at the time of enlistment. At that time equal pay was made retroactive to their date of enlistment. Ira Berlin, Joseph P. Reidy, and Leslie S. Rowland, *Freedom: A Documentary History of Emancipation, 1861–1867* (Cambridge, England: Cambridge University Press, 1982), series 2, 363, 367–368.

70. Virginia M. Adams, ed., *On the Altar of Freedom: A Black Soldier's Civil War Letters from the Front* (Amherst: University of Massachusetts Press, 1991), 83.

71. McPherson, *Negro's Civil War,* 199.

72. Berlin, Reidy, and Rowland, *Freedom,* 365–366.

73. Susie King Taylor, *Reminiscences of My Life in Camp with the 33d United States Colored Troops Late First S.C. Volunteers* (Boston, 1902).

74. Joseph T. Glatthaar, *Forged in Battle: The Civil War Alliance of Black Soldiers and White Officers* (New York: Free Press, 1990), 91.

75. Foner, *History of Black Americans,* vol. 3, 374.

76. Ibid., 375.

77. Ibid., 376.

Index

Note: Page numbers in italics indicate illustrations.

About the Authors

James Oliver Horton, the Benjamin Banneker Professor of American Studies and History at George Washington University, directs the African American Communities Project at the Smithsonian Institution. He is a regular panelist on The History Channel's *The History Center.* **Lois E. Horton** is a professor of history at George Mason University. They are coauthors of several books, including *In Hope of Liberty: Free Black Culture and Community and Protest among Northern Free Blacks, 1700–1860* and *Black Bostonians: Family Life and Community Struggle in the Antebellum North.*